From Privilege to Competition

MENA DEVELOPMENT REPORT

From Privilege to Competition

Unlocking Private-Led Growth in the Middle East and North Africa

THE WORLD BANK
Washington, D.C.

© 2009 The International Bank for Reconstruction and Development / The World Bank
1818 H Street NW
Washington DC 20433
Telephone: 202-473-1000
Internet: www.worldbank.org
E-mail: feedback@worldbank.org

1 2 3 4 12 11 10 09

This volume is a product of the staff of the International Bank for Reconstruction and Development / The World Bank. The findings, interpretations, and conclusions expressed in this volume do not necessarily reflect the views of the Executive Directors of The World Bank or the governments they represent.

The World Bank does not guarantee the accuracy of the data included in this work. The boundaries, colors, denominations, and other information shown on any map in this work do not imply any judgement on the part of The World Bank concerning the legal status of any territory or the endorsement or acceptance of such boundaries.

Rights and Permissions

ISBN-13: 978-0-8213-7877-9
eISBN: 978-0-8213-7889-2
DOI: 10.1596/978-0-8213-7877-9

Library of Congress Cataloging-in-Publication Data

Benhassine, Najy.
    From privilege to competition : unlocking private-led growth in the Middle East and North Africa / [Najy Benhassine, principal author].
        p. cm. -- (Mena development report)
    ISBN 978-0-8213-7877-9 -- ISBN 978-0-8213-7889-2
    1. Economic development--Middle East. 2. Economic development--Africa, North. 3. Public-private sector cooperation--Midde East. 4. Public-private sector cooperation--Africa, North. I. World Bank. II. Title.
    HC415.15.B465 2009
    338.956'05--dc22
                            2009030180

Cover photo: Zoubida Allaoua and Catherine H. Burtonboy
Cover design: Naylor Design

Contents

Tables

Figures

Boxes

Foreword

Times of economic turmoil often overshadow long-term challenges. However, the current global economic crisis could be a historic opportunity for the Middle East and North Africa region. It could open the door for fundamental reforms that will prepare the countries of this region to rebound, embrace the future global recovery, and strengthen their long-term growth prospects.

From Privilege to Competition: Unlocking Private-Led Growth in the Middle East and North Africa complements previous regional reports published by the World Bank by focusing on the role of the private sector as an engine for stronger growth and employment creation. The 2004 report on trade and investment and the 2008 report on education touched on other fundamental ingredients of economic competitiveness and private sector development. This report—focusing on market institutions, the quality of implementation of economic policies, and the credibility of reforms from the private sector perspective—offers a new angle to the growth and development challenges of the MENA region.

Stronger Private Sector Growth is Needed to Create Jobs.

All countries in the region face a pressing employment challenge: about 40 million jobs will need to be created in the coming decade. A young and increasingly well educated labor force is looking for opportunities to use their skills and creativity. Governments will not be able to create these jobs in the public sector—nor will state-owned enterprises in a sustainable manner. The jobs will have to come from the private sector.

The future prosperity and social cohesion of the MENA region rests in great part on the ability of governments to enable the private sector to respond to this job creation challenge. That is what this report is about: enabling new generations of entrepreneurs to play a bigger role in the growth of their countries. It is also about encouraging more investors to believe in the prospects of the region and trust that business-friendly policy reforms will benefit them as well—and not only a minority of privileged entrepreneurs.

Skeptics voicing doubt that the private sector will succeed in generating the needed jobs and growth are legion in MENA, and the global financial crisis may have added to this skepticism. However, the lessons of past crises support the main message of this report: sustained job creation can only come from a competitive private sector, which in turn requires governments to build efficient regulatory capacity. Where regulatory institutions are weak or where regulators are captured, the state cannot play its supportive role effectively.

A more vibrant private sector in MENA countries will also contribute to increased economic integration of the region. With a conducive business environment, new entrepreneurs will emerge to reap the benefits of greater intraregional trade and investment—driven more by business considerations than by political concerns.

While There Have Been Policy Reforms, Their Implementation Needs to Improve to Foster a Stronger Response From the Business Community.

In many MENA countries the institutions that implement private sector policies, need strengthening to make reforms more credible, and to ensure that they are implemented equitably and consistently to the benefit of all entrepreneurs.

This region has made great strides over the last few years in improving its investment climate—even if some countries still lag. Yet the response of the private sector has been muted. Arbitrary implementation of reforms and discretion in enforcing rules explain why too many would-be entrepreneurs believe that the key to success is how connected, or how privileged, they are, which diminshes the importance of competition, creativity, and persistence. Focusing on the credibility of reforms and the consistency of their implementation is what this report recommends. This new agenda for private sector development applies to all countries in the region, even if it translates into different strategies depending on each country's specifics, its progress with business environment reforms, its resource endowment, and its political economy.

This new agenda emphasizes the role of institutional reform as the cornerstone of any credible private sector development strategy, and is therefore in essence a "good governance" agenda. The aim is to increase the effectiveness and consistency in which public agencies and market institutions—customs, tax authorities, investment agencies, courts, industrial land market agencies, and so forth—interact with firms and enforce regulations. The report argues that reforms need to reduce conflicts of interests and target regulations that either restrict competition or erect informal barriers to entry. These reforms will all require visible actions by political leaders to signal that there will be a level playing field. The credibility of these signals will ultimately be the most important driver of private investors' response to reforms.

The Private Sector Also Has a Responsibility: It Needs to Be Better Organized and Be More Inclusive, More Creative and More Dynamic in Order to Be a Credible Partner of Governments in Implementing this Agenda.

The report argues that the private sector and civil society, too, have an important role to play in changing expectations for the better. It shows that in many countries, the dominant private sector—privileged by past policies and remaining distortions—is seldom an agent of change, but tends to defend the status quo. New generations of entrepreneurs, ones that are more open to competition, exports, and innovation, need to voice their interests more prominently. To this end, they need to be better organized. The same is true for civil society. The demand for reforms is often weak in MENA countries—sometimes because channels of voice are muted, but often because these voices are not unified or organized. The report calls on the private sector and civil society to play a bigger role in support of reformers in their governments.

This report offers innovative ideas and recommendations for policymakers, the private sector, and civil society in the MENA region and beyond, and it will generate debates and discussions to help the private sector to grow and create the jobs that are badly needed. The World Bank stands ready to support our MENA client countries in this endeavor.

SHAMSHAD AKHTAR
REGIONAL VICE-PRESIDENT
MENA REGION

Preface

The objectives and intended impacts of this report are threefold: informing policy makers and other stakeholders, proposing a new angle on private sector policies, and provoking a debate.

First, informing. The report brings together new evidence on private sector development across the Middle East and North Africa (MENA), as well as the findings from the literature on this topic, particularly country-specific analysis. Its aim is to present current knowledge on business environment challenges in MENA—at least on selected issues presumed to be most pertinent to the region. It also aims to inform policy makers and other stakeholders of successful policy reforms in the region or elsewhere.

Second, proposing a new perspective on public policies shaping the investment climate. This report is prescriptive, offering new routes for policy reforms. Rather than reiterate the list of standard reforms that might be ongoing in the region, this report will offer different angles to the business environment reform agenda. For example, in the legal and regulatory environment, the report emphasizes the institutional underpinnings of the reform process and its public sector governance aspects. Similarly, for industrial strategies the report will distance itself from dogmatic views on whether such strategies are good or bad. Instead, it will focus on the institutional underpinnings of good industrial strategies, as well as on the design and evaluation of these interventions.

Third, provoking a debate. Ultimately, this report aims to bring public sector governance to the center of the private sector development agenda. Public sector governance, accountability, transparency, credibility, rents, privileges, discretion, and state capture are terms sprinkled throughout the report, much more prominently than the vocabulary usually associated with the private sector—technology, innovation, entrepreneurship, competitiveness centers, small and medium-sized enterprises, incubators, and the like. Another objective of this report is to provoke debate among stakeholders in the MENA countries and to raise awareness that the private sector agenda in this region is mostly one of public governance.

A poll of 3,900 citizens of six Arab countries conducted in late 2005, identified *"Ending corruption and nepotism"* as the third most important concern of citizens after job creation and improving the health care or education systems.[1] Depending on the country, *nepotism* is also cited as the first or second reason why employment opportunities are hard to find. This report in a sense links the two issues by showing that discretionary policy implementation and rent-seeking distortions—both manifestations of nepotism—are constraining private investment and job creation in the region.

The report is intended for multiple audiences: governments, the private sector, and the public at large. For the policy makers in MENA, and particularly the reformers among them—whether in government, in parliaments, or in various ruling circles—the report proposes concrete policy recommendations. It tries to fill a gap by offering a specific content to the public sector reform agenda as it applies to private sector development. It not only emphasizes that the success of private sector development policies rests in great part on more effective, predictable and equitable implementation of these policies by the relevant public agencies. It also offers a menu of measures of public sector reform that would allow this.

The second audience is the private sector. All too often the pitfalls in the business environment are attributed exclusively to governments. As this report argues, the private sector should also play a role in identifying, designing, monitoring, and evaluating reforms. It needs to be enabled to do that, and it needs to build its own capacity to organize and contribute constructively to the policy debate—when it is invited to do so. The private sector in MENA is very diverse, and often its most powerful advocates are not the most reformist. In all countries some in the private sector are active defenders of the status quo—a fundamental problem. The central message of this report—good governance of the public sector—applies to the private sector as well. As much as the report targets reformists in the government, it also targets reformists in the private sector.

The report is also designed for specialists, particularly academics in the region, and nonspecialists—the press, policy commentators, and citizens. Because the quality of public governance is central to private sector development and job creation, this report concerns all citizens.

---

[1]Zogby International, "Attitude of Arabs: 2005" (www.zogby.com). The countries covered and the respective sample sizes are the Arab Republic of Egypt (800), Jordan (500), Lebanon (500), Morocco (800), Saudi Arabia (800), and the United Arab Emirates (500).

In its broadest definition, private sector development would include all economic activities of privately owned firms—from formal manufacturing, trade and services industries, regulated industries in infrastructure or the social sectors, to informal merchants. In view of the stated objectives, the report is selective.

First, the report does not cover issues related to labor markets. They are, of course, an essential part of the growth-employment equation. But MENA's labor markets have already been the subject of two important World Bank regional flagship reports—the report on education in MENA (World Bank 2008c) as well as the 2003 report on employment (World Bank 2003c). This report focuses on the demand for jobs by private firms, because it is dictated by investment and the dynamism of the private sector.

The report does not directly address the issue of the informal sector. Short of reliable data and studies on the informal sector in MENA countries, little is known on this topic. The barriers to entry of new formal firms, however, explain in great part why so many entrepreneurs and laborers decide to stay out of formal markets. With a growing labor force, the informal sector is inevitably poised to grow. The topic is therefore addressed indirectly because only a significant improvement in the business environment in MENA countries will reduce informality.

The report does not analyze specific sectors of the economy, unless they are relevant to the central questions addressed. The rural economy is also not covered. Although there may be specific issues in the rural investment climate (especially in rural land markets), they are not covered in this report. These are complex issues that deserve dedicated analysis rather than a superficial treatment.

The report addresses how one aspect of infrastructure affects the business environment—namely, access to serviced industrial land—but does not address private sector participation in the provision of infrastructure services. Access to investable land is found to be the leading infrastructure issue facing businesses of the region. Private participation as a means to improve the efficacy of public infrastructure is not analyzed, however; that would require specific analysis for different infrastructure sectors, which is not the objective of this report.

Finally, this report will not treat the specific challenges of private sector development in conflict-affected areas. Although building government credibility after conflict is central to private sector reconstruction and recovery, the specifics of economic policy making in politically unstable or conflict situations is so complex that it demands a focus that is outside this report. Instead, the report is about the long-term process of building public institutions to govern markets in the entire region.

A cautionary note on data sources: The private sector's scope is large—informal merchants, microenterprises, restaurants, dentists and hotels, rural firms, manufacturing firms, multinational corporations, and all economic activities owned and managed by private entities constitute the private sector. Naturally, much of the analysis in this report draws on a subset of what constitutes the private sector in each country. For example, World Bank enterprise surveys cover mostly industrial small and medium-sized enterprises. The *Doing Business* data generally refer to a formal manufacturing firm in the capital city.

The report draws on a variety of data sources, including international databases, country-specific databases and reports, World Bank enterprise surveys, original data collection conducted during its preparation, and the published economic literature. Most of the microeconomic evidence rests on a database of about 10,000 firms surveyed in the region using a standard questionnaire. International comparisons of firm-level evidence was done using the same source of survey data collected by the World Bank in more than 80 countries, totaling more than 80,000 firms (see www.enterprisesurveys.org).

The analytical underpinnings in this report rest on these diverse and inevitably partial data sources. The underlying assumption is that the strengths and weaknesses identified among a certain group of private firms (say, manufacturing) reflect on broader issues that affect the private sector at large. Many investment climate issues may be specific to certain groups of firms and sectors, but lacking comprehensive data coverage of all entities that constitute the private sector in each country, the analysis here does not delve into these specifics.

The lack of data availability in this area not only pertains to the diversity and scope of the private sector, it also reflects a fundamental weakness in the statistical systems throughout most of this region. In addition, it reflects the lack of access (for the authors and the general public) to the many data sources that are generated by various government agencies. This lack of public information is a key challenge in the MENA investment climate that this report also emphasizes.

The report starts with an introductory chapter that sets the stage for the issues and provides a short historical background on the development of the private sector in MENA—drawing on anecdotes and stories heard from many entrepreneurs and public officials consulted throughout the region during the preparation of this report.

The core of the analysis is then presented in three parts. Part I assesses the performance of private sector development in the region from a macroeconomic and microeconomic standpoint (chapter 2). It then presents the framework that is used to explain the identified performance gap (chapter 3) and uses this framework in chapter 4 to claim that the lack of private sector dynamism in MENA is not necessarily due to insufficient reforms, but rather to the discretionary way in which rules and policies are implemented, and the lack of credibility of governments to really level the playing field when applying their policies and reforms.

Part II then illustrates how this issue of poor implementation of the policies translates in three key policy areas in the business environment of the region: access to finance (chapter 5), access to land (chapter 6), and the conduct of industrial policies (chapter 7). The aim is to show how the role of the state and its institutions, when diverted from their regulatory and administrative missions by special interests and when subject to discretionary influence, can distort policies that may otherwise be well designed and well intended.

Part III analyzes the political economy of reforms in MENA (chapter 8) and uses this analysis to offer a set of strategic recommendations and concrete policy actions that take into account the region's diversity and political economy (chapter 9).

Acknowledgments

This report was prepared by a team led by Najy Benhassine, principal author, and comprising Andrew Stone (principal co-author), Philip Keefer (political economy chapter and overall storyline), Youssef Saadani Hassani (research assistant and co-author of the finance chapter), and Sameh Neguib Wahba (land chapter), under the guidance and supervision of Zoubida Allaoua.

Since its inception, this project has benefited from the inspiration and guidance of Mustapha Kamel Nabli (during and after his tenure as Chief Economist of the MENA region). He provided continuous support and advice as well as key inputs that shaped the storyline of this report. He also provided detailed feedback on successive drafts of chapters. The report also benefited from the guidance and extensive reviews of Ritva Reinikka, Director of the Social and Economic Development Group of the World Bank MENA region, who oversaw the completion of this project. She provided substantial inputs that led to this final draft, contributing in particular to the overall storyline of the report, its key messages, and the framing of its political economy and governance focus. Daniela Gressani, in her former position as Vice-President of the World Bank MENA region, has provided detailed comments on an earlier draft of the report, which led to very useful reframing of key parts of the text and the storyline.

Other contributors who provided inputs to the various chapters, background papers, or research assistance include Jennifer Keller (background paper on private sector performance and measurement of policy reforms), Philippe de Meneval (legal and regulatory chapter), Patrick Plane, Marie-Ange Véganzonès-Varoudakis, and Tidiane Kinda (background paper on firm-level productivity in MENA), Gael Raballand and Claudia Nassif (background notes for the industrial policy chapter), and Mehdi Benyagoub, Manuela Chiapparino, Sylvie Maalouf, Yasmine Rouai, and Jimena Zuniga (research assistance and data analysis). Sydnella Kpundeh was the team assistant throughout the production of this report, including help with organizing the consultations that took place in the initial and final stages of its preparation. Steve Wan Yan Lun also provided continuous support to the team. Lin Wang Chin desktopped the report. Iya Bouguermouh, Samra Chaibani, Donia Jemail, Hafidha Sahraoui, and Amira Fouad Zaky provided support to the consultations in Cairo, Algiers, Sana'a, Rabat, and Tunis, respectively.

The summary findings of the report were presented to various audiences during a series of consultations that were organized during the winter of 2008–09 in Algiers, Cairo, Rabat, Sanaa, Tunis, and Washington, DC. These consultations included private sector representatives, government officials, civil society and academia, as well as staff from international organizations (the World Bank Group, the African Development Bank, the Organization of Islamic Conference, the European Investment Bank, which contributed to background research work to the finance chapter through the participation of Valerie Herzberg, the European Commission, and the Organization for Economic Cooperation and Development). All participants in these consultations are hereby gratefully acknowledged for their useful feedback and suggestions.

Since the concept stage, successive drafts of this report benefited from inputs and comments of many colleagues at the World Bank Group and among various stakeholders in countries in the region. These include the formal reviewers, Michael Klein (former Vice-President for Finance and Private Sector of the World Bank Group and former Chief Economist of the International Finance Corporation) and Roberto Zagha (as Senior Economic Advisor to the Vice-President of the World Bank Poverty Reduction and Economic Management group, and Secretary of the Commission on Growth and Development); Joseph Saba and Leila Zlaoui, who helped the team sharpen the messages of the report's overview; Ahmed Galal, Managing Director of the Economic Research Forum, who contributed to the concept note and provided comments on successive drafts of the report; as well as Gabi George Afram, Randa Akeel, Mohammed-Cherif Belmihoub, Kevin Carey, Nadereh Chamlou, Ndiame Diop, Anton Dobronogov, Laurent Gonnet, Neil Gregory, Farrukh Iqbal, Omer Karasapan, Auguste Kouame, Anjali Kumar (who prepared a background paper on access to finance, jointly with Mukta Joshi, Ergys Islamaj, and Vidhi Chhaochharia), Nadir Mohammed, Sahar Nasr (who provided numerous inputs to the access to finance chapter and contributed to the survey of banks), Vincent Palmade, Douglas Pearce, Nadjib Sefta, and David Steel. Professor James Robinson commented on the overview. However, none of these contributors are responsible for any errors or omissions in the final version presented here.

The team would like to thank all who provided comments at various stages of production of this report, including members of the MENA management team and other colleagues of the region who reviewed the report on two occasions, and the many stakeholders met in different MENA countries who were consulted at the initial stages of this project, as well as during the draft report consultations. Bruce Ross-Larson and his team at Communications Development Incorporated edited the report. Richard Crabbe, Elizabeth Kline and the Production Services Unit of the World Bank's Office of the Publisher managed design and production.

Glossary of Terms

As its title hints, the thrust of the policy message of the report has to do with issues of governance of market institutions, unequal implementation of the rules and a business environment that favors a few incumbents and therefore less dynamism in the private sector. This diagnostic, and the policy prescriptions that go with it, deserve some clarifications regarding the terms used because it departs somewhat from the standard recommendations in this area. A lexicon of the most important terms used in the report is therefore necessary to clarify what they refer to in the context of private sector development.

Credibility: This term is used to describe the extent to which government policies and reforms—laws, regulations, and how they are implemented—are credible in the eyes of investors and the public at large: credible in the sense that they are expected to be pursued and implemented as enacted and announced, and in an equitable and predictable manner. The extent of credibility also encompasses the credibility of commitment of governments to reform plans it announces.

Governance: The aspects of governance that this report emphasizes pertain to the ones directly affecting the investment climate. In particular, governance refers to the quality of service in public agencies that interact with markets and private firms (for example, the customs, registration agencies, and the tax authorities). It also refers to the quality of the regulatory functions of the state (for example, the capacity of the judiciary to enforce the laws and regulations).

Investment climate and *business environment:* These terms are used interchangeably to describe all the policy areas that affect the incentives of entrepreneurs and investors.

Market institutions, public institutions, and agencies: These terms are used interchangeably throughout the report to designate all institutions that regulate markets, implement the rules and regulations, and interact with firms and investors. This set of institutions includes the judiciary, customs, tax administration, labor inspectorate, local/central government agencies in charge of administering or regulating land markets, financial supervision and regulatory institutions, sectoral regulatory or inspection agencies (in regulated industries like health or agribusiness), investment-related agencies (one-stop shops, registration offices, investment promotion agencies), labor and social security administrations, and others. All these institutions—some are more often called *market institutions*, others *public agencies*—have different functions, but they all share a central role in enforcing the rules and regulations in a consistent and predictable way on behalf of the state.

Predictability: The extent to which the rules and policies are applied to investors and firms in a predictable way—in a way that is consistent with what the rule actually states or how the public institution that implements the rule is expected to perform. Arbitrary implementation of the rules or discretionary behavior in public agencies that lead to unequal implementation reduces predictability in the business environment.

Quality of governance: This is understood as the effectiveness of the administrative and regulatory functions of the state; its equitable nature, or the degree to which rules and regulations are interpreted and applied equally to all economic actors; and its independence from private interests, or the degree to which these public institutions are immune from political and personal influence in the way that they enforce the rules. It is not meant to cover broader issues of civil service reform or public financial management.

Abbreviations and Acronyms

ANSEJ	Agence Nationale de Soutien à l'Emploi des Jeunes
CEO	chief executive officer
CPI	Corruption Perceptions Index
FDI	foreign direct investment
GAFI	General Authority on Free Zones and Investments
GCC	Gulf Cooperation Council
GDP	gross domestic product
GMG	Groupement de Maintenance et de Gestion
ICA	Investment Climate Assessment
IMF	International Monetary Fund
ISIC	international standard industrial classification
MENA	Middle East and North Africa
NPL	nonperforming loans
OECD	Organisation for Economic Co-operation and Development
RPLA	resource-poor, labor-abundant
RRLA	resource-rich, labor-abundant
RRLI	resource-rich, labor-importing
SME	Small and Medium Enterprise
UNCTAD	United Nations Conference on Trade and Development
WTO	World Trade Organization

Overview

What Is This Report About?

Enabling the private sector to become the engine of strong and sustained growth.

Creating jobs for a young and better-educated labor force is a top priority of all governments in the Middle East and North Africa. Better jobs are even more important today as countries face a global economic downturn. What will that take? Sustained economic growth driven by the private sector—and dedicated long-term strategies and the leadership committed to carry them out. The private sector has been central in all countries that have grown strongly over long periods. International experience indicates that relying on state-owned enterprises to create jobs and investment has never been a sustainable substitute for investment by privately owned firms—because no government has been able to expose firms that it owned to real competition and hard budget constraints. This has been the experience across the Middle East and North Africa (MENA) region as well. Governments have realized that the model of state-led development used in earlier decades yielded economic stagnation and have sought a new model, one with a larger role for the private sector. The challenge for policy makers is to align the incentives of profit-maximizing entrepreneurs with the social objectives of shared growth and job creation. The private sector cannot do it all, however. Growth also requires public investment in education, knowledge, and infrastructure. Such public spending does not crowd out private investment, it crowds it *in*. Together with other characteristics such as market openness, stability, good governance, and visionary leadership, these policies have been common to all the economies that have been able to grow fast over the last few decades.[1]

Sustained growth in MENA will require more private investment, higher productivity of firms, and greater diversification— especially for exports. This has not been sufficiently the case in the region so far. Although the private sector has a larger role in MENA economies than ever before, it still falls short of being the engine of strong growth. Private investment has been insufficient to create the necessary jobs, and unemployment remains at double-digit levels in most countries. Weak productivity and innovation have restrained firm competitiveness and the diversification of exports. Clearly growth has accelerated, averaging 5.8 percent over the 2005–08 period, but it still lags behind the developing country average of 7.2 percent, surpassing only Latin America and the Caribbean (5.1 percent). The sustainability of this growth revival remains uncertain—especially in light of recent developments in the global economy. In resource-rich countries it has mainly been driven by the oil boom. The recent drop in oil prices and their volatility is yet another reminder for these countries that the diversification of their economies remains a pressing priority. In non-oil countries, past growth has not been accompanied by a structural transformation of the economy—especially in terms of exports—such as the one witnessed in high-growth East Asia or in Eastern Europe. The ongoing growth slowdown in the Organisation for Economic Co-operation and Development is also a reminder that these countries remain vulnerable to demand shocks to their low-value-added exports.

The role of government policies in ensuring a business environment conducive to private-led growth is central. The role of state and regulatory institutions to ensure proper functioning of private markets is also a key one—as the current financial crisis has shown. Recent developments have led some policy makers to reexamine the respective roles of markets and governments. The crisis has highlighted the need for a stronger role for the state in regulatory oversight. At the same time these events do not imply that a return to failed policies of the past will somehow bring better results. The leadership role of the private sector as an engine of growth is not in question. Instead, the crisis has been a reminder of how capable market regulatory institutions are crucial to ensure an orderly functioning of markets to serve both private (profit maximization) and public objectives (job creation and shared economic growth).

Is the Private Sector Able to Play the Role of a Growth Engine?

New entrants and greater competition will convince the skeptics.

Public-private relations in the MENA region: a story of mutual mistrust. Skepticism about the ability of the private sector to be the engine of growth is legion, and the current financial crisis has reinforced this skepticism. The private-led model is perceived as not having delivered on its promises. Almost 60 percent of public officials interviewed across the region thought the private sector in their countries was *rent seeking and corrupt*.[2] Only 21 percent claimed it is *dynamic*, and 9 percent thought it was *transparent and law abiding*. The distrust is reciprocal. It is rooted in the belief by officials that a small group of rent-seeking firms dominate the private sector—a group that has long been protected by all sorts of barriers to entry. Among the negative behaviors cited are the bribing of civil servants, lobbying for special benefits and tax exemptions, hiding of revenues and salaries to avoid tax obligations, and nontransparent corporate governance. On the private sector's side, it is also rooted in the belief that governments do not act to improve the investment climate for all businesses, but rather for the benefits of politicians and a narrow group of their allies.

This report is also about creating the conditions that enable a more developmental and more dynamic private sector to emerge—one in which fewer entrepreneurs are focused on protecting their rent situations from competition, one that is perceived as wealth and job creating rather than rent seeking. In a more open environment, many new firms and entrepreneurs will come forward. Countries in transition—Hungary, Poland, and Vietnam—show that, more than the expansion of existing firms, a generation of new investors supports growth accelerations. This has been the case in MENA every time policy changes have allowed new entrants. There will be even more dynamic entry if the environment improves further, and this will lead to a more diversified private sector, which will support further reform more strongly and more vocally than protected incumbents.

How Has the Private Sector Performed So Far?

It plays a bigger role—but it is not yet driving the transformation of MENA economies on a high-growth path.

Over the last three decades, MENA countries have moved from a model of state-led growth to one relying more on the private sector. All countries have adopted more prudent macroeconomic policies and increased their openness to trade and private investment. The reforms started in the 1970s in countries such as the Arab Republic of Egypt and Tunisia, gained momentum in the 1980s, and accelerated in the 1990s in other countries such as Algeria, the Syrian Arab Republic, the Republic of Yemen, and more recently in Libya. They have pushed the share of the private sector in (non-oil) GDP in all but a few of these countries to between 70 and 90 percent. This shift followed global trends.

Despite its larger role, however, the private sector still falls well short of transforming MENA countries into diversified, highly performing economies. Whether gauged by the diversification of exports, their technological sophistication, the level and sectoral composition of private investment, or the productivity and innovation of firms, no MENA country exhibits the kind of dynamism and economic transformation witnessed in countries such as China, the Republic of Korea, Malaysia, or Turkey. For example, private investment rates and the number of products exported all appear weaker in MENA (figures 0.1–0.2).

The report does not pretend to offer a standard recipe that would generate strong private-led growth in every country—such a recipe does not exist. Lessons learned from past successes and disappointments with standard reform packages call for humility in this search for the keys to growth. Today this search is even more challenging because short-term global economic prospects are grim. Many characteristics of a good investment climate are common to high-growth countries, such as relative macroeconomic stability, a certain degree of market openness, functioning factor markets, safe property rights, good governance, and

FIGURE 0.1

Stagnating Private Investment Rates
(percent of GDP)

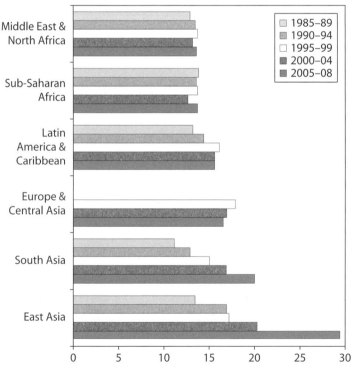

Sources: *World Development Indicators*, national accounts, International Monetary Fund (IMF).

FIGURE 0.2

Lower Diversification of Exports

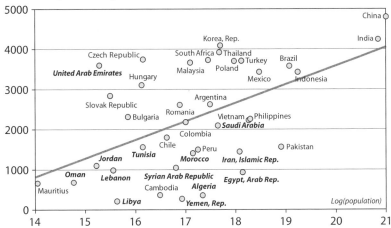

Source: Comtrade, 1995–2007 six-digit data.

increased public spending on education, health, and infrastructure. However, not all need to be perfect at the same time to trigger growth.

Instead, the report focuses on three aspects of policy making that are crucial in shaping investors' behavior:

- *First, the formal rules, regulations, and policies governments formulate in all areas of the business environment.* These range from macroeconomic and trade policies to the microeconomic policies regulating capital, land, labor, infrastructure, and product markets. The focus here is on the rules as they are written and how policies are designed on paper—in other words, *"Is the problem about missing reforms?"*

- *Next, the way the rules, regulations, and policies are actually implemented and enforced.* Whether it is the government or state agencies that directly interact with firms or the institutions that regulate markets and enforce property rights, every area of the business environment is supported by public institutions that should implement the rules and regulations that policy makers enact. Depending on the quality of these institutions—in particular how much they are immune from arbitrary political influence—this is done more or less consistently, equitably, and efficiently. These features of government and state agencies, both actual and perceived, are what matters for firms when they assess how the rules, regulations, and policies will be applied to them. Thus, going beyond standard benchmark indicators of policy reforms, we ask *whether the problem is with* the way *rules and policies are implemented.*

- *Finally, the shaping of investors' expectations about future policies and how they will be implemented.* The credibility of governments and the signals they send to firms are central to entrepreneurs' investment decisions. The current rules and policies and how they are implemented matter for firms, but anticipation about how these will evolve in the future are also crucial to assess the expected risks and returns of investments. Here, the report emphasizes the role of political economy factors—the demand for reforms, as well as their supply as shaped by features of decision-making institutions—in affecting expectations and weakening the credibility of government policies in the eyes of investors of the region.

Is It about Missing Reforms?

Not only. Policy gaps remain, but the private sector's response to reforms has been weak.

Reforms have accelerated, even if wide policy gaps remain in some countries and in some areas. Most governments have improved the business environment by simplifying business regulations, opening up the financial sector, and reducing restrictions to trade and investment. All international indices of the business environment point unequivocally to improvements. For example, in the area of business regulations that are measured by the *Doing Business* report, the average number of reforms conducted in MENA countries has been increasing steadily over the last few years (figure 0.3). Even if the reforms measured by the *Doing Business* report do not span all areas of the investment climate, they are good proxies of reform trends. The same positive trend has happened in the areas of macroeconomic management and trade and investment openness.

The private sector has responded to the reforms and grown— Private investment rates have increased by 2 percentage points on average. The response has been higher in resource-poor countries that have been the most ambitious and consistent in reforming—such as in Jordan, Morocco, Tunisia, and, more recently, Egypt. Foreign investment had also picked up significantly before the current downturn, although the majority has been concentrated in energy, infrastructure, and real estate, much less in technology-intensive ventures. Another reflection of this dynamism is that historically low business entry rates have, over recent years, slightly surpassed that of other developing regions.

—but the response has been far below what similar reforms have produced in high-growth countries. Private investment rates in MENA have on average been less responsive to reforms than elsewhere (figure 0.4). Between 1990 and 2007 private investment rates increased

FIGURE 0.3

The Number of Regulatory Reforms Has Increased Recently in MENA Countries
(average number of regulatory reforms per country, as measured by the Doing Business *report)*

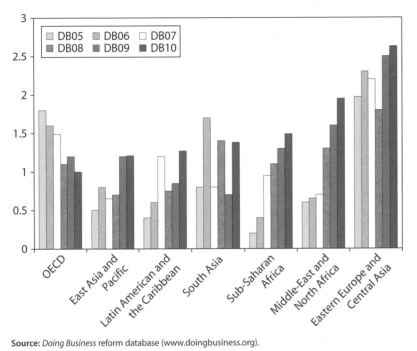

Source: *Doing Business* reform database (www.doingbusiness.org).

FIGURE 0.4

Reform Episodes and Private Investment Response
(private investment, % GDP)

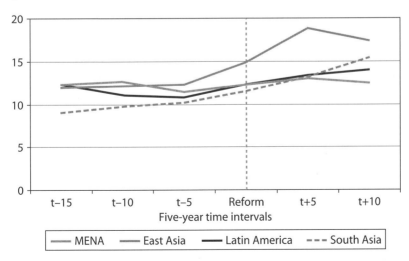

Sources: Private investment rates are from the *World Development Indicators,* national accounts, and IMF and have been averaged over the five-year periods. Episodes of reforms are based on the Economic Freedom Index of the Fraser Institute (www.freetheworld.com), and a reform episode is defined as a five-year episode during which this 0–10 index permanently improved by at least one unit.

FIGURE 0.5

Overall, the Business Environment in MENA Countries Looks "Average," as It Does in Many Fast-Growing Economies

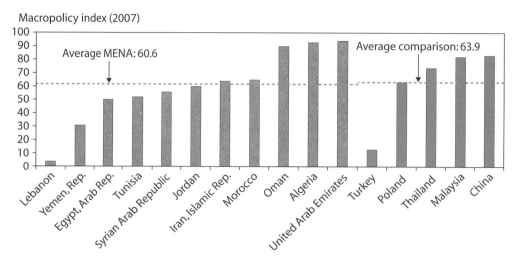

Macropolicy index (2007)

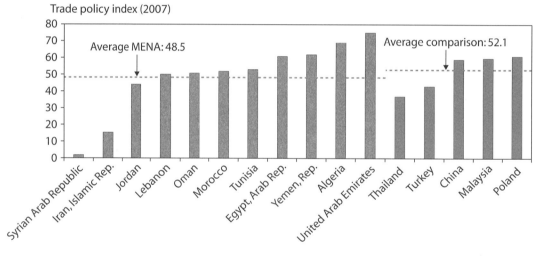

Trade policy index (2007)

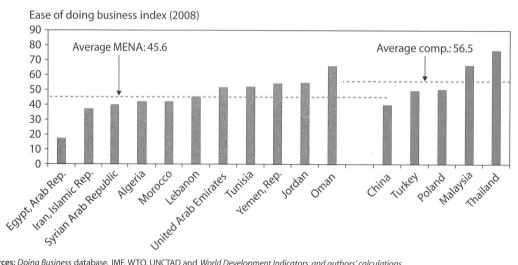

Ease of doing business index (2008)

Sources: *Doing Business* database, IMF, WTO, UNCTAD and *World Development Indicators, and authors' calculations.*

8

slightly in some MENA countries and declined in others—in contrast to other countries such as like China, Malaysia, Poland, Thailand, and Turkey. Is this because those countries reformed more than MENA countries? The answer is *no*.

The lackluster response apparently is not due to insufficient reforms in the region. The usual indicators of market-oriented reforms are not that much worse in MENA countries than those for high-growth countries (figure 0.5). The gaps are too small to explain the difference in performance. With few exceptions, due to the reform deficit in some oil-rich countries, the region's rank in the world is "average," as are those of China, Malaysia, Poland, Thailand, and Turkey.

Is It about the Way Rules Are Implemented?

Yes, the business environment is not the same for all: discretion, arbitrariness, and the unequal treatment of investors abound.

Policy uncertainty and discretion in implementing the rules constrain investment. Investors in MENA—especially managers of small and medium-sized firms—consistently point to policy uncertainty and an uneven playing field that favors some incumbent firms at the expense of new entrants and competitors. Corruption, anticompetitive practices, and regulatory policy uncertainty all rank high in the minds of business managers (figure 0.6). In many countries, businesses also point to reform gaps in the regulatory environment, in access to finance, and in access to land. Rather than policies as they appear on paper, a large part of the problem seems to lie with the unequal, discretionary, and preferential implementation of policies. Surveyed firms often refer to the implementation of rules and regulations as inconsistent and unpredictable (figure 0.7).

Other symptoms of a business environment that is not the same for all can be identified: older firms, lower business density, and little competition point to a prominent role for incumbents. Firms in MENA are much older than in other parts of the world and almost 10 years older than in Eastern Europe (figure 0.8). Business managers are also older than elsewhere. Incumbent firms face less competition. Except in South Asia, fewer registered firms per capita are found in MENA (figure 0.8). These are all symptoms of a discriminatory business environment that prevents the entry and exit of firms.

Although policy reforms are necessary in many areas and many countries, the mix of imperfect rules with the unequal and discretionary implementation and enforcement of these rules is what

FIGURE 0.6

Policy Uncertainty and the Unequal Implementation of Rules Are Leading Constraints to Businesses

Leading constraints to MENA firms
(simple average of a country's percentage of firms ranking a constraint as "major or severe")

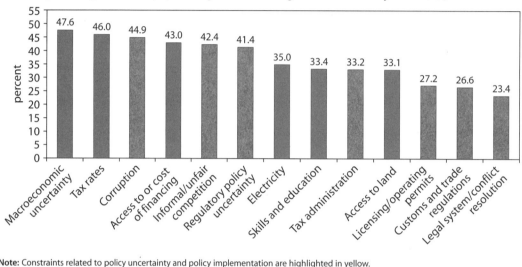

Note: Constraints related to policy uncertainty and policy implementation are highlighted in yellow.

Sources: World Bank Enterprise Surveys of Algeria, Egypt, the Islamic Republic of Iran, Jordan, Lebanon, Morocco, Oman, Saudi Arabia, Syria, West Bank and Gaza, and the Republic of Yemen economies, various years.

FIGURE 0.7

Perceptions about the Consistency and Predictability of Rules and Regulations as They Are Applied in MENA Countries

Interpretations of regulations are consistent and predictable.
(percent of respondents disagreeing)

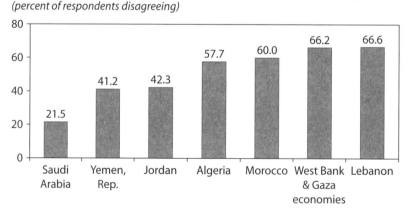

Source: Investment Climate Surveys (2005–08).

FIGURE 0.8

The Lasting Influence of the Business Elite and the Lack of Dynamism and Competition in the Private Sector

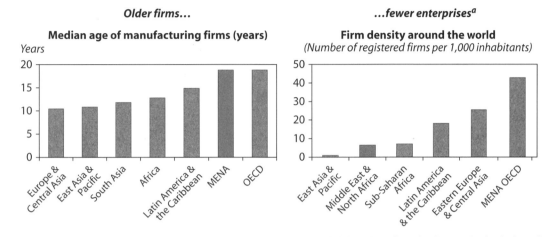

Older firms...

Median age of manufacturing firms (years)
Years

...fewer enterprises[a]

Firm density around the world
(Number of registered firms per 1,000 inhabitants)

a. Note that despite the strong growth, firm density in Asian economies is particularly low. This is driven by China's and India's high (rural) population and the fact that firm density counts only *formally* registered firms per capita.

Sources: World Bank Enterprise Surveys of manufacturing firms in Algeria, Egypt, Jordan, Lebanon, Morocco, Oman, Saudi Arabia, Syria, West Bank and Gaza economies, and the Republic of Yemen (various years) and World Bank entrepreneurship database.

hinders private sector development in the region. The common problem boils down to the role of the state and its institutions in various areas of the business environment. The report goes beyond the laws and the regulatory frameworks in place, to dig into the role of the state in *credit* and *land* markets—access to both is problematic in most MENA countries. It also covers the area of *industrial policy* that has attracted renewed attention lately. It illustrates, in each area, the wide gap between enacted policies and the behavior of institutions that implement them. This is best shown in these three topics, but the argument extends to other areas of the business environment where discretion and favoritism can weaken the public institutions that implement private sector policies and the credibility of government commitments to reform. Both hurt the expectations of investors and limit investment, competition, and innovation.

The challenge for the governments is to implement policies that give clear signals to investors and strengthen their credibility as they work to level the playing field for all investors. Strengthening and sustaining growth in MENA will depend on whether the region's policy makers will be able to convince existing and would-be investors that they are ready to reduce the unequal and discretionary ways of implementing policies. Only then will policy reforms have the expected impact on private investment and growth. However, changing expectations of investors by getting at the root of the rents and privileges is also difficult, because it requires shifting the balance of each country's political economy.

Why Is It Difficult to Improve the Business Environment in the Region?

It requires facing political economy factors that undermine support for reforms and the ability to pursue them.

Weaknesses in the business environment relate, in part, to the extent of discretionary allocation of rents to the private sector. This situation calls for reforms that alter the relations between policy makers and the beneficiaries of privileges. Credibility with investors, public officials, and the broader public will be earned only if political leaders commit to dismantling the rent allocation channels that weaken the regulatory and administrative functions of the state in many areas of the business environment. The rents vary from country to country. They are more prevalent and widespread in oil-rich, labor-abundant countries where the rents are larger and the pressure for reform is easier to contain, but they also remain pervasive in resource-poor countries. Some smaller states of the Gulf Cooperation Council (GCC) have created a more business friendly environment, with Dubai leading the way and Oman and Saudi Arabia catching up. The political economy, however, of these countries—where government leaders may often be the business leaders—does not offer a viable model for imitation in other larger MENA countries, where the political economy is more complex.

The political economy that prevails throughout most of the region limits the willingness and ability of policy makers to reform. First, demand for reform is weak. In transition countries where the private sector has grown more diverse and more vocal (such as in Eastern Europe), pressure on policy makers to extend the reforms has grown. This has not been sufficiently the case in the MENA region, as incumbents and beneficiaries of the status quo are more vocal and better organize to protect their rents. Also, the supply of quality reforms is hindered by policy-making institutions that lack credibility of commitment. The region lacks the institutions that would limit discretion and arbitrariness by public officials.

Weak Demand for Reform: A Private Sector That Has Yet to Become an Agent of Change

The private sector in most MENA countries has not been a loud and unified voice for reform. The part of the private sector described as "rent seeking" has been more vocal in promoting protection and the status quo. Advocacy for reforms has not yet found substantial support from generally weak, unrepresentative, or nonindependent business associations. Depending on the country, the most prominent of these are either government controlled or are dominated by large, old firms that favor the status quo or selective interventions and protection in their favor. In many countries, the "new" private sector of recent entrants and smaller firms has yet to organize to better advocate for change. In many countries they are constrained from doing so because independent organizations are either not allowed (as is the case in at least five countries) or are effectively barred from freely voicing criticisms of government policies. A survey of the most important business organizations in MENA, conducted in 2007, showed that their policy advocacy priorities are narrower and more sector specific than the policy priorities for growth emphasized by the majority of enterprises. Given the limited activity of civil organizations and the lack of a free press in many parts of the region, one finds little counterbalance to official business associations in policy dialogue (where it exists).

Enabling the entry of new investors and allowing more private voices to be heard will progressively shift the balance from the incumbent, often rent-seeking private sector to the developmental, competition-oriented private sector. The private sector in MENA countries has already grown more diverse. New business associations have emerged—some representing new, young entrepreneurs, as in Algeria or Syria; some from specific regions or sectors, as in Algeria, Jordan, and Morocco; and some representing distinct categories of firms such as small and medium-sized enterprises or exporters, as in Egypt. Even the incumbent leadership of large business associations are increasingly challenged by younger, more growth-oriented entrepreneurs—as was the case recently in Algeria. These new voices are often more vocal in demanding pro-growth reforms. If entry barriers continue to be lowered, these private constituencies will grow even more diverse, and pressure for reform will increase. Even partial reforms can trigger a self-sustaining dynamic process. The entry of more new players increases the support for further reform, leading to even more new entrants, which can eventually tilt the political economy equilibrium. This, however, will require a new partnership between policy makers and their private constituencies—one that

guards against capture, that is transparent, and that allows for all voices to
be heard.

Weak "Supply" of Reforms: Policy-Making Institutions That Lack Credibility

*Insulating key institutions from discretion and capture has been
central to the success of East Asian growth strategies.* Differences
in the role given to key institutions, and the rules based on which they
function, explain how apparently similar countries—in terms of their
progress in economic and political reforms—enjoy very different levels
of credibility and confidence in the eyes of investors. In established
democracies, systems of checks and balances—in particular, periodic
elections and the separation of powers—ensure, even if imperfectly, that
political leaders cannot systematically use state institutions at their discretion for the benefit of a few private interests. In less mature democracies or in autocracies, other means can be put in place to guard against
capture. The aim is to ensure that the process of policy making as well
as key government agencies have built-in rules and features that shield
them from arbitrary and discretionary influence by politicians. For example, in some of the world's most economically successful countries of
East Asia, political leaders have allowed an institutionalized ruling party
or a meritocratic public administration to emerge. China, Korea, and
Singapore have devolved authority to the institutions through substantial information flows and a system of incentives that rewards behavior
that promotes growth. Private investment in China soared after the
decision-making institutions undertook major internal institutional
reforms that increased the predictability of career paths of officials, that
rewarded growth-oriented behavior, and that devolved power from the
central rulers to lower level officials. Similarly, the strong central ruler
of Singapore devolved substantial authority over economic decision
making to a professional, merit-based civil service.

*In contrast, in many less successful countries, decision-making
and government institutions that regulate the markets and interact
with firms are subject to arbitrary intervention by political leaders
and public officials, to secure their power and extract rents.* For example, in a number of other East Asian countries with imperfect democratic institutions, political leaders relied more on political strategies
rooted in selective benefits, with policy decisions dominated by discretionary and personal allocations of publicly controlled assets to maintain
loyalty. In the latter group of countries, the size of the entrepreneurial
community that felt insulated from arbitrary decision making is corre-
spondingly smaller, because it includes only groups that are connected to

the political leaders. For historical reasons MENA countries find themselves largely in the latter group.

Policy-making arrangements that substantially devolve authority from central rulers to broad, rule-based institutions find no equivalent in MENA. The region has yet to move away from relationships between narrow political and economic elites that are not transparent and that undermine competition and pro-growth policies. A larger group of civil servants needs to be able to believe their careers will depend on their success in promoting private investment. The locus of decision making and policy implementation in MENA countries—parties and public administrations—are not "institutionalized" when compared to East Asia, for example. They are not rule bound, they do not reward allegiance to those rules and the institutions, and they are often not able to act independently of political interference or to challenge it. Improving the effectiveness of private sector policies will require reforms that change the incentives for all institutions that interact with firms and regulate markets. Only then will policies be implemented more equitably and with less arbitrariness. In turn, for these reforms to carry enough credibility in the eyes of investors, they will require a change in the institutional arrangements for policy making.

Cohesion between stakeholders and mobilization around a clear long-term economic strategy is also lacking in many countries— reflecting in part the lack of a consensual commitment to the growth objective. Few countries of the region have devised a clear long-term economic growth strategy. Sectoral ministries often have strategic plans, but rarely are they part of a consistent comprehensive approach. Coordination and cohesion between ministries is often weak— generally reflecting divided political elites. Some stand as exceptions here, but the mobilization among all stakeholders around a common long-term economic goal—a strong feature of the East Asian growth successes—is rare in the region.

What Should Be Done Differently? Where Should Each Country Start?

Build credibility and support by removing rents and fostering competition, reforming institutions, and promoting more inclusive policy making.

Make investors confident that things are really changing in a sustainable way. Some reform strategies may be appealing but are less useful from a credibility standpoint. If investors fear unequal and discretionary implementation of policy reforms, then they need to be accompanied by administrative reforms for transparency and accountability of the institutions that implement them. Only such reforms will give investors confidence that even-handed implementation will be sustained.

The mix of policies that will carry the greatest credibility in the eyes of investors varies by country. Where to start to signal that "change is real" is usually common knowledge among local stakeholders. Reform priorities and the pace of their implementation must be adapted to local circumstances, but local investors, policy makers, civil society, and the public usually share a common knowledge of what would signal a fundamental change.

To signal their commitment to growth, governments should focus on three things: removing sources of rents and barriers to competition, reforming institutions to reduce arbitrariness, and broadening the process of policy making and evaluation. Short of such a fundamental shift in the way that private sector policies are formulated and implemented, investor expectations that governments are committed to reform will remain weak. Investment responses will be muted by weak government credibility and lack of institutional progress to underpin policy reforms. The impact of any reform will be low if investors do not believe that changes are real, deep, and set to last.

Getting Specific: A Roadmap for Credible Private-Led Growth Strategies in MENA

First and foremost: reduce the major traditional channels of rent allocation, and foster competition.

With the proper regulatory environment, governments can encourage entry in all sectors of the economy by removing formal and informal barriers to competition. This is a prerequisite for reducing rent seeking and fostering the emergence of a more diversified private sector that will, in turn, pressure government for more pro-growth reforms. This applies particularly to oil-rich countries outside the GCC that have had the budgetary means to delay these standard reforms and protect failing (public or private) industries. A priority for them will be to catch up with the rest of the region's more advanced reformers. Short of that, other low-grade reforms or interventions will have little impact on investor expectations.

Specifically, Depending on each Country's Situation, this Reform Agenda Entails the Following Actions

Increase openness to competition, particularly foreign competition, through trade and investment. Examples include: (1) opening protected sectors such as retail and real estate, which have barriers to foreign investors in many Gulf countries, Egypt, Syria, and Tunisia; (2) reducing tariff bands and nontariff barriers; (3) removing protection of state-owned firms by enforcing hard budget constraints and exposing them to open competition; and (4) eliminating anti-export biases, such as the explicit surrender requirements on exports still in effect in a few countries (such as in Algeria, where 50 percent of export receipts need to be surrendered). Such measures will foster more openness and competition and will un-ravel many bastions of rent.

Remove formal and informal barriers to new entry of firms by eliminating entry requirements that give discretion to public officials to exclude some investors (and advantage others)—such as sector-ministry approvals in effect in many activities in Algeria, Egypt, Syria, and Tunisia. Other barriers include high minimum capital requirements and restric-tions on foreign ownership in certain sectors, in effect in Algeria, the Is-lamic Republic of Iran, Libya, Syria, Tunisia, and some GCC countries. The most important policy initiatives to develop small businesses should focus on easing entry and formalization, to increase competition. Beyond formal requirements to business creation, the focus should be on the other barriers to entry that stem from high operating costs, difficulty ac-cessing inputs and factor markets, and difficult exit of firms.

Improve the governance of the banking sector by increasing entry and competition among all banks—public and private. Coun-tries where state-owned banks still dominate should engage in open and transparent privatization transactions. Algeria, the Islamic Republic of Iran, Libya, and Syria should invest much political capital to pursue pri-vatization transactions that would reduce the dominance of public banks. Open and transparent competition in that process will be essential. This increases the value of the transactions and the quality of the investor, but even more important, it signals a change in the way business is carried out with government. Beyond privatization, all countries should increase banking competition and reduce the room for abuse—for example, by limiting the credit single borrowers can receive from public banks, by publicizing the public bank's portfolios and all troubled loans, by removing branching restrictions, and by improving the independent supervision of all banks.

Remove the conflicts of interest between politicians and busi-nessmen—or make them transparent. This is a difficult agenda, but the first steps would be for reformist political leaders to send strong sig-nals that things are really changing in this area. Particularly in countries that have made the most reform progress in MENA, but where these conflicts of interest still hinder competition in important sectors, bold steps by politicians to divest their current shares in major ventures (often in protected sectors) and to declare their assets would be a break from the status quo. A minimal alternative would be to increase transparency about these ventures and make them public. The presence of political leaders and their families in private markets hurts competition and creates serious conflicts of interest. It also damages the beliefs of other investors that the rules of the game are fair—no matter the extent of the reforms promoting openness.

Second: Reform institutions by anchoring elements of public sector reform in every agency implementing private sector policies.

MENA governments should aim at putting in place good public sector reform features in institutions that deal with the private sector. The goal is to instill a culture of equitable and effective public service to businesses, exempt from discretion and interference. This requires building strong rule-bound public institutions, delegated with substantial decision-making power over economic outcomes. It also requires increasing the transparency and accountability of public institutions that interact with the private sector and regulate markets.

This wide-ranging public sector reform agenda could be started one institution at a time, focusing on ones in which discretion and arbitrariness are highest. In some countries of the region, this could be the tax authority, the customs, or the land administration. In others it could be the licensing and inspection agencies.

These Reforms Entail the Following Actions

Put in place a continual process of regulatory and procedural reform that reduces the room for discretionary (and rent-oriented) behavior by public officials. This institutionalized process should continually evaluate and review regulatory and administrative barriers. It would do the following:

- Systematically reduce the number and complexity of administrative steps in every significant interaction between businesses and public officials

- Publicly establish quality standards (legality, efficiency) for new laws and regulations and a transparent system for enforcing these standards

- Ensure that laws and regulations are clear and publicly available, with little room for interpretation

- Systematically introduce simplified, reengineered electronic processes (e-government) in administrative interactions that allow it

Increase transparency and access to information for more account-ability in every public institution that interacts with the market. Implementing measures to improve access to information would signal a serious and significant drive toward increased transparency and account-ability (and a radical change from the status quo). These measures are difficult to reverse. Even if they are implemented partially and applied to just a few institutions, they will begin to have an impact. Transparency is contagious: pressure on other institutions to follow suit would quickly increase. Such measures include the following:

- Launching independent, regular, and publicly available measurement of the performance of public agencies in contact with the private sector. This would help to instill a culture of accountability in these institutions.

- Opening access to business information from various institutional databases—and introducing freedom to conduct independent surveys and research.

- Systematically publishing information on transactions involving privatizations, public land transactions, subsidies, and procurement tenders—particularly information on the beneficiaries—and on court decisions on commercial litigation.

- Creating a unified interagency enterprise identification number, to link the firm-level databases of all public institutions that deal with businesses and making most of the data open and accessible. No MENA country has implemented such an identification number so far, and doing so could be a major step toward more transparency.

Reform incentives in public agencies and encourage institutional innovations to improve effective and equitable service delivery to businesses. Rewarding effort for effective public service (such as performance-based compensation in public institutions) and discouraging discretion in key institutions that affect the business environment in MENA should form the core of private sector strategies. These reforms are part of core public administration and civil service reform agendas. Some could be initiated one institution at a time. Areas in which to start include the customs, the tax authorities, the industrial land administra-tions, and the agencies regulating investment approvals and business entry.

Increase autonomy of state institutions from the control of the executive branch and political leaders. Institutions such as the competi-tion authority, the regulatory agencies of various sectors, the financial reg-ulators (including the central bank), the audit authority, and the judiciary council usually report to the head of state in most MENA countries. The power of appointing senior administration officials is also concentrated with the head of state. Reforms that increase the autonomy of institutions—for example, by shifting reporting requirements and accountability to parliaments—would go a long way to improve their credibility.

Introduce systematic, independent, transparent, and regular evaluation of any selective public intervention, including industrial strategies. Public interventions in support of select groups of firms (exporters, small and medium-sized enterprises, or specific sectors) should systematically include features that will guard against failure and rent seeking:

- Measurable objectives, outcomes, and selection criteria would form the basis of a monitoring system for the intervention. Monitoring reports should be public and, where possible, the subject of consultation with relevant stakeholders.

- Systematic publication of information on beneficiary firms and the subsidies they receive.

- Independent access to data and surveys to evaluate and monitor interventions. When feasible, impact evaluations should be built in at the start of any intervention.

Third: Mobilize all stakeholders around a dedicated long-term growth strategy.

This will require building reform alliances and institutionalizing the reform process. In many MENA countries, reformers are in the minority in a system skewed toward the status quo. In these situations, only broad and vigorous coalitions can sustain successful reform efforts. A new form of partnership is needed between the government and all stakeholders—inside the different parts of government and with the private sector especially. These partnerships should lead to the development of stronger reform alliances and to more open and broader participation in designing, implementing, and evaluating policies. Mobilizing forces inside and outside governments on a credible long-term growth strategy—supported by strong political leadership—has been a common characteristic of all countries that have sustained high growth rates over long periods of time.

This Agenda will Entail the Following Actions

Improve government cohesion and interministerial coordination. Poor coordination is symptomatic of low-performing decision-making processes. It is very hard to tackle, and it takes more than creating multiministerial committees that abound in the region. It requires that the locus of coordination be a politically strong body that has explicit and visible political backing from the top leadership of the country (for example, a high-level reform council chaired by a top-level politician, or a visible interministerial group chaired by the head of state or prime minister). Quite often in MENA countries, the lack of coordination between different ministries dooms multisectoral reforms and encourages a proliferation of uncoordinated actions that are the responsibility of single entities. In some cases, four or more ministries can have prerogatives that are directly linked to the private sector agenda. Reformist ministers of the region are often constrained in the extent of their reform efforts by the limited scope of their ministerial responsibilities and the lack of coordination with other ministers.

Build partnerships between governments and other stakeholders, especially the private sector. This requires the following:

- *Freedom for the private sector to organize in independent organizations, to raise funding from members, to obtain economic and policy information, to inform open policy debates, and to advocate for policy reforms.* Such freedoms are not granted by law or in practice in at least six MENA countries.

- *Capable and inclusive business associations. Most independent business associations in MENA countries are either small—lacking advocacy or organizational capacity—or are controlled by a few prominent members.* Business associations growing out of a rent-seeking business environment tend to be rent seeking. If the freedom is granted to create independent associations, then it will be up to the business community to engage in more active and organized advocacy. The government should have no active role in this area other than to remove barriers to entry and to increase transparency in its consultations with the private sector.

- *An institutionalized, transparent, and inclusive process for private sector consultation in the identification of policy issues, the design of reforms, and the monitoring and evaluation of their implementation.*

- *More freedom of information relevant to economic policy, administrative performance, and markets to allow stakeholders to hold government accountable, to participate in dialogue, and to reduce uncertainty.*

Mobilize all stakeholders around a clear long-term growth strategy. Institutionalizing a reform process requires that it be part of a clear long-term strategy with measurable objectives, action plans, and responsibilities. It also needs to be carried by strong and cohesive leadership. Few MENA countries have communicated such a plan. Communicating the reform strategy, its implementation, and its evaluation should be an integral part of any successful private sector reform effort. Moreover, generating consensus may also require compensation of losers by putting in place an efficient social protection system that dampens the inevitable adjustments involved in economic transformation.

Looking Forward

A time of challenge, a sense of urgency:
seizing on current opportunities to unlock
the region's private sector potential.

MENA is at a crossroads. Reforms have progressed throughout the region, although at different paces. Despite the current global economic crisis, signs of positive expectations about the future and increased attractiveness to foreign investment are visible in almost every country. The coming years will be crucial for the region's economic future. Will the growth revival of recent years and private sector enthusiasm be strengthened beyond the current crisis and sustained? That will depend on the ability of each country's political leadership to commit credibly to change the deep-rooted status quo by pursuing difficult reforms that reduce discretion and inequities in the investment climate.

Despite the complex political economy of each country, opportunities are immense to advance toward sustained growth. Recent reforms that have tackled privileges and rents show the way forward. A more developmental private sector that supports further reform is slowly emerging. Examples can be found in almost every country. Recently successful experiences with regulatory and institutional reforms have reduced entry barriers in Egypt, Libya, Morocco, and Saudi Arabia. Several are leading the way in some areas—banking in Morocco, tax reform in Egypt, business entry in the Republic of Yemen, e-government in Dubai, and customs in Tunisia. Successful liberalization stories abound, such as for telecommunications in Algeria. These reforms have allowed many new businesses to enter the market and have created more diverse constituencies, ones demanding further reform. In Egypt, Jordan, Morocco, the United Arab Emirates, and other countries this new diversity of private sector actors is creating a dynamic of change, pressuring for more reforms. The ability of the rent-seeking private sector to maintain the status quo is diminished—even if it remains powerful in many countries.

All these scattered reform successes show that the key to stronger private sector–led growth is within reach. However, it will take political will—and time—to support sustained reforms that credibly address the real issues holding the region back and meet the expectations of investors and the public. It also will take a renewed and stronger commitment to long-term growth, one that mobilizes all stakeholders. The region's policy makers know the challenges and how crucial a stable and transparent climate for private investment is to growth, job creation, and social stability in their countries. All are endowed with strong human capital, good infrastructure, immense resources for some, and much creativity and entrepreneurship everywhere. The economic and social payoff of embarking on a more ambitious private-led growth agenda could thus be immense, for all.

Notes

1.   These are key messages of the recently released report of the Commission on Growth and Development (2008), "Strategies for Sustained Growth and Inclusive Development" (www.growthcommission.org).

2.   These interviews were conducted during various regional conferences organized by the World Bank in different MENA countries over the last two years on the topic of investment and private sector development. Officials invited at these conferences hold positions in ministries and agencies in charge of private sector development. Although these interviews are not a fully representative survey of officials in the region, they nevertheless represent evidence of widely held views. These interviews do not represent quantitative estimates of the extent of actual corruption and rent seeking in the private sector but are meant to highlight the lack of trust between the public and private sector and the perceptions that each group has about the other. These are important issues that affect the credibility of reforms and their impact.

CHAPTER 1

Voices of Entrepreneurs—Stories of Success, Hope, and Challenge

After independence, most countries in the Middle East and North Africa (MENA) adopted variants of a development model relying heavily on state intervention in all areas of economic activity. The characteristics of that model were state planning, industrial development through protected local markets, nationalizations of private sector assets, and redistributions of wealth through vast public expenditures directed to social development and large-scale public sector employment. Even when the private sector was tolerated (for example, in small domestic trade or services), it remained highly dependent on demand from the large public sector and constrained by the regulatory environment.

Resource allocation and public policies were geared toward public investment, especially in oil-rich countries after the dramatic rise of their hydrocarbon export revenues in the 1970s. Most resource-poor countries—such as Jordan, Morocco, and Tunisia—also adopted a state-driven growth model. Although the private sector (even large enterprises) was more tolerated in resource-poor countries than in resource-rich, labor-abundant ones, it was still severely constrained by regulations on prices, inputs, and trade. In the Gulf countries, the private sector operated mainly in trade and small service activities, but it was heavily dependent on the state through a rigid licensing allocation system, particularly in the lucrative import sectors.

The legacy of these early policy choices shaped the structure of the region's private sector and the pace and sequence of reforms. With sweeping nationalizations of industry, banking, trade, and agriculture resulting in a massive public enterprise sector, the limited formal private sector consisted mainly of small and often rent-seeking firms that benefited from state policies and spending. Many of these firms were protected from external and internal competition. The regulatory environment and exchange rate discouraged private investment and trade and impeded the development of competitive and export-oriented industrial sectors.

Following the collapse of oil prices in the mid-1980s and the subsequent balance-of-payments crises, a handful of MENA economies moved to more market-oriented economies, adopting macroeconomic stabilization programs and undertaking private sector and export reforms. By the 1990s most countries in the region had followed suit. These programs varied but generally included cutting subsidies, reducing public spending, liberalizing trade, reforming exchange rate regimes, encouraging exports, easing restrictions on foreign investment, privatizing state enterprises, and strengthening the institutional foundations of a market-led economy. The expectation was to create an environment for the private sector to expand and support greater job creation. The stabilization succeeded, and growth resumed by the end of the 1990s.

The ownership structure of MENA economies has changed fundamentally. Contrary to widespread belief, the private sector responded to the reforms, and today most MENA economies have moved from being public sector based to private sector based. To get a sense of the private sector, consider nonhydrocarbon gross domestic product (GDP) in oil-rich countries. The energy and mining sectors, consisting of a handful of enterprises, remain in state ownership and account for a significant part of these economies. Beyond these two sectors, however, most MENA countries look much like comparator countries in Eastern Europe or Asia, which have gone through such a transition from public to private, albeit much more rapidly (figure 1.1). Outside of the hydrocarbon and

FIGURE 1.1

Most MENA Economies Are Private Sector Based, 2005 and Previous Decades

(private sector share as percentage of nonhydrocarbon GDP)

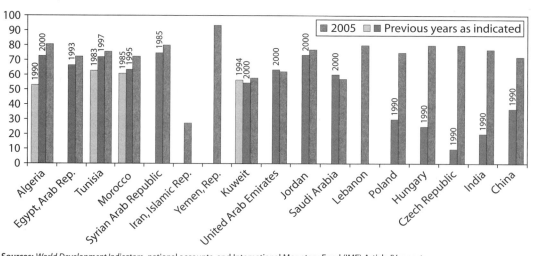

Sources: *World Development Indicators,* national accounts, and International Monetary Fund (IMF) Article IV reports.

mining sectors, the MENA countries are no longer public-sector–dominated economies.

Even if the majority of the productive base in MENA is in private hands, some countries (Algeria, the Islamic Republic of Iran, Libya, and the Syrian Arab Republic) still have manufacturing sectors with significant state ownership, with implications for their performance. Even so, these state-owned firms, expressed as a share of non-oil and nonmining GDP, represent a minority of business assets, and the private sector largely dominates. Except for resource-rich, labor-importing countries (Kuwait, Saudi Arabia, and the United Arab Emirates), where the share of the private sector in GDP lies at about 60 percent or less,[1] that share looks quite similar across the region, averaging 80 percent, close to that of Eastern Europe and Asia.[2]

Listening to Entrepreneurs

This evolution has profoundly shaped the private sector, which has grown more diverse and more dynamic than ever before. Entrepreneurs and private enterprises, ranging from informal street merchants to multinational corporations, are the economic actors that will create the wealth in support of future economic growth and job creation. Listening to their stories and experiences tells us much about the challenges the region faces.

Their experiences include stories of impressive successes on an international scale, less visible but no less remarkable achievements by local entrepreneurs across the region, challenges faced in conducting business, and sometimes tragic problems in conflict-affected areas. They include narratives of hope and enthusiasm, as well as all-too-common allegations of anticompetitive behavior and examples of unlevel playing fields.[3] As in other developing and developed regions, the private sector in the Middle East and North Africa embodies all these experiences and more. It is out of this diversity and these challenging environments that the potential for the future prosperity of the region lies.

Family Conglomerates—Building the Business Elite

From family business to the London Stock Exchange, the Arab Republic of Egypt's Orascom is undoubtedly the largest and most impressive of MENA's success stories. Founded by Onsi Sawiris, it dominates Egypt's telecommunication and construction sectors and is aggressively expanding across the Mediterranean region. A major player in telecommunications in Algeria, Greece, Iraq, Italy, Jordan, Tunisia, and elsewhere, the company is expanding its international reach through its construction subsidiary, Orascom Construction Industries. The family-owned group has been a pioneer in creating a privately owned multinational corporation in the Arab world, with shares of its telecommunications subsidiary publicly traded on the London Stock Exchange.

Orascom's story is a family story, like many in the region. Sawiris's sons Naguib, Nassef, and Samih lead the group's activities in telecommunications, construction, and hotel and real estate development (through its Orascom Hotels and Development subsidiary). Having transitioned to a world-class professionally managed group, this family should inspire many family entrepreneurs across the Arab world.

Other successful family-owned businesses abound in the region, often family groups operating in multiple sectors. Morocco's Ynna Holding is active in construction, tourism, and retail in Europe, Africa, and the Middle East. Owned by its founder, Miloud Chaabi, and his family, it is expected to go public in the medium term. Tunisia's Poulina, founded in the 1960s, operates in agribusiness, tourism, hotel development, and real estate. Cevital—Algeria's largest private enterprise—is another family group aggressively diversifying beyond agribusiness into retail trade, automobiles, media, desalination plants, energy production, glass, and petrochemicals. Nothing seems out of reach for founder Issad Rebrab, who began as an accountant in socialist Algeria in the 1960s. Rebrab, his daughter, and four sons each manage different parts of the group.

Politicians in Business

Many entrepreneurs in the region come from the highest political and country leadership spheres. In some countries, this is transparent and highly visible. In others, networks of businessmen allied with the ruling spheres of society, the military, or politicians dominate the private sector. Albeit less visible and transparent, these relations are often known. Finding a businessman with close ties to the political leadership is common. Although such ties are not always sufficient for success, they can often get things started in a heavily regulated environment. High entry barriers protecting monopolies, privileged positions in highly regulated sectors, preferential access to large public procurement contracts, and other noncompetitive practices made some of the region's most publicized and spectacular successes possible.

Indeed, when looking at the region's dominant business groups, one finds few stories of industrial success in competitive tradable sectors. Instead, real estate, retail, and regulated industries (telecommunications, pharmaceuticals, agribusiness, or trade)—or a combination of them in conglomerates controlled by large family groups—are the region's main source of business growth. Before diversifying, these companies made their fortunes in regulated sectors or when protected by a less business friendly environment (often dominated by state-owned firms). Some were privileged first-comers. Others benefited from lenient support from government in an import-substitution era—with subsidized loans, protected monopoly positions, and exclusive procurement contracts to state-owned enterprises.

Even so, these groups coped with competition, and they often grew independently from their state sponsors in complex environments and sophisticated sectors. Morocco's Banque Marocaine du Commerce Extérieur, now expanding in North and West Africa, is a prominent example. It was founded by the long-time symbol of Moroccan capitalism Othman Benjelloun, head of the Maghrebian Bankers Association, and is active in mobile telephony (Méditel), insurance, retail, transport, and tourism.

Even so, the networks of privileges and the nexus between politics and business hurt the credibility of governments and reformers in particular. The perception that connections are an important source of competitiveness (some say the most important) discourages many would-be entrepreneurs. Even governments that try to aggressively reform the business environment in their countries see the impact of their efforts lessened by the perception that things are not really changing because only connected entrepreneurs will be successful.

Less Visible Successes—Microenterprises and Returning Expatriates

Abounding in the region are smaller, less visible success stories in various sectors across the years, independent of any state-supported or privileged position. Hundreds of thousands of microenterprises (some only semiformal) have flourished in trade, services, and small industry as their economies opened. Emerging from the fastest growing sectors, microenterprises in nontradable industries have produced most of the recent employment growth (World Bank 2007b). Only a few of these firms will grow into small or medium-sized firms or expand to reach a market beyond their area of operations (or even neighborhood), let alone export. They remain vital in three respects, however. First, they provide employment, particularly for low-skilled labor, and are a social safety net for many people who cannot survive in larger firms. Second, those in services and trade support other parts of the economy. Third, some will do well and expand into medium-sized or large ventures.

Getting out of informality: from informal merchant to computer services provider. Such is the story of Abdullah Al Haythem, an entrepreneur from Oman, who started as a small (mostly informal) shop owner in downtown Muscat, expanded his shop to sell second-hand computers, and eventually grew to develop a successful computer repair services venture, employing four software engineers and even more technicians.

Signs of confidence: returning from the diaspora. More frequent are the stories of entrepreneurs from the diaspora who quit successful careers abroad and returned to their home country to launch a business. They reflect the growing confidence in MENA economies. Consider Eskadenia—the story of a Jordanian couple who worked for Ericsson in China, Dubai, Lebanon, and Sweden and decided to return to Jordan in 2000 to launch what grew into one of the largest and fastest-growing software firms in the Middle East. Their network of worldwide industry contacts from 30 years abroad helped them penetrate foreign markets quickly. Unable to tap startup capital from banks demanding high collateral, the partners self-financed the startup investment of about $600,000 and hoped to break even after three years. Today Eskadenia employs about 100 engineers, expects to double in size in the next two years, and exports 80 percent of its products to countries in the Middle East, Eastern Europe, and North Africa.

Government Successes and Pitfalls in Supporting the Private Sector

MENA governments have a long tradition of intervening in markets and supporting enterprises. Some of these interventions may have been useful. Others have benefited a few privileged firms, or have increased the dependence of a "rentier" private sector on government support.

Incomplete Markets and Information as Limiting Factors for the Expansion of Small and Medium-Sized Enterprises

In 2000 a Tunisian female entrepreneur owned a small subcontracting workshop in Sousse employing nine women to make lingerie for a Belgian company. The client exported the goods and provided material and inputs, paying her a fee for her labor. When asked why she did not procure the material herself, design her own products, and sell them directly in foreign markets, she responded:

> I am afraid to do it, because my sole client may learn about it, and I may lose him. You understand, I would need to invest a lot upfront in market research, travel abroad, and so on. Also, there is no one with expertise in Tunisia who could help me overcome these knowledge gaps. The upfront investment is just too high for me when I am very uncertain about the outcome. I just cannot afford it.

Upfront investment in the face of imperfect information about foreign markets and missing market for specific expertise are typical market failures that a well-designed government intervention could correct. That is precisely what a government program, Fonds d'Accès aux Marchés d'Exportation, provides in Tunisia (http://www.famex.org.tn). A public-private partnership, it is a network of consultancies in export market access—filling in the "missing market." Four years later, the Tunisian entrepreneur had enrolled in the program, entered four new export markets, and expanded her business out of subcontracting to get into design and direct exports.

The Heritage of Heavy Government Intervention: Traits of a "Rentier" Private Sector

Another Tunisian garment entrepreneur benefited from extensive state support through investment subsidies and grants to pay for external expertise, enabling him to export his spring collection of ladies' dresses to France and Italy. The collection was designed by a world-class French designer, who worked for two months at the firm's premises in Tunis. Most of the designer's trip and fees—totaling about $60,000—were paid by a government-sponsored program. When asked about the business environment constraints facing his firm, he answered:

> Overall, the business environment is good in Tunisia. The government supports the industry, as it did for the design of my spring collection. My only problem is that we can only benefit from that particular support program once. What am I going to do for the coming fall collection? This is a problem. The government should change its program and allow us to benefit from it more often.

This kind of dependence on government support characterizes many private firms across the region. It is typical of many MENA entrepreneurs who grow accustomed to state protection and support. Indeed, "additional government support and protection" is the dominant advocacy line of many business associations in the region.

Challenges Facing Entrepreneurs—From Regulatory Barriers to Conflict and War

Coping with Stringent Labor Regulations

Of 178 countries, Syria ranks 126th in the rigidity of its labor regulations. Severance pay is 80 weeks of salary for dismissing a redundant worker who has been in a firm for 20 years. When asked about how problematic this was, a Syrian manufacturing businessman replied:

> Not problematic at all . . . that legislation is the easiest to cope
> with. Any new recruit in my firm, from the production line worker
> to my managers, had to sign an undated resignation letter upon
> entry. I have one such letter for each one of my employees. If I
> need to dismiss any of them for whatever reason, I just include the
> appropriate date in the letter. Of course, social constraints prohibit
> me from abusing my employees, and I would never do that unless
> I am forced to by economic conditions or if a worker commits a se-
> rious mistake.

Other regulatory barriers include cumbersome legislation on employing
expatriates. Like other Gulf countries, Oman employs a large share of
foreign workers. To increase employment in the private sector for nationals, the government has launched a policy that encourages firms to recruit
Omanis. It obliges firm owners to recruit a specific share of nationals, a
share set administratively for each activity. This is the story of Mohammed
O., head of a small accounting firm that employs Indian expatriates:

> All my accountants are Indian. They're well trained and experi-
> enced. I understand the goals of Omanization and adhere to them,
> but I just can't replace part of my team like that, and I can't easily
> find these skills today in Oman. To abide by the law and avoid
> paying the fines associated with noncompliers, I had to artificially
> recruit Omanis—some of them friends. I reached the target ratio in
> the professional services sector. I did not need that extra labor as my
> business was stagnant. In theory they're on my payroll for low
> skilled support jobs, but in reality I have an arrangement with most
> of them. Many businessmen in the professional services sector
> do that.

Business-Entry Procedures—Often an Uncertain and Time-Consuming Process

Discretionary business-entry procedures often prevent potential entrepreneurs from realizing their ambitions. In Libya, the administrative
process to create a small, locally owned, and limited liability business is
rather simple. It includes an application form that describes the
envisaged activity and the background of the entrepreneur. The local
council then decides to grant the authorization to exercise the activity—
or not. Ahmed, a statistics graduate from the University of Tripoli,

wanted to open an Internet café in 2003. His recollection of the process reveals the fickle nature of government entities during such processes:

> I applied in March 2003. It was very simple and took me just a few days to get the paper work in, as I had the premises to start working. Unfortunately, my application was turned down in July that year. The local authority told me that my training did not prepare me to manage a small Internet business. I applied again, and again. It was declined three times before I finally could open my business in 2005.

Sector-Specific Constraints

Not all business environment constraints affect all firms. Many aspects of the investment climate are specific to certain sectors and activities. Such is the case in regulated sectors, for example, or in sectors that require specific investments and in the large retail industry. In 1998 a large and diversified family conglomerate in a large country of the region opened the first supermarket of a new chain. In 2005 it had 18 stores across the country. When asked about their business constraints, an executive from this chain replied:

> We would have opened more than 50 stores by now to meet the growing demand if opening branches was not so cumbersome. This is by far our biggest challenge. We have to deal with 11 different authorities at the local level to get approval. Typically, you get only a temporary approval that allows you to start operating, but final approval may be delayed for months and sometimes for years. Their temporary licenses must be renewed every six months. Many of the laws we are subject to date back to more than five decades, when there were no supermarkets, so the actual application is almost entirely discretionary.

Another investor in the growing retail sector of the region—a large international chain—faces a different constraint linked to its foreign ownership. One of its executives explained how the laws in a promising market favoring importers in that country affected the company's prices:

> Our company could not import goods for direct sale because only majority-owned firms from this country can do that. As a result, we had to go through a local intermediary import company. Therefore we could not get the price benefits of our large-scale import orders through our usual international procurement channels.

Gender-Specific Constraints

Some constraints in the business environment can be gender specific. Despite that, very successful women entrepreneurs have been able to rise all across the region. A female chief executive officer (CEO) and founder of an investment bank has secured commitments of multiple billions from investors to finance infrastructure projects across the Middle East and India. However, because the law in her country prohibits women from acting as CEOs, she could not register her bank. Rather than appoint a man to formally run her own company, she decided to register her bank in Bahrain, which has no such constraint on women.

Regulatory Barriers and Rent Seeking

Excessive licensing and unaccountable public agencies are a recipe for corruption, which deters investment. A hotel in the capital city of the region exemplifies the barriers—but variants are heard of everywhere. The hotel, a small operation of 40 rooms, with excellent quality service, had no restaurant. Here is the owner's account of trying to set one up:

> To attract more clients, especially foreign visitors, I really needed a restaurant. The problem is that according to our laws, I needed a separate license for the restaurant. The hotel one was not enough. I eventually got it. I invested $200,000 in furniture and equipment. When I was ready to start, the whole venture collapsed: a representative of one of the four government agencies regulating the tourism industry visited the hotel, claimed that the license for the restaurant was not enough, and requested a large bribe for another license. I refused and decided to go out of the hotel business. I am now leasing my property on a long-term contract—a line of business that is regulated by only one government agency.

Conflicts and War

In some MENA countries the private sector also suffers from instability and war. Conflicts—actual, potential, or residual—greatly affect the uncertainty and type of investments, because entrepreneurs' short-term horizons favor more liquid assets. The following example from an entrepreneur affected by the 2006 war in Lebanon speaks for itself:

> My ready-wear garment factory employed 25 people. It was completely destroyed and burned. It was in a 12-story building that collapsed. Our area in South Beirut was totally destroyed: machines,

merchandise, a complete loss. Since then, I've just filled out applications; there have been lots of visits from officials. All the workers are at home—they haven't left. Their families are there. We want help to begin the business again. We want help for the workers.

Beyond the human cost, wars damage a country's infrastructure and business community—but peace and reconstruction can improve future business prospects. In the West Bank and Gaza economies, the stalemate in the peace process and the constraints on moving goods and people, in addition to the Gaza blockade, have created uninterrupted barriers to Palestinian businesses for years. Many have closed or moved to other areas, such as the leading Palestinian furniture manufacturer, Shawa Furniture Company. Founded in Gaza City in 1990 with an initial investment of $800,000, Shawa's Gaza plant employed 30 workers and produced home furniture exclusively for the Israeli market because of restrictions on access to other export markets. Here is its story:

> Following the closure of the Gaza Strip, the company had to shut down its plant in August 2006 and move to Port Said in Egypt. The business now faces a different type of constraint—mainly through its interactions with public agencies, but that move enabled the firm to enter new export markets in Jordan, Libya, and the United Arab Emirates. Today it employs a skilled workforce of 60 Egyptian craftsmen and women. However, it has no more operations in Palestine, where the 30 skilled employees have been unemployed since the plant's closure.

War and macroeconomic instability hurt most investors equally—but other dimensions of the business environment can hurt some and help others. In such contexts entrepreneurs with connections can turn into highly successful businessmen. Although a recipe for success only for the happy few with the right connections, an unlevel playing field, with high barriers to entry, damages the credibility of economic policies and the prospects for long-term growth.

Privileges, Unlevel Playing Fields, and the Credibility of the Reforms

The private sector in the Middle East and North Africa is full of stories of privileges and unlevel playing fields. These stories are symptoms of poor governance in some public agencies and in the private sector. They hurt the credibility of reforms that governments might be struggling to implement. They also reflect the unlevel playing field in the business environment across the region, as well as the daunting challenges that genuine reformers face in the region. The political economies in these countries are not monolithic. Different interests and ambitions compete. The instances of state capture by business reveal the strength of opponents to profound and credible reform.

Partners and Invisible Shareholders—When Powerful Officials and Good Connections Matter

Consider the story of a young entrepreneur in the region, who in 2004 inherited his late father's construction business:

> My father's business was quite successful and depended heavily on bidding for public construction contracts. Eager to take it on, I discovered after he passed away that he had an invisible partner, a high-ranking officer from the army, who secretly owned 50 percent of the shares of the family's venture. I decided to disinvest from that enterprise and run my own business in another sector. I may not be very successful, but I figured I did not have any heavy connection or any value-added to bring to that business partner.

Here is the story of two prominent entrepreneurs who hold strong ties to the ruling circles in their countries. In 2001 both were investing in each other's country in different sectors. Such privileged cross-country investment, although profitable for the well connected, can hinder opportunities for reform. One investor recalled their encounter:

> As I was going through the investment process in that country and had already transferred the initial capital, I was contacted by a local entrepreneur whom I knew was close to the country's leadership. He offered to take part in my venture with a 25 percent share, bringing in a free land plot . . . and assurances that the investment would proceed smoothly with "no administrative hassle." I knew what that meant, of course, and the risk it involved for my control of the enterprise. Fortunately, I knew of ongoing investment in my own country. I made him understand that we would both gain in our respective countries to have our investments proceed smoothly, but also by staying away from each other's businesses as I could also make things difficult for him in my country, thanks to my own connections.

These cross-country investments proved successful for both well-connected entrepreneurs. That is good news for them, but they probably have further eroded the credibility of reforms in their countries in the eyes of other local and foreign investors who are not as well connected.

Tariffs, Market Institutions, and the Rule of Law—Not the Same for All

Corruption, privilege, and unfair competition are also reflected in the all-too-common story of groups of importers—some known to hold close ties to political leaders, (officially) bringing in Asian consumer goods at zero tariffs, only to flood their local markets and reap the difference with the official tariff rate on such goods at the expense of consumers and the supposedly protected local industries. Consider a conglomerate controlled by one powerful family—through a complex web of cross-ownerships—that dominates most sectors of the economy (banking, telecommunications, retail, automobile, media, agribusiness, mining, insurance, and fuel distribution). Consider, too, the foreign investor accused of dumping by the suddenly active antitrust agency because a firm indirectly owned by a political leader is competing in the same sector. These are stories that resonate in many places in the region.

Corruption: *Wasta, Pistons,* and Other Innovative Means to Get Things Done

The private sector also includes widespread but less visible stories across the region of large discretionary powers in the hands of local officials.[4] Such is often the case in the allocation of subsidized public land (industrial or commercial)—a source of large rents that produces corruption, inefficient asset allocations, and high barriers to entry. Corruption in public banks, directed credit to political clientele, forgiven nonperforming loans, and numerous scandals involving unaccountable politicians and noncompetitive procurement of large public contracts are common, notwithstanding greater policy maker attention to reforming governance systems.

Interviews with entrepreneurs in medium-sized manufacturing industries in MENA countries reveal how they perceive such influence as unfairly hurting their businesses:

> By corruption I mean the use of influence. People stealing public resources and taking bribes. People in the ruling party wear two hats—they are a key party member and they are in the private sector. Corruption affects your productivity. For example, if you send a driver with goods, the police stop him and take bribes.

The government overlooks tax evasion and behind-the-scenes workshops, yet we receive sharp punishment for trivial mistakes.

There is unequal opportunity. If someone has influence, he gets infrastructure and paved roads, an electric transformer, and water supply. It depends on your name.

Any error in the product labeling—for example, a smudged expiry date—is considered a misdemeanor with a penalty of up to one year in prison. This is why we have two factory operations managers: one to manage the factory, and one to show up in court throughout the year. Unless you're ready to pay bribes, there's no way out of this harassment.

We have a factory that has been operating for 12 years. Until now, we still have not been able to register the land. The threat of eviction that hangs upon us is used to extract bribes from us once or twice a year.

Such stories and experiences are well known in the region. Widespread in both developing and developed countries, they are not unique to MENA, but each adds to the deficit of trust many citizens have in their governments. These stories hurt the reputation of the private sector, and, most important, they hurt the credibility of reforms and those who pursue them. They reinforce the (often justified) perception that competition in the private sector is not on a level playing field and that connections are the most important asset for business success, not management skills or innovation.

Hope and Enthusiasm for the Future

The region is at a turning point in expectations. Investors—local and foreign—are betting that the wind of economic reform will be sustained. Governments face the challenge of meeting these expectations.

Credible Reforms Tilting Expectations

Egypt's Azza Fahmy illustrates this renewed enthusiasm and how positive expectations about government commitments to reform can spur investment. Thirty years after founding a small jewelry design workshop, she manages an organization of more than 160 employees, with marketing, sales, design, planning, and quality control departments. Internationally recognized, Azza Fahmy Jewelry has recently expanded to become a leading designer in the Arab world and Egypt's first designer label, with a presence in Bahrain, Dubai, Jordan, London, and Qatar. Says Azza:

> The Egyptian government's commitment to reform is one of the most important ingredients to our recent success. Before 2004, a number of obstacles regarding property registration, taxation, and trade barriers hindered our expansion. With the appointment of a reform-oriented government that tackled these obstacles aggressively, I thought that the time was ripe to bet on the future and expand. Since then, our sales have grown at about 30 percent annually, and we now export 35 percent of output.

Azza adds, "We benefited from the corrective measures taken [by the new government] to enhance the investment climate, including amendments of a number of legislations related to tax, land registration, and simplification of the business registration process." These reforms raised her expectations about the future, leading her to invest heavily. She is also a member of the jewelry sector's steering committee, working with the government to develop the industry. Greater collaboration between the public and private sectors is also a sign of changing times. As she says, "We are part of the reform process. We sit with the policy makers and contribute to the formulation of new laws and regulations. The government now listens to the concerns of the private sector, and this has made a big difference."

Signs of Greater Trust and Better Public-Private Cooperation

Improving relations between the government and the private sector is key to building coalitions for reform. The recent partnership between the government of Algeria and window maker BKL Industries could mean that the tumultuous and distrustful relationship between the Algerian private sector and its government is improving. BKL Executive Vice President Samy Boukaila initiated the partnership. To expand BKL's distribution franchise—Dar BKL—Boukaila approached the head of the government-sponsored youth entrepreneurship program Agence Nationale de Soutien à l'Emploi des Jeunes (ANSEJ), which provides seed capital and credit guarantees for young entrepreneurs. Created in 2008, the partnership includes an agreement among ANSEJ, BKL, and the Banque Extérieure d'Algérie. ANSEJ and BKL jointly select young entrepreneurs applying to launch a BKL franchise in their region. ANSEJ provides the seed financing for the new venture, as well as a credit guarantee. The bank partner supplies the rest of the financing, and BKL provides the franchise contracting arrangement and trains the new franchisees, in partnership with the Ecole Supérieure des Affaires d'Alger business school. This innovative public-private partnership can be a model for improved relations between the state and the private sector in the whole region.

Signs of Growing Interest from International Companies

Positive expectations are also tilting the perception of international companies—renewing their eagerness to invest in the region. Consider automaker Renault-Nissan, which announced in summer 2007 its plan to invest nearly $1.5 billion in Morocco in what is to become the largest auto plant in the Mediterranean region and Eastern Europe. Major suppliers to the automobile industry followed suit and announced their intension to invest in Tangiers, where the French automaker will be producing 200,000 cars starting in 2010, and twice that number starting in 2012. With direct and indirect employment creation of about 30,000 workers, this investment will spur an important industrial cluster in the region.

What Does It Take to Tilt the Priors on a Country?

What led CEO of Renault-Nissan Carlos Ghosn to choose Morocco instead of other locations in North Africa or competing locations in Romania or Turkey? The opening of TangerMed's world-class port infrastructure is one reason. A dedicated terminal in that port, as an export platform for the automaker at (subsidized) preferential rates, is another. A free land plot and other subsidies must have helped. Help from the highest authorities to make that deal happen was another key. The series of reforms over the last few years (in customs, trade liberalization, transport and logistics, the banking sector, and so on)—a strong positive indication of the government's commitment to making Morocco more business friendly—must have been another crucial factor. Amid rumors that the global recession may cause Renault to cancel its investment, the CEO confirmed in June 2009 that the plant would start production on time, even if Nissan decided to put its (small) share of the deal on hold.

This story illustrates what it can take to tilt investor expectations: a mix of consistent and sustained policy reforms, world-class infrastructure, public-private consultation, strong signals and commitment from government, and, where justified, a dose of targeted support. Although they are not found everywhere nor are they simultaneous, signs of enthusiasm about the private sector, positive expectations about the future, and increased attractiveness to foreign investment are more visible in MENA.

Together, these stories paint a picture of the private sector in MENA. Entrepreneurs are exploiting the opportunities offered by reforms and are betting on future improvements as well as looking beyond their borders. Connected businessmen have benefited from past (and sometimes continuing) protection and regulations. Some have built large conglomerates spanning many sectors and are now major players in their economies. Many have grown less dependent on the connections and privileges that spurred their initial success and are embracing international competitors in their countries and beyond.

The MENA private sector, however, is also the story of smaller entrepreneurs coping with difficult investment climates and unlevel playing fields. Too often, inequitable business environments make it easier for some insiders to conduct business and harder for outsiders. The private sector is seldom able to advocate for its collective interests, either because it is not allowed to organize or because the few businessmen that speak for it pursue personal interests.

Even so, the private sector is more diversified and maturing in a more competitive environment, and it sees the benefits of less government intervention and smarter government initiatives to correct for market failures. The agenda for MENA governments should include improving the business environment, confronting the costs of poor public governance by increasing market accountability and reducing the discretionary behavior of public administration, and implementing well-designed interventions to address market failures. If reformers embrace this agenda with commitment and credibility, the private sector, in all its diversity, will respond and invest in the future.

Notes

1. These lower shares in Gulf Cooperation Council countries possibly reflect the fact that they do not include state-owned enterprises, which in their governance setup behave more like private entities. Examples include sovereign investment funds, construction service conglomerates such as Dubai World Ports, and airlines. The line between public and private ownership is quite difficult to draw in this subregion because many members of the ruling families are in high-level official positions in the government or the public sector, and at the same time are shareholders in major private ventures.

2. The exception is the Islamic Republic of Iran, where this share is estimated at 28 percent (IMF Article IV Report 2006). That number should be taken with caution, however, and may underestimate the actual share of private sector in GDP. One explanation is that many Iranian

enterprises are part of parapublic conglomerates owned by religious and charitable foundations called *Bonyads*, which are not counted as private sector.

3. Some of these stories are reported with no mention of the name of the firm or the country when they touch on sensitive governance and corruption issues.

4. Terms for corruption, privilege, and connections to "get things done" vary across countries. *Wasta* (Arabic for *intermediary*) is often used in the Middle East; meanwhile *piston* (French for *plunger*, meaning *to push things*) is common in the Maghreb.

Private Sector Performance in the MENA Region: Explaining the Untapped Potential

Is there really a performance problem with private sector development and growth in the MENA region? If yes, what holds back the private sector in sustaining stronger growth? Is it about insufficient reforms or something else? Part I offers some answers.

First, chapter 2 tries to assess the performance of private-led growth in MENA from different angles: macroeconomic performance, export growth and diversification, private investment, foreign direct investment, firm-level productivity, and so on. Although private investment rates have risen recently and the precrisis growth rates have also increased across the region, the macroeconomic and firm-level evidence does not offer signs that the countries in the region are on paths of sustained growth accelerations—especially in their export growth and diversification.

To explain this inadequate performance, chapter 3 introduces a simple framework that distinguishes between the different areas of the business environment that firms face in rules, regulations, and policies as enacted and the way that these rules, regulations, and policies are actually applied to different types of firms by different public agencies and institutions. The larger the gap between the two, the lower the credibility and impact of government reforms. The framework helps to distinguish between how the business environment is usually benchmarked and measured and how different investors experience it in the field.

Chapter 4 shows that the business environment in most MENA countries does not appear much worse than that in several high-growth countries. Apart from a few lagging countries and specific areas, the lackluster overall performance of the private sector cannot be fully attributed to missing policy reforms. The problem has been more the inadequate response of the private sector to reforms, due to a gap between the rules and the way they are implemented. Policy uncertainty linked to inconsistency and discretion in the way regulations and policies are actually implemented is an issue for investors, much more than the lack of good rules and policies.

The chapter offers evidence of symptoms in the structure and dynamism of the private sector that are consistent with a business environment that is not the same for all firms. Barriers to competition limit the entry and exit of firms, leading to older firms, older businessmen, fewer registered firms, and less competitive pressure than elsewhere. This is all consistent with rules and regulations that are implemented in a discretionary and inconsistent manner, for the benefit of some, while keeping the business environment difficult for many.

CHAPTER 2

Searching for Signs of Sustained Private-Led Growth in MENA

All MENA countries have enjoyed a growth revival over the last few years before the current global crisis, fueled mainly by the oil boom in resource-rich countries. Even the nonhydrocarbon sectors have been expanding quickly—faster than the oil sector in some cases. Non-oil economies have exhibited the strongest growth outside the Gulf Cooperation Council (GCC) countries. Over the long term, however, the performance has been disappointing, and the recent surge may not be sustained. In addition, the current crisis has affected the enthusiasm for private-led growth across the region over the last few years, and uncertainty about the sustainability of the recent growth is palpable among policy makers, private businessmen, and analysts.

The recent growth boom differed from previous episodes in that it was driven much more by the private sector—a reflection that private investors have responded to reforms. However, few signs can be observed of a sustained and structural transformation of the economy. The private sector does not exhibit the usual features that sustain high growth, as in Asia and other parts of the world: economic diversification, especially through exports, increased private investment rates, and a dynamic process of creative destruction by which firms enter and exit the market much more rapidly.

The private sector's contribution to total investment, although increasing over the years, remains the lowest among developing regions. Private investment rates are the lowest in non-GCC oil countries (Algeria, the Islamic Republic of Iran, Iraq, Syria, and the Republic of Yemen). They are higher in resource-poor and GCC countries but far below the rates in high-growth countries of East Asia and Eastern Europe. Rising foreign direct investment (FDI) over the last few years went disproportionally into nontradable sectors in resource-poor countries and into the energy sector in oil-rich countries. There is evidence of Dutch disease contagion from oil-rich GCC countries to other parts of the region. The share of manufacturing in investment is declining almost everywhere, and the share of manufacturing in gross domestic product (GDP) is lower than that in all other developing regions, except Sub-Saharan Africa.

Using export performance and diversification to assess the private sector's competitiveness, the chapter highlights the poor performance of non-GCC oil-rich countries. Resource-poor countries have improved over the last decade, but they still fall far short in export diversification. The poor performance of firms confirms this trend.

The region's economies are diverse, with significant variation in the development of the private sector. Resource-poor labor-abundant economies (Egypt, Lebanon, Morocco, Tunisia, and West Bank and Gaza economies), early reformers in the region, have made more progress in encouraging private sector development than have the region's oil-rich countries, measured by a range of indicators, including size, employment, and investment, as well as small business development, non-oil export market development, and productivity. Among the oil economies, there is also substantial variation in the performance of the private sector between the resource-rich, labor-importing economies (Bahrain, Kuwait, Oman, Qatar, Saudi Arabia, and the United Arab Emirates)[1] and the resource-rich, labor-abundant economies (Algeria, the Islamic Republic of Iran, Iraq, Syria, and the Republic of Yemen), which have been far less successful in most aspects of private sector development.

This chapter looks first at the overall growth performance of the region—with the understanding that this performance is not solely attributable to the performance of the private sector, especially in previous decades when the state dominated economic activities in many countries. It then looks at the performance of the private sector at the firm level and at a more macroeconomic level.

The Growth of MENA Economies

Almost all MENA economies were growing quickly over the years before the current global slowdown. All were creating jobs at an increased pace. Private sector dynamism seems to have risen everywhere. Will this be sustained beyond the economic crisis? Have countries in the region joined the select group of developing economies that are on the path to convergence with high-income countries? These are the difficult questions this section aims to address. As the main source of sustained growth is the private sector in each MENA country, assessing its capacity to sustain the growth acceleration is the fundamental question addressed here.

Average real GDP growth in MENA rose from 3.6 percent a year between 1996 and 1999 to 4.6 percent between 2000 and 2003 and to 5.8 percent between 2004 and 2008. It is expected to ease to 3 percent in 2009, given the global financial crisis and economic slowdown, and to bounce back to 5.5 percent by 2010 (World Bank 2009). The precrisis revival has been remarkably widespread. Fueled by high hydrocarbon prices, it has been strongest in resource-rich, labor-importing countries of the GCC and Libya, with growth fluctuating around 7.6 percent between 2003 and 2008.

This was not just an oil-boom story: resource-poor countries also grew at 6.3 percent in 2006, with a slight drop to 5.3 percent in 2007. Even in resource-rich, labor-abundant countries, the annual growth of their nonhydrocarbon GDP, 5.6 percent between 2004 and 2006, surpassed overall GDP growth of 4.6 percent.[2]

The resource-poor countries have also grown between 2004 and 2008 despite higher energy prices. This is thanks in part to a better business environment. The reforms that started in the mid-1990s are paying off, but uncertainty remains about their sustainability.

Also supporting the precrisis growth revival is an increase in total factor productivity: the region's human and physical assets are being used more efficiently, with an average annual increase of about 0.5 percent since 2000, probably reflecting the greater openness to local and foreign competition. This contrasts with the long-term negative trend in productivity in the oil countries (more than −1 percent annual decline between 1970 and 2000) and the flat trend in non-oil countries. Parts of the region may thus be at a turning point in their growth and development.

So growth is strong in the region (even with the current crisis, growth is expected to rebound in 2010), total productivity is up, and unemployment is down in all but four countries. Will this be sustained when the crisis is over? Is the region converging to high-growth countries and catching up with the Organisation for Economic Co-operation and Development (OECD) economies? Putting the precrisis growth acceleration in a global and long-term perspective suggests that it is not.

Stepping Back: A Long-Term International Perspective on the Region's Growth

The growth acceleration looks more modest when compared with East Asia, Eastern and Central Europe, and even Sub-Saharan Africa over 2000–07 (figure 2.1). Of the developing regions, only Latin America and the Caribbean are weaker than MENA over the long term and in recent years.

Labor-abundant countries, whether resource-rich or resource-poor, on average underperformed over the last few decades in relation to what their country characteristics, investments, and policies would have predicted.[3] Resource-rich, labor-abundant countries grew, on average, at

FIGURE 2.1

Middle East and North Africa's Weak Growth in International Perspective
(percent)

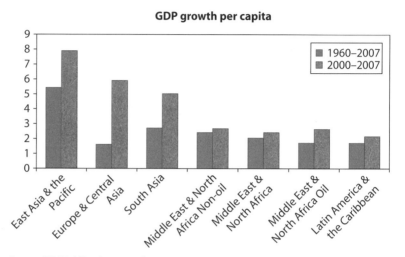

Sources: IMF, *World Development Indicators.*

1 percentage point below what international experience would have predicted, and resource-poor countries, at 1.6 percentage points below (figure 2.2).

By contrast, resource-rich, labor-importing countries of the GCC performed well given their endowments and policy choices. This is all the more remarkable because large natural resource endowments on average reduce long-term growth—the resource curse. This performance reflects the better business environment in these countries, particularly the credibility of policies. Many of these countries have also put in place the sectoral policies and infrastructure investments to build strong comparative advantages in regional financial services, air transport, business travel, real estate, media, construction services, and even port services. Good business environment policies and well-designed sectoral strategies proved to be a successful recipe for the economic diversification of the United Arab Emirates and, later, Bahrain, Qatar, and other GCC economies. Whether these success stories can be replicated to other bigger MENA countries remains questionable.

Using decade growth rates for 88 countries since the 1960s, one can try to see how the MENA region performed relative to the world economy, given its large investments in social and physical infrastructure over the last few decades. The analysis also accounts for the rate of private investment and the policies in each country, such as trade

FIGURE 2.2

Middle East and North Africa's Growth over the Long Term

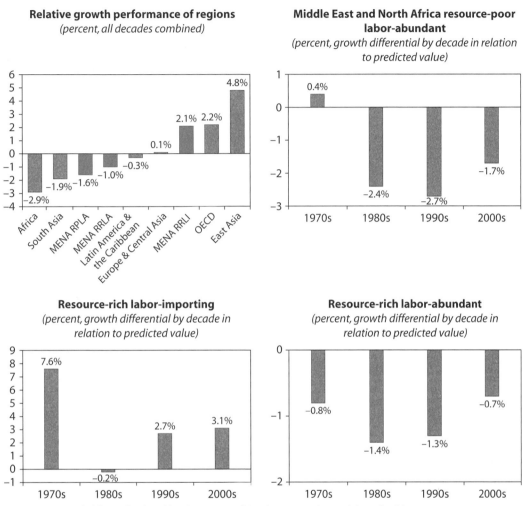

Relative growth performance of regions
(percent, all decades combined)

Middle East and North Africa resource-poor labor-abundant
(percent, growth differential by decade in relation to predicted value)

Resource-rich labor-importing
(percent, growth differential by decade in relation to predicted value)

Resource-rich labor-abundant
(percent, growth differential by decade in relation to predicted value)

Note: Average growth differential with world performance, conditional on country characteristics and policies.

Sources: Authors' calculation using the *World Development Indicators,* national account sources for private investment; International Country Risk Guide indicators.

openness, inflation, the black market premium, government consumption, as well as other country characteristics, such as the population growth rate or indices of the rule of law. Because many countries are rich in hydrocarbons, the regression also controlled for that, as well as for changes in the terms of trade of commodities across decades. Obviously, not all factors affecting growth are included, so the estimated overperformance or underperformance of each economy reflects the contribution of other variables that could not be observed or measured over time.

The Recent Growth Acceleration Raises Hopes and Uncertainties about Its Sustainability

The region has enjoyed growth booms before. In the 1960s and 1970s, it was among the fastest growing in the world. The difference today is that growth is led far more by the private sector. In fact, private investment rates have been rising in all parts of the region since 2003. Outside mining and hydrocarbons, the economies of the region now rely much more on private enterprises operating in relatively open and unregulated markets. This is especially apparent in resource-rich, labor-abundant countries, which went furthest with the state-driven model of development.

Uncertainties about the sustainability of this surge are no longer directly related to state ownership of firms. No single factor can account for the growth surge. What clearly did not drive it—exports—raises doubts about its sustainability.

The growth in recent years (unlike that of other fast-growing regions such as East Asia or Eastern Europe) appears to rest on domestic non-tradables. Private consumption and domestic investment provided the bulk of the regional GDP growth in 2007, with government consumption contributing 2.6 percentage points in resource-rich, labor-importing countries and one percentage point in resource-rich, labor-abundant countries (figure 2.3). Domestic demand is clearly fueled by higher oil revenues. Resource-poor countries also benefit from windfalls that support domestic demand and investment. The most important factors behind this growth in demand include the foreign investment in real estate and tourist resorts that comes in great part from oil-rich countries, the exceptionally high growth of world tourism since 2003, and the steady rise of immigrant remittances, reflecting greater confidence in their home countries.

An Economy-Wide Perspective

This section assesses the private sector from an economy-wide perspective, looking at the share of private investment in total investment, the share of private investment in GDP, the inflows of FDI, the returns to private investment in relation to productivity growth, and the growth, composition, and diversification of exports.

The World's Lowest Share of Private Investment in Total Investment

One measure of the role of the private sector in the economy is its investment as a share of total investment. Since the early 1980s the shares

FIGURE 2.3

Contributions to the Growth of GDP in 2007—Insufficient Role for Exports

(percentage point contribution)

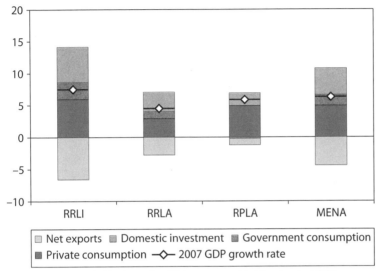

Note: RRLI = resource-rich, labor-importing; RRLA = resource-rich, labor-abundant; RPLA = resource-poor, labor-abundant; MENA = Middle East and North Africa.

Source: World Bank 2007b.

of the private sector in total investment for MENA oil and non-oil countries followed the worldwide trend (figure 2.4). They have been higher in non-oil countries than in oil countries, and they have leveled off since the mid-1990s, while increasing steadily in both Europe and Central Asia and Latin America and the Caribbean. Those shares, however, have consistently been the lowest in the world. Despite the fact that the private sector produces most of the value-added in MENA economies, public investment in the region remains higher as a share of total investment than elsewhere.

Encouraging Trends—But a Long Way to Go

Private investment as a share of GDP is clearly lagging in the region (figure 2.5). Except in the Republic of Yemen, it is lower in resource-rich, labor-abundant countries than in resource-poor countries, which started private sector reforms earlier and went much deeper than the oil-rich countries. Resource-rich GCC countries (except Saudi Arabia) enjoy rates of private investment similar to those of the resource-poor economies. They have better investment climates, and their private

FIGURE 2.4

Private Investment as a Share of Total Investment
(percent of total investment, four-year moving average)

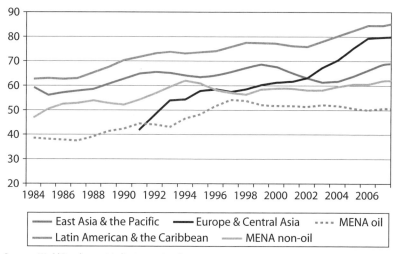

Sources: *World Development Indicators*, national accounts.

investments include those by foreign oil companies. With the hydro-carbon sector being very intensive in capital, the higher shares proba-bly also reflect the predominance of oil in these economies. They also include domestic investments of sovereign wealth funds in some countries.

The gap in private investment shares between MENA countries and the fast growers in Eastern Europe and Asia largely reflects the differ-ences in growth rates. Between 1995 and 2006 private investment shares increased only in Djibouti, Egypt, and Morocco—and to less extent in Tunisia.[4] This contrasts with the large jumps in comparator countries.

The growth of private investment over the last two decades has also been the slowest in the developing world, averaging 1.2 percent a year between the early 1980s and the mid-2000s, compared with more than 2 percent in Latin America and the Caribbean and Europe and Cen-tral Asia,[5] more than 3 percent in Sub-Saharan Africa, more than 6 per-cent in South Asia, and more than 11 percent in East Asia and the Pacific (figure 2.6). Since 2000 the region's private investment has risen by an average of 11 percent a year, below the developing world's aver-age of 16 percent a year and below that of all other regions but Latin America.[6]

FIGURE 2.5

Private Investment as a Share of GDP, 1995–2006
(percent)

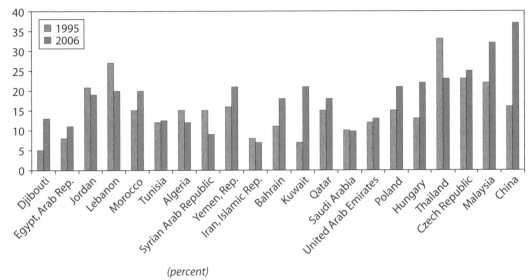

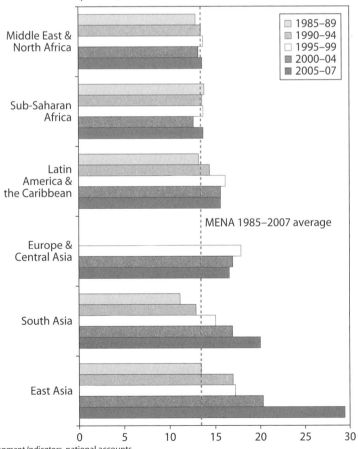

Sources: *World Development Indicators,* national accounts.

FIGURE 2.6

Gross Private Investment, 1980–2006

(average percent growth per year)

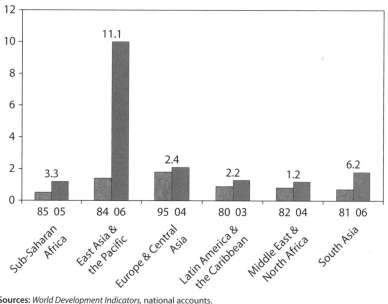

Sources: *World Development Indicators,* national accounts.

Foreign Direct Investment and Signs of the "Contagion" of Dutch Disease

MENA countries have also been much less successful than others in attracting FDI, which has barely risen as a share of regional GDP over the last 35 years (figure 2.7). This signals the lack of opportunities

FIGURE 2.7

Net FDI Flows as a Share of GDP, 1970–2005

(percent)

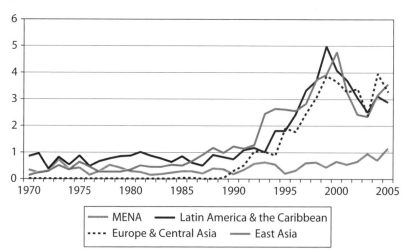

Sources: *World Development Indicators,* national accounts.

FIGURE 2.8

Structure of Foreign Direct Investment, Cumulative 2000–07
(percent of FDI)

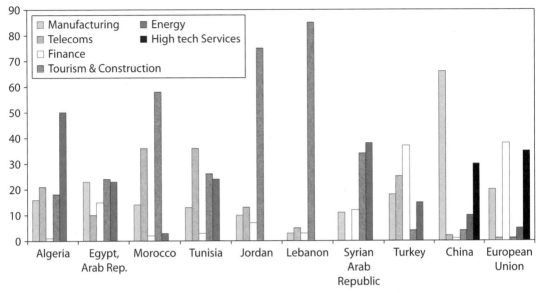

Sources: United National Conference on Trade and Development, *World Development Indicators,* national accounts.

for foreigners to invest, the unattractiveness of the local business environment, and the perceptions of higher risk in some countries. Intraregional variation exists on these, but the lower flows of FDI over the years (outside the hydrocarbon sectors) are evidence of a region that is perceived as less business friendly.

Most FDI outside of the energy sector has been directed to nontradables: typically tourism, telecoms, and real estate, with little to export-oriented manufacturing (on average less than 20 percent) or high-tech services (except telecoms) (figure 2.8). Domestic investment also flowed predominantly into nontraded sectors, such as housing and real estate, with only a fraction into manufacturing and services that have export potential.

These trends in FDI suggest that the region's countries—oil and non-oil—may be suffering from Dutch disease with investment flowing to nontradables because of the declining competitiveness of tradable manufacturing sectors. Contrary to fast-growing Eastern Europe and Asia, FDI in resource-rich and resource-poor countries is not driving MENA's exports. This does not necessarily mean manufacturing is less open to foreign investment, but nontradables look more attractive to foreign investors than manufacturing. This is particularly the case in oil-rich countries,[7] which traditionally have low export competitiveness.

The sectors disproportionally benefiting from foreign and local investment—real estate, tourism, and so on—are not to blame. Tourism can be a formidable source of job creation, of learning by doing, and of human capital formation. The growth of real estate and construction is also creates jobs and demand for new services. But the lack of balance in the allocation of investments suggests that Dutch disease may be at play.

The Dutch disease syndrome is unsurprising in resource-rich countries, but it seems also to affect resource-poor countries, at least in the sectoral composition of FDI. One hypothesis is that, in this era of exceptionally high oil prices, the "disease" has become contagious and is being transmitted to resource-poor countries because of the oil revenue surpluses of the GCC countries, part of which are being invested in the region. In recent years the Gulf countries have become the largest foreign investors in the MENA region with 36 percent of investments, ahead of Europe (25 percent), North America (31 percent), Asia (4 percent), and the other MENA countries (3.5 percent). In 2006, 56 percent of FDI came from developed countries (United States and Europe) and 44 percent from "new players" (four-fifths from Gulf countries).

This increase in intraregional investments is positive. Even if it comes mostly from the oil boom and may not last, the greater integration of the MENA region reflects the improved business environment and attractiveness of these countries. Other factors include the fast growth of the world tourism industry, especially in Egypt, Jordan, Morocco, and Tunisia. Tourism growth has positive effects on construction, real estate, and services in these countries—fueling high returns at the expense of the tradable manufacturing. Increased remittances from migrants (from the GCC to Egypt and from Europe to the Maghreb) also present a windfall of external resources,[8] which may last for some time. They, too, are a result of the reforms and the greater attractiveness of the recipient country—a sort of price of success. For tourism the benefits may more than compensate for the costs. Tourism provides foreign exchange to the recipient countries, is a strong source of job creation and learning, and offers opportunities for innovation and expansion.

Export Trends, Composition, and Diversification

Among all indicators, weak exports are the most reliable reflection of the limited potential of the current MENA private sector to sustain economic growth. Based on the surge in research on this topic over the past years, it is now beyond doubt that more—and more diversified—exports were consistently part of the stories of countries that sustained strong growth in recent decades (box 2.1). With the possible exception of resource-rich countries such as Botswana or India—which was able to

BOX 2.1

An Emerging Consensus on the Link between Export Diversification and Growth

Recent literature has shown a strong positive relationship between export diversification and growth. Lederman and Maloney (2003) find a negative correlation between export concentration and GDP growth. Klinger and Lederman (2004) find robust evidence that a country's export basket becomes more diversified as its income rises.

The relationship between export diversification and growth operates through three channels. First, export diversification leads to higher productivity through knowledge spillovers. Second, a more diversified export structure stimulates new industries and expands existing industries elsewhere in the economy, particularly if diversification takes place through adding new exports to the existing export basket. Third, export diversification reduces the volatility of export revenue.

Does This Mean That All MENA Economies Have to Follow the "Manufacturing Exports" Route to Economic Development?

For *resource-poor, labor-abundant* countries that have some diversification (Egypt, Lebanon, Jordan, Morocco, and Tunisia) the answer is most likely yes. Even if a few niches of nontradable service sectors could provide long-term growth (for example, in health services, or in financial services in countries such as Lebanon), competitiveness in a diversified tradable sector (particularly manufacturing, but not exclusively) will most likely be the path that these countries will need to embrace, to follow the Republic of Korea, Malaysia, Poland, and other "growth stars," and to sustain high growth rates and converge to OECD incomes.

For *resource-rich, labor-abundant countries* (Algeria, the Islamic Republic of Iran, Syria, and the Republic of Yemen) the transition to such a growth path may be slower and more difficult because of the pressure of hydrocarbon resources on their competitiveness. For growth to be sustained, it will also need to rest on strong diversified nonhydrocarbon exports. Indonesia, Mexico, and Norway offer examples of the diversification successes that these countries will need to follow. Several countries are running out of oil and need to build new sources of income and growth (Syria and the Republic of Yemen).

In *small resource-rich, labor-importing* countries (not including Saudi Arabia and possibly Libya)—where Dutch disease is chronic, and where resources that could give the countries an edge in manufacturing exports are lacking—high-value-added services (tradable or not) would be non-oil sources of growth if the training and qualifications of their labor force are up to the international standard needed to develop such niches.

Note that the export diversification challenge of the region cannot be analyzed independent of global trends in production patterns, particularly the rise of China and India

(continued)

BOX 2.1 (continued)

as dominant manufacturing locations in the global economy. The two countries offer
challenges as well as opportunities for many MENA countries to join the global production chains (Pigato 2009).

Note that this consensus on the export-led model of growth has been challenged recently by the global crisis that has hit more export-oriented countries harder. Relying
solely on exports may have gone too far in some countries, and greater diversification
(toward exports but also the local market and nontradables) can lessen these risks of over-
exposure to a single sector.

Source: Authors' report.

---

rely more on a large, protected domestic market to develop its industries
before opening up in the mid-1990s and finally entering the global export
race—every episode of long-term sustained growth had exports as a driver.
This has enabled the developing countries of Asia, for example, to benefit
from the size of the world markets and not to be handicapped by weak domestic demand. This process was usually accompanied by a real depreciation of the exchange rate and strong growth in private investment. Beyond
China, examples abound from East Asia, Eastern Europe, and the OECD
convergence countries (Ireland, Portugal, and Spain) of economies that
have followed such trends (Hausmann, Pritchett, and Rodrik 2005). During the episodes of sustained growth, the export to GDP ratio increased
by 10.7 percentage points on average, the investment rate increased by
16 percentage points, and the average real exchange rate depreciation was
21.7 percent (Hausmann, Pritchett, and Rodrik 2005).[9]

Growing MENA countries exhibit signs of higher investment rates,
but they do not yet show strong signs of the non-oil export growth and
diversification that increase competitiveness in global markets. If export
dynamism of the private sector is used as a metric to assess whether a
country seems, structurally, to be on a path of sustained strong growth,
no MENA country passes the test so far. MENA's manufactured exports
have increased only marginally over the last 40 years. Despite improvements in trade regimes, manufactured exports as a percentage of GDP
remain far below those of other regions (figure 2.9). Country by country, the gap is even more striking with other growing middle-income or
Asian countries.

As with investment trends, much variation is found in the region.
Before the sharp increase in oil prices that started in 2003, the resource-
poor countries had done more to develop their non-oil export sectors—
on average, about 16 percent of GDP in 2003, only slightly off the world

FIGURE 2.9

Manufactured Exports to GDP, 1965–2006
(percent of GDP)

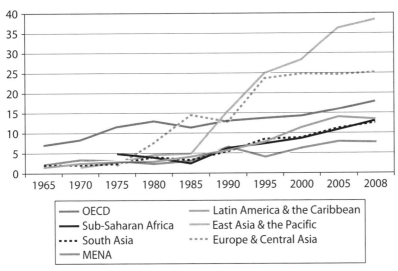

Sources: *World Development Indicators,* national accounts.

average of 17 percent.[10] In resource-rich, labor-importing countries, non-oil exports accounted for only 9.1 percent of GDP, and in resource-rich, labor-abundant economies (including Libya), for a mere 3.5 percent of GDP, about a fifth of the world average.

So far, no MENA country has sustained high export growth—even though resource-poor countries, and more recently Egypt, have shown stronger signs of export dynamism in the last decade. Indeed, the export growth for this group[11] outperformed the world average in 1990–99 and jumped to annual averages of 4–12 percent between 2000 and 2007, thanks in part to a more favorable external environment.[12] Yet most of them reached only half the export growth recorded by other emerging economies (figure 2.10). They have not strengthened their positions in the world market, with their share in global exports being at less than 0.2 percent. Moreover, export growth in MENA is volatile, relying on a few export sectors vulnerable to changes in the external environment.

Beyond the dollar amounts of exports, the content of what a country sells in foreign markets matters as well. In the process of development, countries move up the technology ladder and start exporting more sophisticated, higher value-added products. In addition, the number of products exported and the associated diversification of exports increases. Both have characterized the growth pattern of all but a few countries that have converged—or are converging—to high incomes. On both metrics, however, and despite recent encouraging signs from the resource-poor

FIGURE 2.10

**Recent Export Growth among MENA's Resource-Poor,
Labor-Abundant Countries**
(percent)

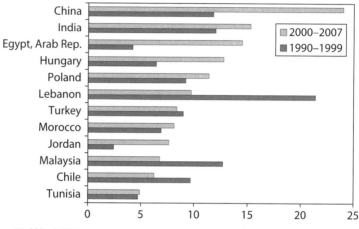

Source: World Bank 2007a.

countries in the region, MENA clearly falls behind its East Asian, Latin American, and Eastern European comparators.

Technology content. The technological structure of exports from the MENA region is weighted toward resource-based and low-technology products. The share of medium- to high-technology exports in total exports has stagnated around 20 percent since 1990 for the resource-poor economies, while growing spectacularly in East Asia, Eastern Europe, and to a lesser extent Latin America. This share is also stagnant in resource-rich economies, at much lower levels, below 5 percent. Today only 21.2 percent of exports from resource-poor economies are high- and medium-technology products (and this share is much lower in oil-rich economies). Contrast this with nearly 37 percent in Latin America, more than 55 percent in Eastern Europe and Southeast Asia, and more than 60 percent in Korea and Taiwan, China (figure 2.11).

These averages hide diversity that tells a better story for some countries. For example, the share of medium- to high-tech products in Jordanian and Tunisian exports lie around 25 percent, thanks mainly to their pharmaceutical exports. In contrast, this share was only 6.2 percent in Egypt's 2004 exports, nearly 80 percent of them resource based. Oil-rich Algeria almost exclusively exports hydrocarbons or products derived from it. A positive development is the rise in service exports in resource-poor countries: to up to half of their exports (and 83 percent

FIGURE 2.11

Technology Content of Exports: Medium- and High-Technology Exports

(percent of total exports)

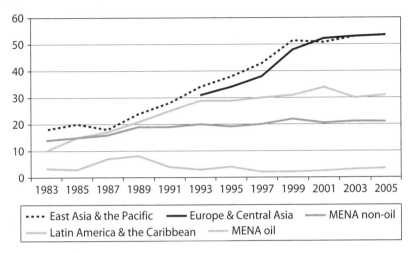

Source: World Bank 2007a.

in Lebanon). Service exports have grown at an exceptional annual rate of 42 percent in Lebanon, close to 18 percent in Morocco, and 7 percent on average in Egypt, Jordan, and Tunisia.

The weak performance of the private sector in high-value-added, high-technology products is not explained by the level of development. The region has done worse than what its structural conditions would predict based on international experience. Econometric analysis for this report shows that—conditional on world average GDP (indicating potential demand), GDP per capita income, secondary school enrollment, and terms of trade (indicating supply and price factors)—high-tech exports in MENA countries are, on average, much below their predicted levels.

Export diversification. One way to measure diversification is simply to count the number of products exported. Using a sufficiently fine definition for the export industries (six-digit international standard industrial classification [ISIC]), figure 2.12 shows the number of products exported by MENA countries in 2005 and 2006 (with the value of exports above $100,000). The gap with other middle-income countries is clear. It is also wide for oil countries, except Saudi Arabia and the Islamic Republic of Iran, which perform surprisingly well.[13] Of course, the number of products exported is also a function of country size. Even controlling for

FIGURE 2.12

Number of Products Exported
(greater than $100,000 in 2005 and 2006)

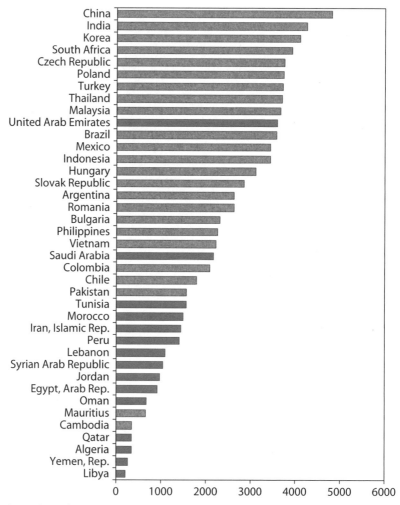

Source: Comtrade 1994–2006 six-digit data.

population, however, most MENA countries are below countries of comparable size (figure 2.13).

On the positive side, countries in the region actually started exporting more products over the last decade. Liberalization and greater openness increased the capacity of the domestic private sector to export, with a more diversified basket of goods. The proportion of products that started to be exported over the last decade is much higher in the 2006 basket in MENA countries—particularly in oil-rich ones—than in the comparator countries (figure 2.14), reflecting greater export dynamism.

FIGURE 2.13

Lower Diversification of Exports

(number of products exported)

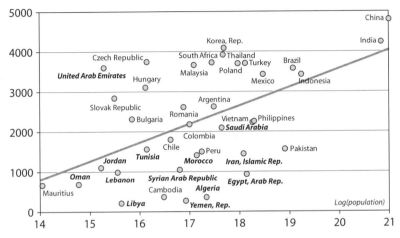

Source: Comtrade 1994–2006 six-digit data.

The question is whether this reflects a sustained underlying trend of diversification or a one-time adjustment from very low diversification in the early 1990s.

Firm-Level Productivity

Firm-level analysis of productivity confirms the economy-wide evidence on the performance of MENA economies and their private sectors. Comparisons with fast-growing East Asia and with middle-income Brazil, South Africa, and Turkey offer meaningful benchmarks. First, the intraregional differences are striking: except for Egypt, resource-poor countries perform consistently better than resource-rich, labor-abundant countries (figures 2.15 and 2.16).[14] Whether in total factor productivity or labor productivity,[15] the average performance of resource-rich, labor-abundant countries in the region (Algeria, Syria, and the Republic of Yemen in the sample) is lower than for the comparators. The average manufacturing firm in the resource-rich, labor-importing countries of the GCC (Saudi Arabia and Oman in the sample) outperforms those of all other countries in the region, with performance similar to high-productivity China, India, and Turkey, possibly reflecting heavily subsidized energy inputs.

FIGURE 2.14

Proportion of New Products in 2006 Export Basket

(exports greater than $100,000 in 2005 and 2006 and 0 in 1994–96)

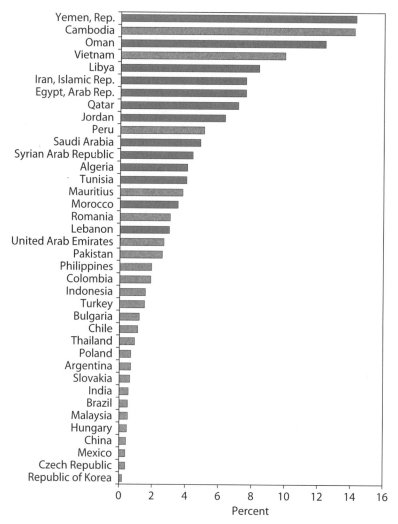

Source: Comtrade 1994–2006 six-digit data.

MENA productivity is close to that of many middle-income countries of Latin America and surpasses Sub-Saharan Africa (except South Africa),[16] but the comparison with high-growth East Asian countries, Brazil, and Turkey shows that gaps in total factor productivity and in labor productivity are enormous in non-GCC countries. In every country world-class enterprises integrated in the global economy coexist with low-productivity firms that serve a small local market.

FIGURE 2.15

Total Factor Productivity: MENA Countries and Comparators

(percent of the average total factor productivity level in Brazil)

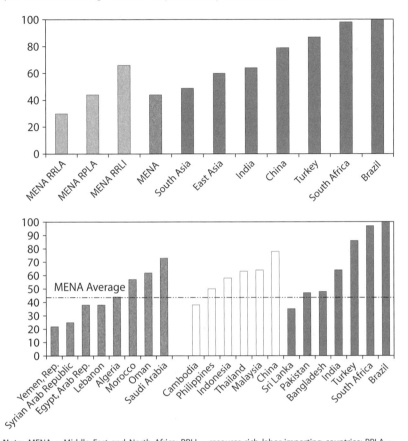

Note: MENA = Middle East and North Africa; RRLI = resource-rich labor-importing countries; RPLA = resource-poor labor-abundant countries; RPLA = resource-poor labor-abundant countries.

Source: World Bank enterprise surveys, various years.

Summing Up

The private sector, despite its larger role, falls short of putting MENA economies on paths to strong, sustained growth. With a few—arguably nonreplicable—exceptions from the Gulf, no country of this region has witnessed in recent years a growth led by a structural transformation of the economy. Gauged by the diversification of exports, their technological sophistication, the level and sectoral composition of private investment, or the productivity and innovation of firms, no MENA country exhibits the kind of dynamism and economic transformation witnessed in, China, Korea, Malaysia, Poland, Turkey, and other fast-growing economies.

FIGURE 2.16

Labor Productivity: MENA Countries and Comparators
(percent of the average labor productivity in Brazil)

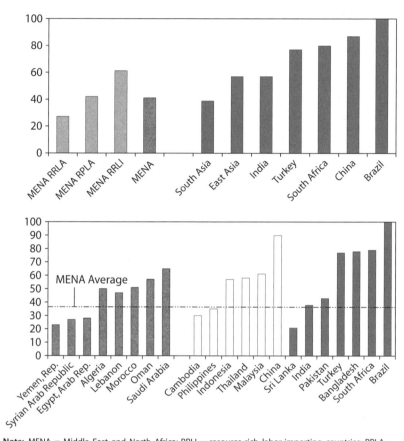

Note: MENA = Middle East and North Africa; RRLI = resource-rich labor-importing countries; RPLA = resource-poor labor-abundant countries.

Source: World Bank enterprise surveys, various years.

The diagnosis varies across countries, but overall, dynamism, competition, and productivity are lacking in the MENA private sector. Understanding why and offering routes for governments to spur private-led growth are the subject of the rest of this report.

Notes

1. Libya is also in this group, although it more closely follows the patterns of the resource-rich labor-abundant countries.

2. In Algeria, the Islamic Republic of Iran, and Syria, the growth in nonhydrocarbon sectors (such as construction) is fueled in great part by

the higher public investment that the oil-price rises in fiscal surpluses are financing.

3. Cross-regional benchmarking of growth rates is useful, but growth is such a complex phenomenon, affected by so many variables, that drawing conclusions on the performance of a given country or region can be made only when one controls, as much as is feasible, for other variables that affect economic growth: initial income, human capital, the infrastructure, macroeconomic stability, governance, and policy variables. All these factors, and many others, some of them visible and measurable and others not, affect a country's growth rate year after year. A standard exercise in the growth literature is replicated here using the robust econometric techniques now standard in this field.

4. The large increases in Bahrain, Kuwait, and Qatar reflect the increasing investments in the booming oil and gas sectors—when compared with the mid-1990s, when oil prices were depressed.

5. Europe and Central Asia's private investment growth measured over 1995–2004.

6. Since 2000, private investment (in GDP deflated U.S. dollars) has grown by 12 percent a year in Sub-Saharan Africa, 25 percent a year in East Asia and the Pacific, 16 percent a year in Europe and Central Asia, 14 percent a year in South Asia, and 3 percent a year in Latin America.

7. The pattern is exacerbated in labor-abundant, oil-rich countries (Algeria, the Islamic Republic of Iran, and Libya), which have been slow to privatize their industrial sectors—sales of state-owned enterprises are often an entry point for foreign direct investment.

8. Another likely factor is the deteriorating terms of trade of MENA countries with China, which has experienced exceptional manufacturing export growth over many years. "It's all going to China, there's nothing we can export competitively anymore," complains one Egyptian businessman.

9. Of course, one should not read these as causal effects on growth, but rather as a characterization of the average sustained growth acceleration.

10. Non-oil exports to GDP were evaluated at the start of the oil boom rather than currently. Because GDP is heavily affected by the oil price, the 2003 share of non-oil exports to GDP more closely represents the state of non-oil export development.

11. Here including Egypt, Jordan, Lebanon, Morocco, and Tunisia, but not Djibouti.

12. This paragraph, and part of this section, draws from parallel work on diversification; see World Bank (2007a).

13. The high number of products apparently exported by the United Arab Emirates actually reflects, in great part, transshipping rather than a

diversified manufacturing production base: tariff-free goods enter through the Dubai port and are reexported to the neighboring GCC countries.

14. Note that the 2008 enterprise survey of Egypt showed that both labor productivity and total factor productivity increased recently.

15. For a description of the methodology used to compute firm-level total factor productivity and labor productivity, see Kinda, Plane, and Véganzones-Varoudakis (2007).

16. See Kinda, Plane, and Véganzones-Varoudakis (2007).

CHAPTER 3

Explaining the Private Sector's Weak Performance—An Organizing Framework

Explaining the weaknesses of private sector development in MENA economies takes more than identifying lists of missing reforms in each country or pointing to international benchmarks of indicators. The report does not offer a standard recipe of reforms that would generate diversification and sustained growth in every country of the region—such a recipe does not exist. Lessons from past successes and disappointments with standard reform packages call for some humility in a search for the keys to strong sustained growth.

Instead, the report introduces a simple framework to focus on three aspects of policy making that affect investor expectations: the rules, how they are applied, and the credibility of government in its commitment to reforms. First, it looks at the policies, rules, and regulations as they are enacted—asking whether the problem in MENA is missing reforms. Second, it looks at the way these rules, policies, and regulations are actually implemented and enforced—asking whether the problem is with uneven and discretionary policy making. Third, it asks whether the problem is with the credibility of government commitments to policy reforms and better implementation of policies—credibility as much as policies determine the expectations of investors of what they will cope with in their business activity. The three are linked. This focus emphasizes that the quality of reforms and their implementation, as well as the credibility of governments, are as important as the reform content and quantity—and all are shaped by each country's political economy.

The Need for Humility in Prescribing the Keys to Private-Led Growth

Identifying the most important constraints to private sector development is a challenge in any country. Many factors affect investor behavior, and current understanding of how these factors combine to trigger strong private-led growth is imperfect. One of the most important lessons from the diverse country experiences with growth is that there is no recipe—no list of standard reforms—that would trigger sustained growth accelerations with certainty.[1] These experiences demand humility in applying standard reform packages that would guarantee a growth takeoff. Many things matter for growth. This report focuses on the credibility of reforms and the quality of their implementation.

What comes out of the success stories and disappointments of the past decades? Sustained growth accelerations rest on strong private sector investment and growth. Public investment matters too—particularly in providing the infrastructure and enabling environment for private investment—but it is not the primary source of wealth creation: "Government provides the environment for growth, but it is the private sector that invests and creates wealth for the people" (Commission on Growth and Development 2008). What is much less clear is how this happens. There is a basic list of prerequisites. Very few economists or policy makers would deny today that a country is very unlikely to sustain growth if its economy is highly unstable, if it is excessively closed to international markets, if it lacks a certain level of infrastructure (at least in some areas of the country), if private property rights do not enjoy a minimum protection, or if some of its products or factor markets (labor markets and skills, land, and credit) are severely undeveloped or distorted. Each of these areas is a dimension of the investment climate that affects investor incentives (figure 3.1). Severe weaknesses in any of them could prevent private firms from growing and entrepreneurs from investing.

Much less consensus is to be found, however, on the minimum conditions needed in each area of the investment climate to trigger sustained private-sector–led growth.[2] No systematic method exists to identify this critical mass of conditions and to understand how they all combine to give private entrepreneurs the incentives to invest.

Many countries have entered periods of sustained growth with far-from-perfect investment climates. India, in the midst of a sustained period of high growth, ranked 132 in the 2007 "Doing Business" ranking of 155 countries rated that year and more recently in the Doing Business 2010 report, India was ranked 133 out 183 countries. In the 2010 rankings China, after decades of sustained high growth, ranked 180 out of 183 in the indicator for construction permits, 130 for taxation, and 151 for business start-up procedures (World Bank 2006, 2007c, 2009b). So countries clearly do not have to get everything right to grow. Some policies tend to work better than others, but it is hard to say what constitutes the perfect combination of policies, because countries have found success with varied policy, regulatory, and institutional arrangements.[3] Even so, countries lagging in some key areas do not succeed unless they more than make up for shortcomings in other areas. For example, the huge domestic markets of China and India are attractive targets for investors, offsetting regulatory inefficiencies.

FIGURE 3.1

The Firm and Its Investment Climate

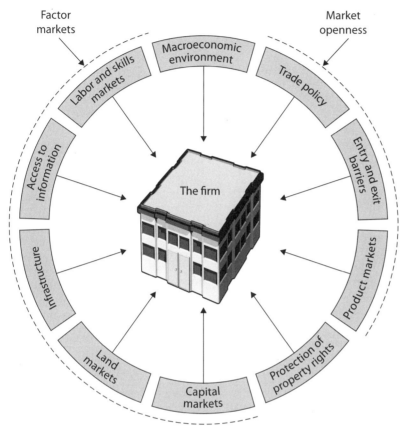

Source: Authors.

Policies, Institutions That Implement Them, and Expectations about the Future

The Firm and Its Environment

The business decisions to invest, innovate, develop new products, adopt a new market strategy, recruit and train staff, and implement productivity-enhancement measures all depend on myriad factors. Investment climate policies include all the external factors that a government can influence through its institutions, macroeconomic and microeconomic policies, investments in public goods, and power to legislate. Firm decisions are affected by the following factors:[4]

- *The macroeconomic environment*—inflation, interest rates, domestic demand, and the terms of trade

- *The degree of market openness*—trade openness,[5] the regulatory barriers to entry and exit of firms from the market, the product markets (including how freely prices are set in product markets), and the regulations governing different business activities[6]

- *The protection of property rights*—the judiciary and the enforcement of court decisions

- *The nature of factor markets*—particularly for labor markets and skills, capital, land, infrastructure, and information; in particular they depend on access to laborers with the skills to compete[7]

- In each of these areas the government sets the rules and regulations and is expected to enforce them fairly and consistently (figure 3.1).[8]

These factors affect a firm's performance and behavior through different channels. First, they affect the costs of doing business at various stages of the firm's life cycle (entry, operations, and exit)—such as administrative and regulatory costs, input costs, production costs, and taxes. Second, they affect the uncertainty that investors face, which can be more costly to managers than predictable costs and delays. Such uncertainty is associated with macroeconomic instability, discretionary behavior of public agencies, unpredictability of laws and their implementation, the lack of protection of property rights, and the unpredictability of demand. Third, they affect the competition that firms face and thus the market structures and the incentives to innovate and respond to competitive pressures. The regulations governing investment and business creation directly affect competition. Beyond the formal barriers to entry and exit, the poor functioning of factor markets and the unequal protection of property rights can create an uneven playing field that favors incumbents and reduces competition.

Rules, Policies, and How They Are Enforced—The Role of Institutions

In each of these areas, government policy consists not only of the rules and regulations adopted, but also of the way that they are implemented and enforced. What matters for business managers is not just the rules, but the way that they expect them to be applied to themselves and to their competitors. This depends on the government agency or institution in charge of administering and enforcing the rules. Investors' assessments of how these institutions will enforce and interpret the rules in a consistent, honest, predictable, and equal manner for all firms affects their incentives much more than the rules themselves. Beyond the laws and regulations enacted, policy making for private sector development is mostly about public sector management of the institutions in charge of enforcing the rules and interacting with businesses, a central theme of the report.

Most indicators of the business environment reflect the rules as written—or (at best) are proxies for how they are applied on average for a typical firm.[9] The weaker the quality of public sector governance, however, and the greater the arbitrariness and discretion in implementing rules, the wider the wedge between how the business environment appears in a reading of the rules and policies, and what most businesses really have to cope with. The investment climate framework of figure 3.1 therefore needs to be enriched to illustrate the possible wedge between how things look on paper and how they are enforced by the institutions that businesses and investors face (figure 3.2).[10]

Assessing the Business Environment Today and into the Future—The Role of Expectations and Credibility of Reforms

Today's rules, policies, and regulations matter for firms. The that way they are applied and enforced by the relevant public institutions matters even more. However, expectations about the future and the credibility of governments in reforming the rules and implementing them matter as well. Indeed, expectations about future government actions, the path of reforms, and the consistency of policies all are important for the behavior of firms and the decisions of investors. Experiences of sustained growth accelerations are very informative in that respect, whether China in the 1980s, India in the 1990s, or Eastern Europe after the fall of the Berlin Wall. The private sector—domestic and foreign—did not wait for all aspects of the business environment to improve to invest. Early, credible signals that reforms were to come and to be sustained were enough to align the expectations of investors and trigger a self-fulfilling dynamic of growth and rising expectations for further reforms.[11]

Many things may affect investor expectations. Low credibility based on experience with a government undoubtedly comes into play and is perhaps the hardest to change. It is no surprise that many growth accelerations follow changes in the political regime (Eastern Europe), a significant change of leadership, or a major change of government with the appointment of credible reformists (India in 1991, Egypt in 2004, or the enthronement of new leaders in Morocco and Jordan in 1999) (Hausmann, Pritchett, and Rodrik 2005). Credible signals by governments followed by bold, irreversible reforms—such as changes in ownership (privatization),

FIGURE 3.2

The Firm and Its Investment Climate: Rules and Policies and the Institutions That Implement Them

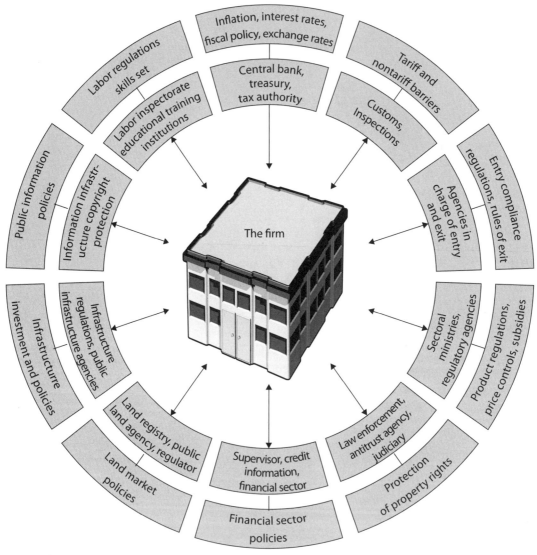

Source: Authors.

major sector liberalizations, or important trade agreements—can also help.[12] Yet building credibility and positive expectations can take time. These arguments are not new: government policies, the way that they are implemented, and how their credibility sets expectations form the core message of the World Bank's World Development Report 2004a, *A Better Investment Climate for Everyone.*

Measuring Rules, How They Are Applied, and Expectations about the Future

For most areas of the business environment, one finds tools to measure the first "layer," the rules, policies, and regulations—particularly using international benchmarks. This has been the case for a long time for macroeconomic policy—and more recently for trade policy and the markets for products, labor and skills, as well as financial markets. It remains to be made standard for infrastructure, information, and land policies. For example, the World Bank Group's *Doing Business* project, among others, has recently made great strides in improving the ability to measure the regulatory environment. Other international benchmarks can be used in the other areas of the business environment. All in all, however, measuring the first layer of the business environment is feasible for getting a first sense of the reform gaps between countries.

Measuring the second "layer"—how policies are implemented in reality—is much harder. First, although rules and policies are the same for all, the experiences with institutions and public agencies can be very diverse depending on the type of firms, the connections of investors, and the specifics of the "microenvironment" of each firm. Second, not every institutional aspect can be benchmarked and compared across firms, let alone across countries. For example, the complexity of the administration of land markets and the differences in the land markets between countries (publicly owned or private) make it next to impossible to construct meaningful comparators.

When available, proxies can be used to diagnose the functioning of institutions. For example, prices or measures of the liquidity of land markets are good indicators of the efficacy of institutions supporting them. Firm-level surveys (such as the World Bank enterprise surveys used extensively in this report) offer good indicators of the diversity of interaction with administrations and the average associated costs and delays. In particular, the variance of the costs and delays among firms offers a good indicator of the extent of uncertainty or discretionary behavior associated with public agencies.

Chapters 5 to 7 show how state institutions implement rules and policies in the areas of access to finance, access to land and industrial policy. Rather than providing benchmarking of where MENA countries stand, they analyze in detail the barriers that investors face, focusing on institutional weaknesses and the role of the state.

Expectations and the credibility of the government's reform efforts are the hardest to measure. Some surveys ask business owners about their expectations about future economic prospects, but rarely about their expectations about their government's reform agenda. Expectations explain investors' responses to reforms—especially in the early stages of reforms, but by nature they are intangible. There is no recipe for influencing them—they depend on the credibility of the authorities, the "irreversibility" of commitments, the nature of the signals that government sends, and other intangibles.

Short of directly measuring government credibility, some governments have better armed themselves to make credible commitments of reforms to investors—by well-established institutions (such as political parties and public agencies) or entrenched electoral processes (chapter 8). This line of argument can explain the difference between the development paths of many countries in the MENA region and those in Asia, such as China, Korea, or Singapore. Looking into the political economy of private sector reforms is essential to understanding the credibility of governments in really implementing the reforms they enact—and thus understanding the expectations of investors about how the rules as they appear on paper will be applied to them and about future reforms.

Understanding the political economy of reforms in MENA is also important for setting priorities for policy prescriptions, by focusing on ones that will have the greatest impact on private sector development and investors' expectations. This will be the subject of chapter 9, which offers strategic recommendations that apply quite uniformly across the region, mirroring the three aspects of the business environment in the framework. They touch on policy reforms to reduce barriers to entry and rents, institutional reforms of the state, and measures that should improve government credibility and reduce the interference of political economy factors on the business environment.

Notes

1. See, for example, Commission on Growth and Development (2008) and its background papers (www.growthcommission.org); World Bank (2005); Hausmann, Pritchett, and Rodrik (2005).

2. Brazil grew over a sustained period with fairly high inflation. India has been growing quickly for more than a decade, even though its standing in most international benchmarks of the investment climate put it in the bottom quartile of countries (see, for example, www.doingbusiness.org), and it has had consistently high fiscal deficits.

3. In the absence of a single right path, see, for example, World Bank (2004a); Zagha and Nankani (2005).

4. This standard representation of the investment climate has been used, for example, under a different variant, in World Bank (2005).

5. See, for example, Sachs and Warner (1995); Frankel and Romer (1999); and Dollar and Kraay (2001).

6. Palmade (2005) makes the case that many business environment constraints are sector-specific or product-specific regulatory constraints.

7. See, for example, World Bank (2008a).

8. Note that in many of these markets, market failures could require some sort of intervention by government. This is implicitly included in this framework, and interventions in markets are policy instruments that governments can use to improve the investment climate.

9. The *Doing Business* indicators do not use averages but rather responses of informed professionals about what would apply to a hypothetical firm with specific characteristics (see www.doingbusiness.org).

10. The list of institutions is indicative and could be expanded. For the macroeconomic environment there is no institution with which firms interact. However, institutions such as the central bank and the treasury establish the credibility of macroeconomic policy and therefore its impact on the business environment.

11. For case studies that trace the reform and growth paths of high-growth countries in recent decades, see, for example, Rodrik (2003).

12. Such as joining the World Trade Organization or entering into trade agreements with the European Union, which many MENA countries have done.

CHAPTER 4

Policy Reforms in MENA, Their Credibility, and Their Implementation

Using the framework to distinguish between the business environment as it is usually measured and benchmarked, and how it is actually experienced by investors, this chapter makes four arguments:

- *The business environment in most of MENA does not appear much worse than that in high-growth countries. Room can be identified for significant improvement in some areas and countries, but the lackluster overall performance of the private sector cannot be fully attributed to missing policy reforms. In fact, the investment climate has improved significantly in recent years, and the private sector has started to respond.*

- *Reforms similar to those in high-growth countries have not yet produced strong and sustainable responses. Why?*

- *The problem in MENA is not so much missing reforms or bad regulations— except in lagging countries and some areas of the regulatory environment— but one of a lack of response of the private sector to reforms.*

- *The diagnostic evidence points to a gap between the rules and how they are implemented—hence the lack of investor response to policy changes "on paper." The chapter offers firm-level, indirect evidence that inconsistency and arbitrariness in the way regulations and policies are actually implemented are issues for investors, more so than a lack of good rules and policies.*

- *Symptoms in the structure and dynamism of the private sector show that the business environment is not the same for all firms in MENA countries. Barriers to competition limit the entry and exit of firms, leading to older firms, older businessmen, fewer registered firms, and less competitive pressure than elsewhere.*

Explaining weak private sector development in MENA requires understanding the role of the state in shaping and interfering with public institutions that regulate markets, implement policies, and interact with firms.

Is the Problem with Missing Reforms?

Not really. Some policy gaps remain, but the business environment looks "average," and the reforms have accelerated over the years. For many of the key elements of the economy affecting the expected returns to investment, MENA countries stand somewhere in the middle—neither star reformers nor complete laggards. Even if regional indicators mask the substantial diversity in areas of the investment climate between countries (and even subnationally), all countries in the region have both stronger and weaker areas in their business environments and, overall, MENA looks average.

The usual indicators of market-oriented reforms are not that much worse in MENA countries than those for high-growth countries (figure 4.1). Even if wide policy gaps remain in some countries and in some areas, the gaps are too small to explain the differences in performance. With few exceptions, due to the reform deficit in some oil-rich countries, the region's rank in the world is "average," as is that of China, Malaysia, Poland, Thailand, and Turkey. It is clear that some countries have achieved sustained high levels of growth with indicators no higher than the MENA norm. Yet each MENA country still has weaknesses in its policy environment.

It should be emphasized that these indicators of macroeconomic, trade, and business environment reforms provide measures of the policy environment in these areas. They do not, however, reflect how these policies are actually implemented for individual firms, particularly for trade and the business environment. Indicators of trade openness—even when they include nontariff barriers—do not capture the quality of service at customs or at the ports of entry. They do not capture the uncertainty that firms face when clearing their imported goods or when they export. This is even more so for business environment indicators, such as the *Doing Business* indicators.[1]

Overall, reforms have accelerated in recent years (figures 4.2 and 4.3). Most governments have improved the business environment by simplifying business regulations, opening the financial sector, and reducing restrictions to trade and investment. All international indices of the business environment point unequivocally to improvements. For example, in business regulations measured by the *Doing Business* report, the average number of reforms conducted in MENA countries has been increasing steadily over the last few years—from 0.65 regulatory reforms in 2004 to 1.95 in 2009, the second most reformist region after Europe and Central Asia, according to this report (figure 4.2). Even if the reforms measured by the *Doing Business* report do not span all areas of the investment climate, they are good proxies of reform trends. Indeed, in trade policy

FIGURE 4.1

Overall, the Business Environment in MENA Countries Looks "Average," as It Does in Many Fast-Growing Economies

(ease of doing business index 2008, macro-policy index 2007, trade policy index 2007)

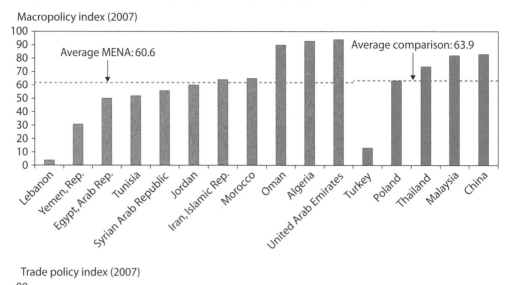

Macropolicy index (2007)

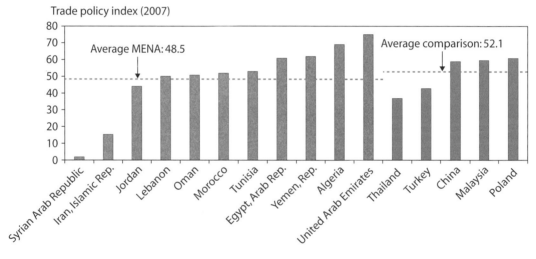

Trade policy index (2007)

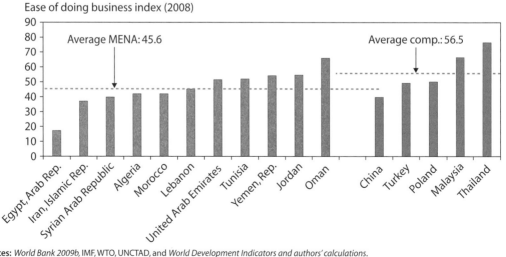

Ease of doing business index (2008)

Sources: *World Bank 2009b,* IMF, WTO, UNCTAD, and *World Development Indicators and authors' calculations.*

FIGURE 4.2

The Number of Regulatory Reforms Has Increased Recently in MENA Countries
(average number of regulatory reforms per country, as measured by the Doing Business *reports)*

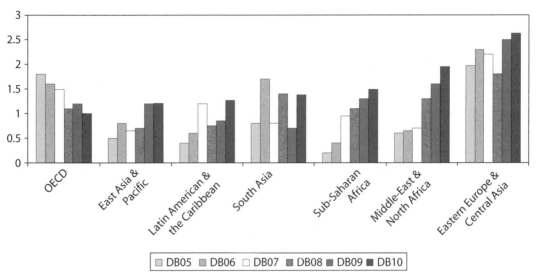

Source: *Doing Business* database.

FIGURE 4.3

MENA Tariff Reductions Top Those of All Other Regions, 2000–07
(scale: 0 = lowest improvement to 100 = highest improvement)

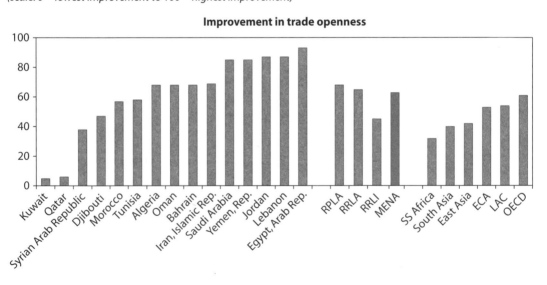

Sources: World Bank 2007b, WTO, and UNCTAD TRAINS database.

the region's tariff reductions since 2000 top all other regions (figure 4.3), reflecting that MENA has been opening up later than others, as current tariffs remain higher than the world average. Even so, this is a strong indication that reforms have progressed over the last few years.

Even MENA countries that lag badly in their overall trade policy have generally reduced tariffs in recent years. Average tariffs have been slashed in most, and the dispersion of rates (from highest to lowest) has also declined sharply. The Islamic Republic of Iran, Lebanon, and the Republic of Yemen—three countries that fare poorly on the trade policy index—are among the leaders in tariff reductions. Regionwide, un-weighted average tariffs have been cut from 20.4 percent in 2000 to 13.2 percent in 2007, allowing South Asia to displace MENA as the region with the highest average tariffs. Clearly, as tariff rates are addressed, the agenda must shift to nontariff barriers and to trade facilitation and logistics.

On macroeconomic uncertainty, after a period of significant imbalances after the collapse of oil prices in the 1980s, MENA countries undertook extensive macroeconomic reforms. The programs varied but generally included improving fiscal balances (including reductions in some expenditures and privatization), reforming exchange regimes, and liberalizing trade and financial flows. In the 1990s a number of MENA countries underwent successful stabilization efforts of varying intensity. Budget deficits narrowed from an average of 13 percent of GDP in 1991 to less than 1 percent of GDP by 1997. The continued improvement in MENA's macroeconomic policy environment for investment is apparent in summary indicators of macroeconomic stability.

Despite the positive trend, stability can still be improved in some macroeconomic areas. Some countries are burdened with high debt (Lebanon stands out). Others are vulnerable to their continued reliance on dwindling oil production (Syria and the Republic of Yemen). Regional and internal conflict creates macroeconomic uncertainty in several countries and economies (Iraq and West Bank and Gaza economies). In other countries macroeconomic stability is vulnerable to the need for further reforms (for example, to reduce expenditures on energy subsidies) and global economic conditions, with the economic health of several Mediterranean countries linked strongly to European economies.[2]

Although standard measures of policy reforms are not available in every area of the business environment (as described in the framework), the trends for the available measures (macroeconomic, trade, and regulatory indicators) also apply to other areas. *Doing Business* spans a number of them: business entry, exit, construction permits, legal issues, finance, trade logistics, and labor markets. For example, in the financial markets most countries have progressed well in opening the banking sector, reforming entry requirements and prudential regulations, and improving credit information and collateral legislation. Regulations for foreign direct investment have also been liberalized in most MENA countries. This does not mean that no more policy reforms are needed.

The list of standard reforms remains long in some parts of the region, especially in large oil-rich countries.

The Problem Is the Insufficient Private Sector Response to Reforms

The private sector has responded to these reforms and grown, but timidly and far below what similar reforms have produced in high-growth countries. Private investment rates have increased by 2 percentage points on average (figure 4.4). The response has been higher in resource-poor countries that have been the most ambitious and consistent in reforming—as in Jordan, Morocco, Tunisia, and, more recently, Egypt. Foreign investment has also picked up, although the majority remains concentrated in energy, infrastructure, and real estate, much less in manufacturing and technology-intensive ventures. Another reflection of this dynamism is that historically low business entry rates have also increased to 8 percent a year, slightly surpassing that of other developing regions (figure 4.5).

The response, however, is far below what similar reforms have produced in high-growth countries. The performance of the private sector has been weak in MENA countries, despite reforms. In particular, private investment rates in MENA have on average been less responsive to reforms than elsewhere (figure 4.6). Between 1990 and 2006 private investment rates increased slightly in some MENA

FIGURE 4.4

Private Investment Has Been Rising
(percent of GDP)

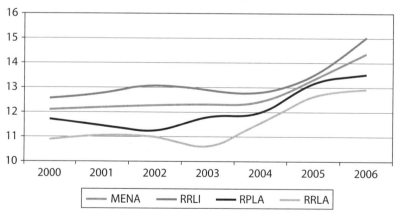

Note: MENA = Middle East and North Africa; RRLI = resource-rich labor-importing countries; RPLA = resource-poor labor-abundant countries; RRLA = resource-rich labor-abundant countries.

Sources: *World Development* Indicators, national accounts, IMF.

FIGURE 4.5

**MENA Business Creation between 2002 and 2005
Leads the Developing World**
(percent increase in registered firms)

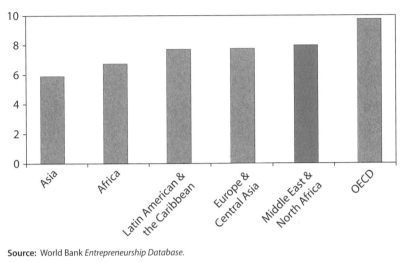

Source: World Bank *Entrepreneurship Database.*

FIGURE 4.6

Reform Episodes and Private Investment Response
(percent GDP)

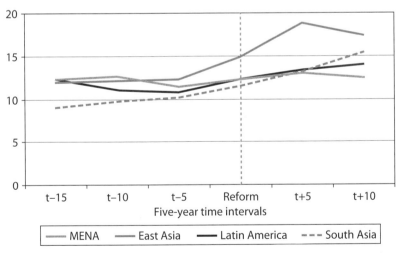

Sources: Private investment rates are from the *World Development Indicators,* national accounts, and IMF
and have been averaged over the five-year time periods. Episodes of reforms are based on the *Economic
Freedom Index* of the Fraser Institute, and a reform episode is defined as a five-year episode in which this
0–10 index permanently improved by at least one unit.

countries and declined in others. By contrast, they rose sharply in
countries such as China, Malaysia, Poland, Thailand, and Turkey
(figure 4.7). Is this because those countries reformed more than
MENA countries? No.

FIGURE 4.7

Private Investment's Response to More than a Decade of Reforms Has Been Relatively Weak, 1990 and 2006

(Private investment rates 2006 versus 1990 percent of GDP)

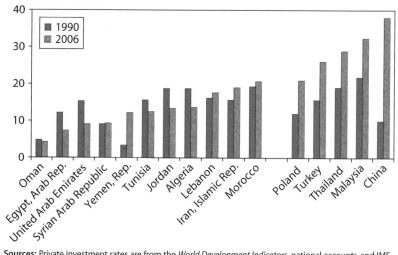

Sources: Private investment rates are from the *World Development Indicators,* national accounts, and IMF.

Is It about the Way Rules and Policies Are Implemented?

One possible explanation for this private response gap is that the combination of reforms has not been correct. Some reforms complement others. For example, the beneficial impact of trade liberalization may be altogether missed without complementary liberalization of factor markets, and it can be greatly amplified by reform in trade facilitation (Wilson 2003; Bolaky and Freund 2004; Dennis 2006a, b). Government policies that distort incentives or restrain the mobility of labor and capital to higher value uses can impede the private response to macro- and trade reform. So, although there is no one path to sustained growth, some of the roads not taken may have yielded better results.

A second explanation could lie in weak implementation of reforms. In many countries in the region a central problem is the opacity and unpredictability of laws and regulations affecting enterprise investment, operation, and employment. If public administration is weak, improved policies "on the books" may not overcome inept, inadequate, or discretionary application. Most indicators do better at evaluating policies in place than policies in practice. Survey responses suggest that the application of rules can be inconsistent for a substantial minority of firms in some countries and the majority of firms in others (figure 4.8). Anecdotally, countless

FIGURE 4.8

Large Proportions of Investors Complain That the Regulations Are Interpreted Inconsistently and Unpredictably

(percent of respondents disagreeing with "interpretations of regulations are consistent and predictable")

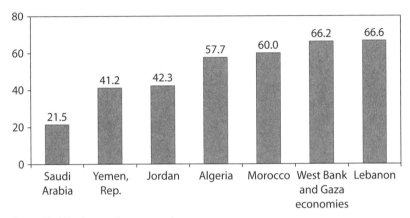

Source: World Bank enterprise surveys, various years.

examples are given of administrative weakness, ranging from inconsistent and unpredictable interpretation of rules and regulations to petty (and not-so-petty) corruption. These perceptions are important, because they can influence individual investors' decisions. The large proportion of entrepreneurs who believe that rules and regulations will not be consistently and predictably applied explains why policy reforms may not have a strong response from investors. The same goes for any area where the application of policies depends on the arbitrariness and discretion of the public agencies implementing them.

Enterprise surveys conducted by the World Bank over recent years in 10 countries in the region show that issues related to the rule of law and how it is applied—including informal and anticompetitive practices, collateral issues, and property rights—are among the top concerns. Corruption is cited as one of the top five constraints in seven of these countries. Regulatory constraints (labor, licensing, tax administration, regulatory policy) are top issues in six countries (table 4.1). This suggests a strong need to address a general lack of clear, predictable, and well-enforced "rules of the game" for market activity. These issues are found in many areas of the business environment, but they are all more related to the way policies are implemented, not the actual policies and rules.

Investors in MENA—especially managers of small and medium-sized firms—consistently point to policy uncertainty and an uneven playing

TABLE 4.1

Private Sector Priority Constraints from Enterprise Surveys, 2003 and 2005–08

Algeria	Egypt, Arab Rep.	Jordan	Lebanon	Morocco	Oman	Saudi Arabia	Syrian Arab Republic	West Bank and Gaza Economies	Republic of Yemen
Corruption	Macroeconomic instability	Macroeconomic instability	Corruption	Tax rates	Labor regulation	Labor regulation	Tax rates	Political instability	Macroeconomic instability
Anticompetitive or informal practices	Corruption	Tax rates	Cost of finance	Access to land	Skills, education of workers	Business licensing/ permits	Tax administration	Macroeconomic instability	Tax rates
Access to land	Anticompetitive or informal practices	Business licensing and permits	Tax rates	Electricity	Cost of finance	Skills, education of workers	Electricity	Corruption	Corruption
Access to finance	Regulatory policy uncertainty	Corruption	Electricity	Anticompetitive or informal practices	Access to land	Access to land	Corruption	Electricity	Tax administration
Electricity	Tax rates	Tax administration	Legal system	Access to finance	Access to finance	Access to finance	Business licensing and permits	Transportation	Antiompetitive or informal practices

Note: The dates associated with the surveys are Algeria (2007), Egypt (2006), Jordan (2007), Lebanon (2006), Morocco (2008), Oman (2003), Saudi Arabia (2005), Syria (2003), West Bank and Gaza economies (2007), and the Republic of Yemen (2005).

Source: World Bank enterprise surveys, 2003 and 2005–08.

FIGURE 4.9

Policy and Regulatory Uncertainty Are Leading Constraints to Businesses

(percent; simple average of a country's share of firms ranking a constraint as "major" or "severe")

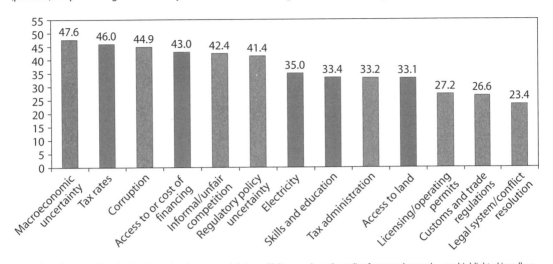

Note: The policy areas linked to implementing the rules and their credibility—and not the policy framework as such—are highlighted in yellow.

Source: World Bank enterprise surveys of Algeria, Egypt, the Islamic Republic of Iran, Jordan, Lebanon, Morocco, Oman, Saudi Arabia, Syria, West Bank and Gaza economies, and the Republic of Yemen, various years.

field that favors some incumbent firms at the expense of new entrants and competitors. Despite a favorable macroeconomic environment for the last decade, macroeconomic uncertainty remains a leading concern for business (figure 4.9). Corruption, anticompetitive practices, and regulatory policy uncertainty all rank high in the minds of business managers. In many countries, businesses also point to reform gaps in the regulatory environment, access to finance, and access to land. A large part of the problem seems to lie not with policies as they appear on paper, but with the unequal, discretionary, and preferential implementation of policies.

Another source of policy uncertainty comes from the way that policies are prepared and announced by governments. Opacity in reform design and lack of consultation lead to unpredictability and lack of visibility for investors. Policy reversals are common and reduce the credibility of reforms.[3] Policy changes are often unannounced—leading to a lack of clarity for both investors and administrations implementing newly enacted rules.

Legal and regulatory ambiguity expands the space for discretion in public agencies—a key element in the variation in firm outcomes. In numerous investment climate assessments, legal and regulatory conditions introduce unwanted uncertainty. First, there is the question of legal drafting: is the law unambiguous and specific enough, and consistent with other laws? Unclear laws can tie private parties up in litigation. They can also put undue discretion in the hands of the administration official who applies a rule.

A 2007 legal and judicial sector review of Lebanon, and a similar review in 2004 for Algeria, found that poorly drafted legislation often creates uncertainty for judges over whether new laws supplement, amend, or replace existing laws (World Bank 2004b, 2007d). Similarly, in Morocco the 2003 legal and judicial sector review found that "[t]he law-making process is weak, resulting in poorly drafted laws, and legal dissemination is inadequate" (World Bank 2005, 2003a). In the Republic of Yemen the lack of clarity in land laws is said to account for the fact that 40–50 percent of court cases concern land disputes. In many countries ambiguous tax regulations contribute to administrative burden, corruption, and evasion.

Arbitrary Implementation of the Rules Leads to Discretion, Harassment, and Unfair Discretionary Treatment of Investors

The unequal implementation of policies can appear in all areas of the business environment presented in the framework: trade, entry and exit regulations, product market regulations, factor markets, and even labor markets. Firms can face arbitrariness and discretion in their interaction with each public administration that implements the rules and policies. The firm-level evidence in this section points to the implementation of business regulations, competition issues, and corruption. More broadly, part II of this report shows that policies for finance, land, and industrial strategy also suffer from a disproportionate role of government in markets, leading to discretion and unequal treatment of investors.

Unclear rules and discretion can also enable harassment, as with frequent inspections, beyond what is needed to ensure compliance with rules and public health and safety. MENA firms undergo anywhere from seven inspections a year to 31, depending on the country (figure 4.10). Although some inspections are genuinely necessary, it is hard to believe that countries with three times the inspections are three times more compliant or three times safer.

Inspections touch on many areas of the business environment. They can happen at customs (trade). They can be related to regulations in product markets. They are often linked to the infrastructure in industrial zones (fire safety inspections or environmental inspections) and even to labor markets. The objective here is not so much to pinpoint particular areas of the business environment (as illustrated in figure 3.1 of the

FIGURE 4.10

Days Spent in Inspections or Required Meetings with Officials
(number of days)

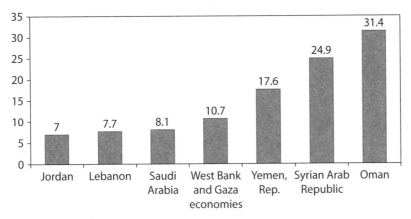

Source: Investment climate assessment surveys.

framework) but to show that discretionary implementation of the rules can "hit" investors in any area in which they interact with the state and regulatory agencies. Corruption is a symptom of this. When it develops, it often touches more than one area. Evidence that corruption is an issue in the business environment is a reflection of discretion and rents in state-business interactions in general.

The cumbersome implementation of regulatory requirements occupies senior managers who might otherwise devote more time to their core business operations. Researchers asked firms about the management time devoted to regulatory compliance activities, and MENA firms gave widely divergent responses—ranging from 7.1 percent in the West Bank and Gaza to 19.5 percent in Algeria (figure 4.11). For several countries this compliance time would translate into at least half a day each week. If governments streamline regulations and seek the most efficient alternatives, they can continue to pursue valid social goals (such as health and safety) while imposing fewer burdens on business.

Firms report that many inspections involve informal payments or gifts, which can add up to a substantial informal tax. Anywhere from a tenth to more than half of inspections can involve such payments, depending on the country (figure 4.12). Country data suggest, depending on local policies and practices, that the most frequent inspections can be by tax or customs officials, police, health inspectors, or even fire and building safety officials.[4]

FIGURE 4.11

Senior Management's Time Spent Dealing with Regulations
(percent)

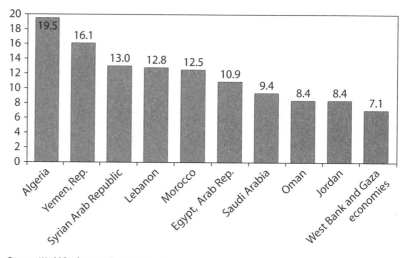

Source: World Bank enterprise surveys, various years.

FIGURE 4.12

Inspections in Which an Informal Payment Is Requested or Expected
(percent)

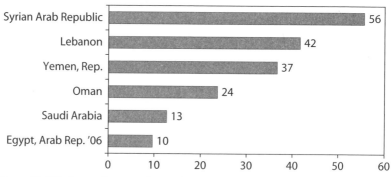

Source: World Bank enterprise surveys. Data are for 2005, except for Egypt, whose data are for 2006.

Corruption is a leading problem in several countries, but it is far from uniform. Enterprise surveys suggest that it ranks second among leading constraints to enterprise operation and growth, but this ranking varies widely between countries (figure 4.13). Where corruption prevails, it can

FIGURE 4.13

Perception of the Corruption Constraint among MENA Firms

(percent of firm managers who rate corruption as a major or severe constraint to their business)

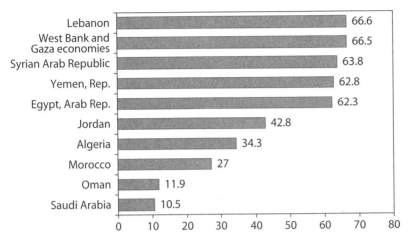

Source: World Bank enterprise surveys, various years.

impose a substantial and often arbitrary tax on businesses. Dealing with corrupt administration officials can distract managers from running their businesses, impede certain areas, or make types of operation more vulnerable to rent seeking. Conversely, corruption presents some opportunities for some businessmen, diverting them from pursuing fair competition (through improved efficiency and innovation) to seeking advantage and protection.

In perception-based indices, oil-rich countries of the Gulf tend to rate better than other countries on governance measures. When adjusted for per capita income, however, most countries lag behind the international norm in their corruption ranking (figure 4.14).

Perceptions of Unfair Competition Prove That the Rules of the Game Are Not the Same for All

Administrative (petty) corruption or bribe taking forms part of this picture. In several countries informal payments are expected to speed approvals or access to services—or to ease the burden of taxes and regulations. Interviews and focus groups suggest, however, that an important part of the corruption picture is also higher-level corruption and political capture (see chapter 8). As much as petty corruption, capture explains the distress that many businesses feel when they say that the influential and powerful benefit from discretion and from preferential public policies, or are first in line for public benefits.

FIGURE 4.14

Most MENA Countries Lag behind International Norms in Their Corruption Ranking
(Corruption Perception Index: 0–10)

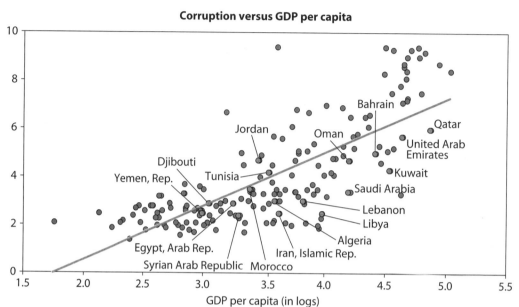

Note: A country's CPI Score relates to perceptions of the degree of corruption as seen by business people and country analysts and ranges between 10 (highly clean) and 0 (highly corrupt). The 2007 CPI ranks 180 countries and draws on 14 polls and surveys from 12 independent institutions. Countries' relative positions on these indicators are subject to indicated margins of error that should be taken into consideration when making comparisons across countries.

Source: Transparency International *Corruption Perceptions Index* (CPI) 2007.

Businessmen not receiving such treatment develop an understandable sense of unfairness and in several countries see their competitors' ability to evade the rules as a leading constraint. Anticompetitive and informal practices figure among the top 10 constraints identified by businesses in seven of 10 countries surveyed. The ability of competitors to evade the rules is a leading business constraint. In four of 10 surveyed countries, more than half of the firms identified "anticompetitive and informal practices" as a "major" or "severe" constraint, and three more countries saw it identified as serious by more than a third of firms (figure 4.15).

Perhaps the most common concern in countries where most people are getting away with something is that they fear that their competitors are getting away with more. Whether for evasion of tax, labor, or trade rules, in countries where the application of rules is negotiable, there is always a concern that someone else got a better deal. Concern about unfair competition is often about privileged large competitors evading the burden of taxes and regulations or getting favorable treatment and access to privileges—or about small informal firms operating at low costs and, with few tax and regulatory burdens, undercutting formal firms. The

FIGURE 4.15

Anticompetitive/Informal Practices
(percent of firms identifying this constraint as "major" or "severe")

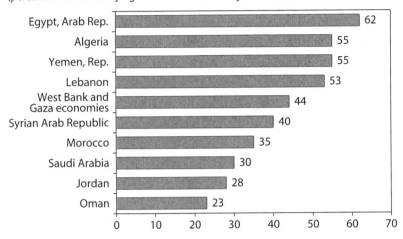

Source: World Bank enterprise surveys, various years.

prevalence of informality in MENA is linked to investment climate failures that reduce the benefits or increase the costs of formal participation in the economy (chapter 5) (Schneider 2005).

In Lebanon entrepreneurs complain about several modes of unfair competition—from privileged firms with special subsidies or protection to informal firms operating in blatant disregard of the law (figure 4.16). Entrepreneurs acknowledge that typical firms engage in substantial degrees of informality, concealing part of their income or their workforce to avoid taxes and regulations (figure 4.17). They estimate that firms such as theirs hide anywhere from 4 to 49 percent of their sales to avoid taxes.

Unfair competition and anticompetitive practices do not necessarily point to an inadequate legal framework. Most countries in the region have competition laws. Some have competition councils or antitrust agencies. The problem is more that in all areas of the business environment, the rules are not the same for all. This unlevel playing field is a consequence not of specific entry or exit regulations, but of the different treatment that firms receive in every area of the business environment. This is especially so where the state's administrative role or intervention in markets is strongest. For example, issues of preferential treatment often appear in access to land where (local) governments often administratively allocate individual plots (see chapter 6). They also appear strongly in access to finance when banks are state owned, and they appear in the implementation of business regulations by different agencies.

FIGURE 4.16

Entrepreneurs from Lebanon Complain about Competitors' Practices

(percent of firms claiming that competitors . . .)

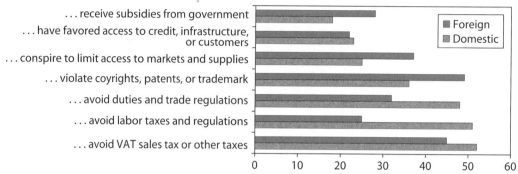

Source: World Bank enterprise surveys.

FIGURE 4.17

Revenue Reported by Typical Establishment for Tax Purposes

(percent of revenue)

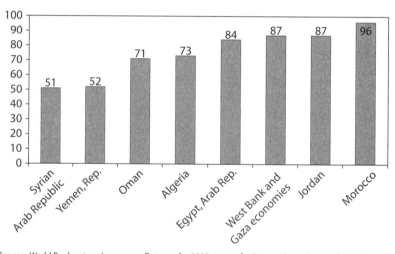

Source: World Bank enterprise surveys. Data are for 2005, except for Egypt, whose data are for 2006.

Going back to the framework presented earlier, the message of this chapter—and the report—is that, in general, no single area of the business environment can be singled out as particularly binding to businesses in the region. In some countries, some areas are more problematic (quite often land or finance) than others. The main issue is cross-cutting: it lies with the public agencies in charge of implementing and enforcing the rules and policies. This applies to every area of the business environment in figure 3.1. It will bind more strongly in areas where discretion is higher, but it is an underlying issue that goes beyond any one policy area.

Symptoms of a Business Environment That Is Not the Same for All

Creative destruction, a phrase coined by Joseph Schumpeter, refers to the dynamic entry of innovative new firms that drive less productive established firms out of the market, a force for economic growth (Schumpeter 1942). This process is especially active during the transition from a state-led to a market-based economy. Research has shown that the largest part of increases in productivity and private sector performance in transition economies came from new entrants in the market and exit of inefficient firms (see, e.g., McMillan and Woodruff 2002). Constraints in the business environment that limit the fluidity of this process—such as entry barriers—also limit growth and productivity gains. By contrast, high levels of entry and exit of firms contribute to a dynamic and healthy economy.

The gap between the rules and how they are implemented—the discretion and unequal treatment of investors in MENA—reflect different forms of high barriers to entry and competition. This section shows that these barriers have reduced creative destruction and dynamism in MENA's private sector.

As explained above, it is important to reiterate that these barriers to entry and competition are not due specifically to regulations of firm entry and exit. They are found in every area of the business environment in which firms are exposed to discretionary implementation of the rules. For example, accessing land is difficult because of the need for connections to receive a subsidized plot in an industrial zone—a barrier to entry.

Older Firms

Firm-level evidence suggests that exit is weaker in MENA than in other regions, because the industrial sector is disproportionately dominated by older firms. The old business elite seem to stay in business longer than in other regions, as evidenced by the median age of local manufacturing firms in developing countries as well as OECD countries (figure 4.18).[5] Older incumbent entrepreneurs in this region seem more likely to survive economic transitions and reforms.

At 19 years the median local manufacturing firm's age in MENA is the same as that in the more mature OECD economies—and almost twice the median in East Asia and Eastern Europe and Central Asia. Old firms that emerged in previous decades continue to dominate business, and the renewal of the industrial structure is slower than elsewhere. Taking into account the old business elite and its origins, this characteristic is important for policy development, particularly from a political standpoint.

FIGURE 4.18

The Lasting Influence of the Old Business Elite in MENA: Older Firms
(years)

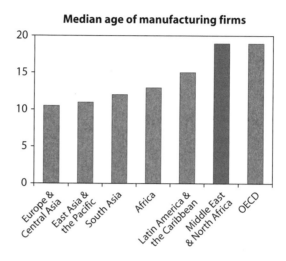

Source: World Bank enterprise surveys, various years. Only private domestic manufacturing firms are included.

Unsurprisingly, the more recent the growth acceleration or the transition, the younger the average firm: the median firm age is 10.5 years in Eastern Europe and Central Asia, 11 years in East Asia, and 12 years in South Asia. This is a reflection of the structural changes in Asia and Eastern Europe, where many new entrants are replacing incumbent firms. More stagnant economies of Latin America and MENA have older firms, reflecting weaker entry-exit dynamism.

The Persistence of Old Generation Entrepreneurs

Not only are the domestic manufacturing firms older than in comparable developing countries, but the managers of these firms appear to be older as well. The difference is even more striking than firm age: the average number of years of previous experience in the sector of managers of local manufacturing firms (usually the business owners) is close to 14 years in MENA, compared with nine years in Africa and seven years in East Asia. This is particularly noteworthy in a region with one of the world's largest proportions of youth (figure 4.19).

A recent World Bank study of 211 semiformal microenterprises in Morocco illustrates the generational gap between the two types of private sector (World Bank 2008b). Although the median experience (a proxy for age) in formal small and medium-sized firms is between 16 and

FIGURE 4.19

The Lasting Influence of the Old Business Elite in MENA: Older Entrepreneurs among Younger Populations

(average years of previous experience of firm managers)   *(percent of population under age 15)*

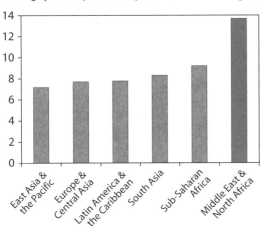
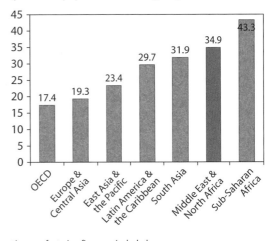

Source: World Bank enterprise surveys, various years. Only private domestic manufacturing firms are included.

18 years, that in microenterprises is eight years. This reflects the more vibrant entry and exit in microenterprises than in formal small and medium-sized enterprises. The average age of the microenterprise owners is 32 years.

The educational profile of business owner-managers is another consistent piece of evidence showing that exit is weaker in MENA and that the old business elite is more dominant than elsewhere. The region has made impressive progress over the last few decades in increasing educational attainment (World Bank 2008c), but the added years of education and the increase in university graduates are not yet reflected in the profiles of manufacturing business owners and managers. Compared with other regions, MENA has the highest percentage of manufacturing business owners who have not completed secondary school: 13 percent, more than the 6 percent in Eastern Europe and Central Asia, 5 percent in East Asia, and 3 percent in South Asia (figure 4.20). Not reflecting the population of the region, this is simply evidence that renewal of the business elite with a generation of younger, better educated entrepreneurs seems to have been slower in the MENA countries than in other parts of the developing world.

Most countries in the region have abundant pools of talented entrepreneurs. What they have lacked is the creative destruction essential for productivity and economic growth. In fact, new entrants in MENA seem

FIGURE 4.20

Less Educated Business Owners
(percent of managers not completing secondary school)

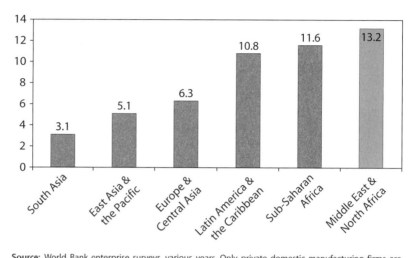

Source: World Bank enterprise surveys, various years. Only private domestic manufacturing firms are included.

more likely to be successful in exporting than older firms. Among manufacturing exporters, the median time between firm creation and the first export—two years—is much lower in this region than elsewhere, except East Asia (figure 4.21).

FIGURE 4.21

Business Creation and Entry into Export Markets
(average number of years between business creation and first export)

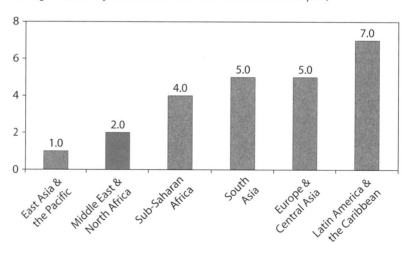

Source: World Bank enterprise surveys, various years. Only private domestic manufacturing firms are included.

Weaker Entrepreneurship—But Things Are Changing

The World Bank Entrepreneurship Database[6] shows that the average firm density in MENA is one of the lowest in the world (figure 4.22). The average firm density in Algeria, Egypt, Jordan, Lebanon, Morocco, Syria, Tunisia, and the Republic of Yemen is a third to a quarter of that in Latin America or Eastern Europe and Central Asia. The difference is consistent with the evidence on the average firm age—reflecting slower entry rates over time and slower exit rates of old incumbents.

FIGURE 4.22

Entrepreneurship in MENA and Other Regions
(number of registered firms per 1,000 inhabitants)

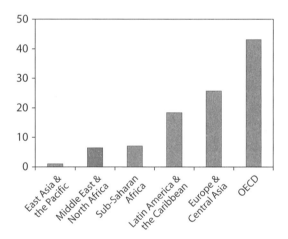

(percentage point increase in registered firms)   *(percentage point increase in registered firms)*

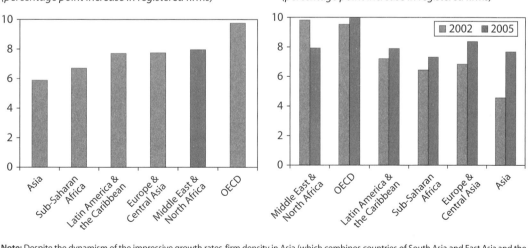

Note: Despite the dynamism of the impressive growth rates, firm density in Asia (which combines countries of South Asia and East Asia and the Pacific) is particularly low. This is driven by China's and India's high (rural) population and the fact that firm-density counts only *formally* registered firms per capita.

Source: World Bank Entrepreneurship Database. MENA countries with data are Algeria, Egypt, Jordan, Lebanon, Morocco, Syria, Tunisia, and the Republic of Yemen. Simple averages are used.

The situation is changing. For business creation rates (averaging between 2002 and 2005), MENA stands out as the most dynamic region after the OECD countries. This reflects the fact that the recent, precrisis growth boom and the reforms from the first half of this decade are creating opportunities for new and smaller businesses. This dynamism may be tempered by the current crisis, but these new waves of entrepreneurs will be at the forefront of the recovery. Anyone who has wandered the streets of Cairo, Algiers, Tripoli, Tehran, Damascus, or Casablanca since the early 2000s has witnessed this greater private sector dynamism. This is good news, especially for employment creation.

Less Competition

One of the most telling indicators of competitive markets in a country is the productivity dispersion of firms in a given industry. If markets are competitive, with reasonably free entry and exit, the dispersion should be quite low, because efficient competitors (and new entrants) drive less competitive firms either to raise their productivity or to exit. Higher dispersion indicates that less efficient producers are not being forced to improve their productivity or exit the market. Firm studies bear this out: a lower productivity dispersion is associated with increased openness and greater competition with foreign firms (Haddad 1993; Haddad and Harrison 1993; Harrison 1994; Hallward-Driemeier, Iarossi, and Sokoloff 2001).

Subsidies or strict regulations that impede entry or exit can bolster high-cost producers. With such firms still in the market, more productive firms may not have an adequate incentive to further increase their productivity or to expand. As competition increases, however, firms face greater incentives to innovate and greater penalties for not doing so. As a result, the productivity dispersion should shrink as productivity rises in the face of greater competition.

Consistent with limited competition and the slower exit of less successful older firms, the dispersion of value-added per worker in the garment industry is higher in MENA countries than in comparator countries (figure 4.23).[7] The productivity dispersion is considerable in Algeria, Egypt, Syria, and the Republic of Yemen—at levels comparable only to Pakistan. In resource-rich, labor-abundant countries the average value-added per worker of a firm near the top of the distribution (80th percentile) is almost seven times higher than an average firm near the bottom (20th percentile). Compare this with 2.4 times in Malaysia and 3.8 in Turkey. The measured dispersion in resource-poor countries, at around 5, is lower. They exhibit a better business environment and greater openness to trade and competition.

When managers are asked how many competitors they face in their sector, those in MENA report fewer competitors than in South Asia and

FIGURE 4.23

Dispersion in Value-Added per Worker

(ratio of 80th percentile to 20th percentile of value-added per worker in the garment industry)

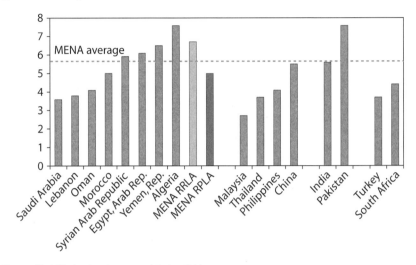

Source: World Bank enterprise surveys, latest available year.

Nore: RRLA: resoure-rich labor-abundant; RPLA: resource-poor labor-abundant

FIGURE 4.24

Competition in Manufacturing

(median number of local competitors in industry)

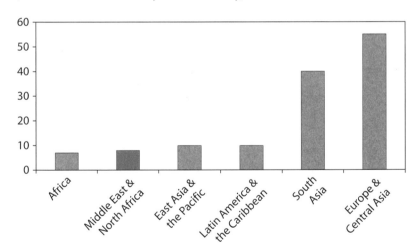

Source: World Bank enterprise surveys, latest available year.

Eastern Europe (figure 4.24). The median number of competitors, eight, is also slightly smaller than in East Asia and Latin America (10). Only Africa (with a median of seven) seems to exhibit less domestic competition than MENA countries.

Summing Up

For many countries in the region, the main problem is not reforming more rules and regulations, but improving their implementation. The evidence in this chapter—both from firms' complaints and from firm-level characteristics—showed that barriers to entry and competition are pervasive in the region. The business environment as it appears on the books is not applied equally to all in each country. This is indirect evidence that discretion and arbitrary implementation of policies reduce the credibility of reforms for most investors, who consequently mute their response.

Understanding the real issues holding back entrepreneurs requires looking beyond policies as they are enacted to understand the role of the state and its institutions in the way that they implement these policies more or less consistently and predictably. Part II of this report examines the role of the state in the credit, land, and industrial policy.

Notes

1. Note that compared with other global indicators that use perception measures, *Doing Business* probably gets the closest to what firms—especially small and medium enterprises—actually face, because it focuses on the complexity of regulatory barriers in different areas of the business environment. Still, it does not measure actual delays and uncertainties facing different types of firms—or the inconsistencies and discretion associated with the actual implementation and enforcement of rules.

2. See, for example, Dobronogov and Iqbal (2005) on the links of the Egyptian GDP growth to OECD economic performance.

3. For example, in December 2008 Algeria enacted rules limiting foreign participation in all new investments to 49 percent and forcing foreign-owned firms that import consumer goods to open at least 30 percent of their capital to local shareholders. Both measures constitute a policy reversal in a trade and foreign investment environment that had been quite open.

4. In a 2006 survey of Egyptian businesses, floating hotels reported that they received 38 inspections by three types of police—river, tourism, and municipal—in a single year.

5. Since 2000, random sample surveys have been conducted by the World Bank in more than 60 countries. These differences in the median age of firms are greater when comparing averages instead of medians.

They are not due to sample bias due to size, because the differences are similar when comparing medium-sized firms.

6. Available online at http://www.ifc.org/ifcext/sme.nsf/Content/ Resources.

7. Dispersion is measured here as the ratio of the 80th percentile to the 20th percentile in the distribution of value added per worker in the garment industry. The garment sector, available in all samples, is generally used for international benchmarking of productivity because its products are reasonably comparable.

PART II

Policies and How They Are Applied: State Intervention and Discretion in Credit, Land, and Industrial Policy

In closing the first part of this report, chapter 4 argued that countries share a common problem of weak, unpredictable or discretionary implementation of policies in all areas of the business environment in which public agencies and the state hold residual discretionary power. It provided indirect evidence in support of this conclusion—complaints by firms point to policy implementation uncertainty; competition, entry, and creative destruction is weak; and neither can be totally explained by a lack of policy reforms. Hence the insufficient response to past reforms by most private investors, which do not expect these reforms to really improve their business environment, especially in areas in which they depend on state institutions for their implementation or they need to interact with public agencies when new policies are applied.

The common problem boils down to the role of the state and its institutions in various areas of the business environment——the topic of part II. It goes beyond the laws and the regulatory frameworks in place—and the common indicators that assess them—to dig into the role of the state in access to credit, land, and industrial policy. It illustrates, in each area, the wide gap between enacted policies and the behavior of institutions that implement them.

Chapter 5 shows how state ownership of banks is the most important determinant of the (in)efficiency of credit markets across the region. Even if the corporate governance rules of state-owned banks have improved, with greater independence on paper, discretion and interference in credit allocations clearly hurt firm access to credit. Even, as well, if most countries have lifted many regulatory restrictions to entry of new banks, in reality, competition in the banking sector is weak. Similarly, collateral legislation may be comparable to that in other emerging markets. Most credit, however, requires collateral far exceeding that in comparable countries—a symptom of a judicial system and enforcement mechanisms that are not working and not trusted.

Chapter 6 shows how state ownership and management in industrial land markets leads to distortions that make access to land a particularly severe problem across the region. Although land policies are intended to facilitate investment, spatial development, and clustering, their implementation is distorted by the discretionary power of many administrative agencies, particularly at local levels. Land is a key rent distribution mechanism in many countries, and allocating subsidized plots creates artificial shortages that hurt economic efficiency and investment. Because full land market liberalization is not a realistic option in the short or medium term, improving access to industrial land will require reducing the discretion of government in managing industrial zones and allocating individual plots to investors. Again, it is not so much about changing the rules or procedures of land access, as about reinventing the role of the state as a key player in land markets to reduce the distortions.

Chapter 7 focuses on a range of widely popular policies that have recently grown in importance: industrial policies. Avoiding a dogmatic stance on government interventions, the chapter argues that the lack of transparency in implementation, the lack of credible evaluations, the excessive reliance on direct subsidies, and the discretionary allocation of benefits limit the potential for successful industrial policies in MENA. Features that made them successful in East Asia and elsewhere—particularly the capacity to shut down failing programs based on credible and transparent criteria—are mostly absent in MENA. They are also absent in the new industrial strategies recently launched in some countries.

CHAPTER 5

Access to Credit in MENA: Toward Better Supervision and Less Interference

An efficient and competitive financial system channels savings and capital inflows to productive investment, stimulating growth and employment. International experience shows that more open and competitive banking systems are associated with better access to finance over the medium term. Such systems are usually characterized by private ownership of banks, including foreign ownership, by strong legal, informational, and financial infrastructure, and by regulatory and supervisory frameworks that manage risks and prevent crises while protecting consumers and ensuring transparency.

This chapter shows that barriers to entry are pervasive in many countries in the region; however, barriers reduce competition and efficiency and exclude enterprises from the financial services that they need. Barriers arise from widespread state ownership of banks and a lack of transparency and accountability in financial systems. Low transparency in the operations of both enterprises and banks are linked to high collateral requirements, fairly high levels of nonperforming loans, and low rates of access to bank loans. Banks too often use collateral requirements as a credit-rationing tool rather than allocate credit based on risk analysis. The collateral required is among the highest in the world, suggesting that the enforcement of collateral legislation is inefficient and not trusted by lenders.

Although some countries still have explicit laws that prevent entry and competition, the legal and regulatory environment of financial markets in MENA cannot explain the poor access to finance in the region. Consistent with the framework in chapter 3 and the diagnosis in chapter 4, this chapter shows that the core of the problem lies with the discretion of the state in credit allocation, less than independent supervision institutions, inefficient and unequal enforcement of the laws and regulations by the judiciary, and a lack of transparency in the system.

Public banks have traditionally served as channels of political patronage—by supporting inefficient state-owned firms or by channeling credit to well-connected private businesses. State ownership of banks tends to be associated with less financial sector development, slower growth, and lower productivity. Reforming the public banks is thus critical to financial sector reform. Private banks in the region are not immune to the inefficiencies of state banks, however, because the supervision and regulation of credit markets is open to political interference and poor enforcement.

Surveys show that 39 percent of the region's enterprises, the highest in the world excluding Sub-Saharan Africa, consider limited access to finance to be a major constraint to their operations. Access to finance may be further constrained by the economic impact of the global financial crisis on enterprise profitability and bank loan portfolios.

To increase access to finance for enterprises in the region, governance, transparency, and accountability each need to be improved. Where state-owned banks still dominate, transparent and competitive privatization to strategic investors should be a priority, as market conditions allow.

Even where the presence of public banks is smaller, the reform agenda rests on increasing competition by allowing new entrants (particularly foreign banks), strengthening supervisory and regulatory institutions, and building financial infrastructure. As the current global financial crisis has shown, the same competition that can broaden access to finance can also result in imprudent lending binges—and in systemic instability—if it is not accompanied by transparency and a strong and enforceable regulatory and supervisory framework. Each of these reforms requires improving risk management, extending access to finance, and curbing discretion and arbitrariness.

Private sector development in MENA countries depends on the capacity of entrepreneurs to design and implement viable, innovative, and productive projects—and to obtain finance for starting them up and sustaining them. Bank lending is the main source of outside finance for most enterprises in MENA countries, although capital markets, remittances, and trade finance can also be important.[1]

This chapter assesses the efficiency of enterprise credit markets along five dimensions, based on country and firm data (table 5.1). Three

TABLE 5.1

Efficiency of Credit Markets

	Depth	Use	Intensity of use	Access	Perception of access	Total
Jordan	2	0	2	2	2	8
Lebanon	2	2	2	2	0	8
Oman	1	2	1	—	2	7
Morocco	1	1	2	1	1	6
Saudi Arabia	2	2	0	1	0	5
Egypt, Arab Rep.	1	0	1	0	2	4
Syrian Arab Republic	0	0	0	—	2	3
Republic of Yemen	0	0	0	—	1	2
Algeria	0	1	0	0	0	1

Note: Each of the five dimensions was rated using a scale of 0 = low, 1 = medium, 2 = high. To obtain an overall ordinal ranking of countries, these ratings were added for each country—and a neutral score of 1 was used for the few missing data items.

Source: Authors' calculations.

groups of countries emerge: in Jordan, Lebanon, and most GCC countries, enterprises have higher access to credit; Morocco, Saudi Arabia,
and Tunisia have moderate access; and Algeria, Egypt, the Islamic
Republic of Iran, Libya, Syria, and the Republic of Yemen have low
access. MENA has a deeper banking sector than most other emerging
markets, but it has a small client base and is vulnerable to nonperforming loans. Overall, access to credit for enterprises is lower than the
average for other emerging markets—and most of this lackluster
performance is driven by the countries that have not reformed their
banking sector.

Credit Markets and Banking Systems in MENA

In 2007 private sector credit was 42 percent of GDP (figure 5.1), the
median among five regions, so MENA compares fairly well with other
developing regions except East Asia. However, the region's banking
systems differ widely across countries (figure 5.2). Those in the GCC are
generally more developed and have a ratio of private sector credit to non-
oil GDP above 80 percent, close to East Asia. Resource-poor countries
are at 60 percent, and non-GCC oil-rich countries below 20 percent.

A high ratio of private sector credit to non-oil GDP can obscure
distributions of credit to a minority of beneficiaries—which leaves most
enterprises facing credit rationing. This ratio does not distinguish
financial depth and breadth and perhaps hides excessive concentrations of

FIGURE 5.1

**Total Credit to the Private Sector Compares Well with Other
Developing Regions, 2007**
(percent of GDP)

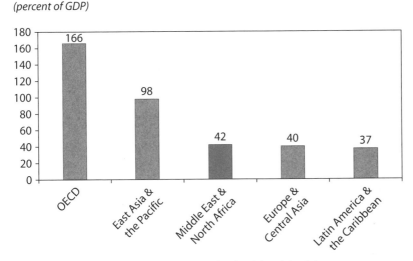

Sources: Database of Financial Sector Indicators, World Bank; IMF financial statistics.

FIGURE 5.2

Beyond Regional Averages: Diversity in the Efficiency of MENA Credit Markets, 2007

(percent of non-oil GDP)

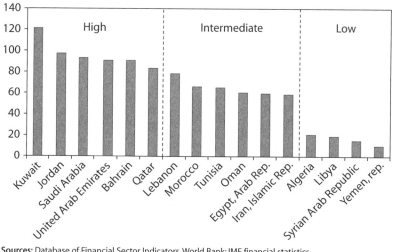

Sources: Database of Financial Sector Indicators, World Bank; IMF financial statistics.

credit. Banks in most countries in the region extend fewer loans and have smaller branch networks than in comparable countries (figure 5.3). If taken with the comparatively higher aggregate levels of credit to the private sector, this may be one reflection of excessive concentration of credit.

FIGURE 5.3

Banking Sector Penetration Is Low

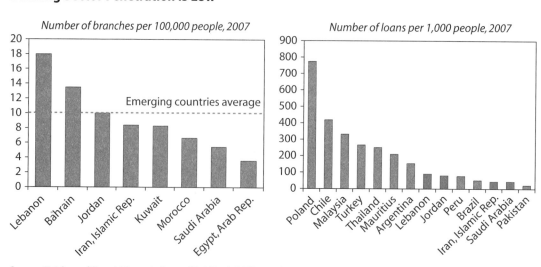

Sources: Database of Financial Sector Indicators, World Bank; IMF financial statistics.

Business Manager Perceptions of Credit Constraints

The perception of financing constraints varies widely depending on economic conditions, the banking system, and the demand for credit. In Egypt, Syria, and the Republic of Yemen, where credit use is low, entrepreneurs complain less about access to finance. But one would expect displeasure with financing constraints to grow proportionately with the demand for credit. Investment Climate Assessment (ICA) surveys in 10 MENA countries reveal that 39 percent of the region's enterprises consider limited access to finance a major or severe constraint on their operations, dissatisfaction exceeded only in Sub-Saharan Africa (figure 5.4).

Dissatisfaction is directly related to the demand for credit and inversely related to the supply. In countries with advanced banking intermediation, enterprise demand for bank credit is high and more sensitive to loan terms—such as the interest rate, maturity, and collateral required. In Lebanon, Morocco, and Saudi Arabia high dissatisfaction is linked to the intensity of demand for credit. The moderate dissatisfaction in Egypt, Syria, and the Republic of Yemen indicates weaker enterprise demand for credit (Figure 5.5). Enterprises with no need for credit, or enterprises with secure bank credit, complain the least about financing constraints.

Changing perceptions of business between 2004 and 2007 illustrate that these constraints are sensitive to overall economic conditions. The ICA surveys of Morocco show that 80 percent of enterprises complained about access to finance in 2004, but only 31 percent did so in 2007. The first survey was conducted in an environment characterized by weak

FIGURE 5.4

Dissatisfaction with Access to Finance
(percent of firms identifying access to finance as a "major" or "severe" constraint)

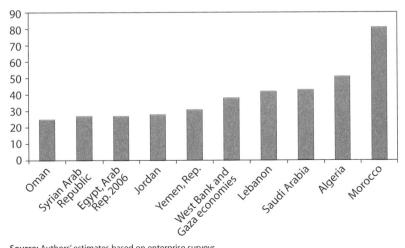

Source: Authors' estimates based on enterprise surveys.

FIGURE 5.5

Dissatisfaction Increases with the Demand for Credit
(percent of firms identifying access to finance as a major constraint)

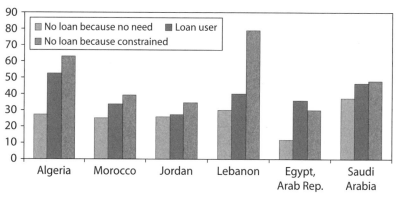

Source: Authors' estimates based on enterprise surveys.

economic growth while the banking sector was restructuring. Enterprise cash flow deteriorated, and demand for credit increased when banks were tightening lending conditions. During the economic recovery of 2007 surveyed firms had better cash positions and clean balance sheets. Perceptions of access to finance improved greatly, even though the use of bank credit by enterprises had not changed to the same extent.

Beyond Perceptions and Complaints: How Many Firms Are Really Credit Constrained?

Twenty-nine percent of surveyed MENA enterprises use bank lending to finance their working capital needs, and 22 percent for their investments, about the average for emerging countries (figure 5.6). How many can be considered to be credit constrained?

Firm-level data on the demand for and access to bank loans allow estimates of the proportion of firms that can be considered credit constrained. The estimates reflect an upper limit on the percentage of firms likely to be excluded from the credit market despite being creditworthy. As with other measures of the credit market efficiency, credit rationing is high among MENA countries that have undertaken few financial sector reforms (figure 5.7).

A survey of 37 banks conducted by the report team in five countries[2] showed that small enterprises face greater difficulties accessing finance, because banks perceive them as less financially transparent than large enterprises. They also lead to higher transaction costs per loan extended. Small enterprises are also less able to come up with the collateral required by conservative lending practices. In MENA countries small enterprises of fewer than 20 employees are twice as likely to be credit constrained as

FIGURE 5.6

How Firms Use Bank Credit
(percent)

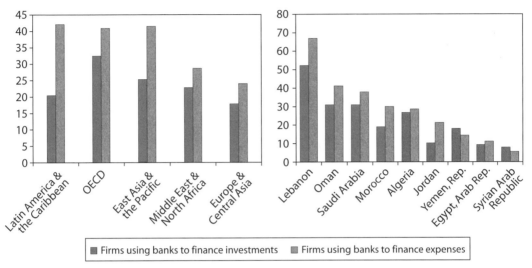

■ Firms using banks to finance investments   ■ Firms using banks to finance expenses

Source: Authors' calculations based on enterprise surveys.

FIGURE 5.7

Credit Constraints Are Stronger in Countries That Have Reformed Less
(upper limit of the percentage of credit-constrained firms)

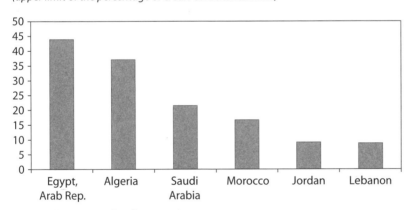

Source: Authors' estimates based on enterprise surveys.

large firms (figure 5.8),[3] but firms with audited financial accounts are less likely to be credit constrained (figure 5.9).

Banks in much of the region generally did not embark on the same expansion of lending into riskier assets as banks in Western Europe and the United States and therefore have not been as immediately exposed to the global financial crisis that began in September 2008. Their portfolios, however, could still be affected by the impact of the crisis on their

FIGURE 5.8

Smaller Firms Are More Credit Constrained Than Larger Firms

(percent of firms that are credit constrained)

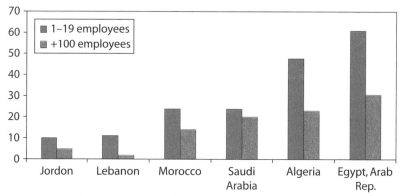

Source: Authors' estimates based on enterprise surveys.

FIGURE 5.9

Transparency in Financial Statements Helps to Enter the Credit Market

(probability of being credit constrained)

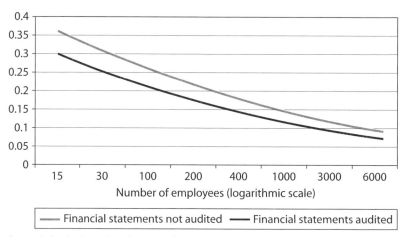

Source: Authors' estimates based on enterprise surveys.

enterprise and individual clients. Such an economic downturn would lower both supply and demand of finance, reducing levels of access to finance. Countries with strong economic links to Europe, such as Morocco and Tunisia, could be particularly affected through lower demand for their exports (or through lower tourism receipts and trade-related revenues for countries such as Egypt). Enterprises in Egypt, Lebanon, Jordan, the Republic of Yemen, and other countries that have had significant investment flows from the Gulf economies may become more reliant on bank lending as those other sources of finance become harder to access.

What Can Governments Do to Increase Access to Credit?

The journey toward efficient credit markets can be sequenced in four stages: ensuring the stability of the banking sector, building market infrastructure, creating the framework for competition and innovation, and correcting for potential market failures through risk sharing with the private sector.

Governments should pursue policies that discipline and harness the market to prevent instability (Beck and de la Torre 2006). Only a stable banking sector can broaden access to finance. But a stable banking system is not necessarily one that provides improved and open access to credit. Governments should remove unnecessary regulations and policies that raise the cost of bank lending to enterprises, while requiring sound risk management practices to be followed. As the current global financial crisis has shown, the failure of bank (or other financial institution) internal controls and the regulators' inability to assess the risks associated with financial innovation compromised financial stability.

Before planning interventions to correct market imperfections, governments must establish the fundamental institutions of the financial sector (see, e.g., World Bank 2007b). If the legal framework for collateral does not ensure creditor security, for example, a costly government-backed guarantee system would not raise bank lending in the long term. Similarly, credit bureaus will not sustainably raise lending levels and reduce borrowing costs if banks are basing lending decisions on criteria other than risk and return.

State Ownership and the Inefficiency of the Banking System: The Need to Credibly Reform the Governance of Public Banks or Privatize Them

MENA governments own higher stakes in banks than do governments in other developing regions. Algeria, the Islamic Republic of Iran, and Syria own more than 90 percent of bank assets. Among smaller countries only Jordan, Lebanon, and Oman have a privatized banking sector. A significant risk of instability in the region's financial systems comes from state-owned banks' lack of independence and market discipline due to political interference. MENA state-owned banks perform worse than private banks overall. The repeated failures to ensure acceptable levels of nonperforming loans are symptoms that their risk management systems are weak. They often support insolvent state-owned enterprises, and

FIGURE 5.10

MENA's Nonperforming Loans—Highest in the World

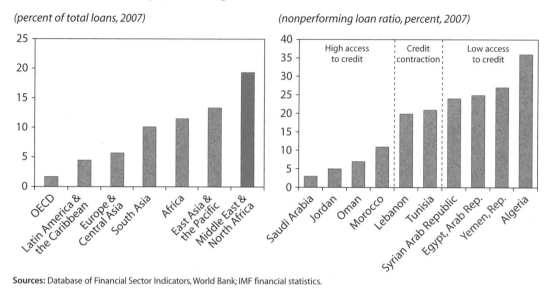

(percent of total loans, 2007)   (nonperforming loan ratio, percent, 2007)

Sources: Database of Financial Sector Indicators, World Bank; IMF financial statistics.

they provide poor services: state-controlled banks can take three times longer than countries with private banks to process an application for a line of credit (World Bank enterprise surveys).

In 2007 MENA banks had the highest rate of nonperforming loans (NPLs) in the world—about 20 percent. This high rate curtails the efficiency of intermediation (figure 5.10). In countries with high rates of NPLs, such as Algeria, Egypt, Syria, and the Republic of Yemen, enterprises have limited access to finance. With their capital bases thus impaired, many banks require new capital injections from government—often renewed over the years. Algeria has the most vulnerable banking sector, with more than 35 percent of NPLs, and Saudi Arabia the least, with 3 percent, similar to OECD countries. Four of the 10 banks with the world's highest NPL rates in 2007 were in the MENA region.[4]

The extent of NPLs is directly related to the prominence of state-owned banks (figure 5.11) and in some cases connected lending. Historically, governments of the region have used state-owned banks to attain socioeconomic goals or for connected lending (to state-owned enterprises or to private businessmen with preferential access). The state's social mandate pushes banks to lend to insolvent borrowers or those likely to default because of their connections or their knowledge of the lack of enforcement. Bank restructuring can claim a sizable share of government budgets—more than 10 percent of GDP in Egypt and 4.3 percent of GDP at year-end 2005 in Algeria. Yet the large outlays to restore financial and operational soundness did not bring sustained stability to the banking sector. Why? Because a public bank with poorly enforced governance rules, if

FIGURE 5.11

The Risk of Nonperforming Loans—Higher with State-Owned Banks

(nonperforming loan ratio, percent, 2007)

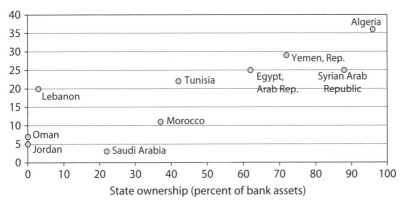

Sources: Database of Financial Sector Indicators, World Bank; IMF financial statistics.

bestowed with fresh capital, may have an incentive to revert to its lax lending habits.

Shifts in corporate governance—such as management contracts—have only rarely improved the efficiency of public banks, and that inefficiency can push state-owned banks to the brink of insolvency. Governments inevitably face pressure to rescue failing public banks. As with the current bailouts of private banks in Europe, the United States, and elsewhere, the political as well as economic costs can seem too high to impose market discipline on these failing banks—too many depositors, debtors, and (state-owned) firms depend on them (box 5.1). The moral hazard associated with these bailouts is much stronger with state-owned banks, because the state is the owner, the manager, the supervisor, and ultimately the lender of first and last resort. Many countries in the region—Algeria, Egypt, and Tunisia, for example—have suffered from successive bailouts of the same public banks over the years. Management contracts and other reforms of their corporate governance have not solved the fundamental moral hazard underlying state ownership.

So governments should, as a priority, improve the governance of the banking sector and reduce discretion in credit allocations. This should increase competition along with more effective regulation and supervision. Where state-owned banks still dominate, transparent and competitive privatization to strategic investors should be given precedence. This applies particularly to resource-rich Algeria, the Islamic Republic of Iran, Libya, and Syria, which have not significantly improved the independence and governance of public banks.[5] Even where the presence of public banks is smaller (Egypt, Jordan,

---

BOX 5.1

Bank Bailouts and the Financial Crisis—A Return to Nationalizations or a Temporary Cure?

What Went Wrong?

The burgeoning literature that tries to explain the current crisis points to a variety of long-standing issues and policy decisions that, together, led to the financial debacle in the United States and elsewhere.[a] Among them are a long period of expansionary monetary and fiscal policy, particularly in the United States, abundant liquidity, low interest rates, rising asset prices (bubble), a persistent and overconfident belief that markets would ultimately correct mispricing and that regulators should stay away from intervening to correct for market failures, and financial innovation on Wall Street that was not matched by progress in risk management and supervision. In fact, much of the financial innovation was by firms whose activities were not regulated (investment banks and hedge funds). Research and debates are still ongoing to determine exactly the root causes of the crisis, but very few attribute it to private ownership of banks.

Some of the lessons from this crisis are not directly relevant for MENA because they relate to the U.S. financial system with its distorted incentives system in the mortgage market, complex mortgage financing value chain, opaque securitization structure, and complex and fragmented supervisory architecture. Useful lessons are relevant, however, for the region's policy makers. For example, the role of government-sponsored mortgage finance companies—Fannie Mae and Freddie Mac—in the U.S. financial crisis is another reminder of the potential distortions caused by political interference in financial institutions with dual (public-private) mandates.

Are We Experiencing a Paradigm Shift on State Ownership?

Given the extent of several government interventions to bail out troubled private banks and key financial institutions to stabilize financial markets, many observers wonder whether this response has not ushered in a paradigm shift—putting the state rather than the private sector in charge of financial markets.

The current bailouts of banks by many OECD governments are part of short-term strategies to contain the crisis. These include plans for recapitalization—the injection of new capital. This does not mean, however, that the state will remain indefinitely in control of the banks: past crises have shown that the state needed to intervene in situations in which markets are unable to value distressed assets. The state needs to provide the necessary lifeline to avoid a contagion effect that leads to unsustainable losses in output and employment. None of the current government strategies, however, aim at regaining permanently control of private banks. To the contrary, the bailouts explicitly include exit

(continued)

BOX 5.1 *(continued)*

strategies for governments. Although the presence of the state in the financial sector may temporarily increase in these countries in the short term to respond to the crisis, the overwhelming evidence on the inefficiency of state ownership of banks remains valid—including those in MENA and elsewhere in developing nations.

a. For a review of recent literature on the current financial crisis, see World Bank (2009) and references therein.

Source: Authors' report.

Morocco, and Tunisia), the reform agenda rests on increasing competition by allowing new entrants (particularly foreign banks) and strengthening supervisory and regulatory institutions and the associated infrastructure. That requires strengthening the (independent) supervisory capacity of central banks.

MENA countries have privatized banks at varying rates. Since 2004 Egypt has forged ahead with financial reform. It privatized the fourth largest bank—the Bank of Alexandria—in 2006 and is expected to do the same with the third largest bank—the Banque du Caire—as soon as international financial markets recover. The state also divested its holdings in 15 joint venture banks that account for 20 percent of banking system deposits. Its share of deposits in total banking system deposits is now below 50 percent. Algeria's progress has been much slower, with several reforms repeatedly postponed, and with not a single state bank privatized by 2008. Syria allows foreign banks to enter the local market—private banks have grown rapidly since first licensed in 2004—but state banks still account for about 80 percent of financial system assets. In Libya two large state-owned banks were privatized in 2007 and 2008, and two of the three remaining public commercial banks were merged in April 2008. Most regional banks have also been merged into one bank, and agreement has been reached with financial institutions from Qatar and the United Arab Emirates to establish two new banks (International Monetary Fund 2008).

Privatizing state-owned banks can reduce access to finance for enterprises in the short term if investors do not commit to maintain a level of access—for example, to include small and medium-sized enterprises as clients, or to keep open a proportion of branches. Otherwise measures may be introduced to boost short-term profitability at the expense of enterprise clients. Banque du Caire, with its successful microlending program, may face this challenge. Two state banks in Iraq account for 450 of the total banking sector network of 550 branches and are therefore key to wider access.

Building Credit Market Infrastructure

Even financially sound well-managed banks face obstacles to efficient lending, chiefly information asymmetries and high transaction costs. A sound and well-functioning credit market requires better information about borrowers and stronger legal protections for creditors and borrowers, which in turn requires efficient, transparent, and well-governed institutions. The global crisis has also underscored the centrality of better financial reporting and disclosure to allow market participants to assess risks and allow supervisors to scrutinize more closely the accuracy and integrity of banks' financial disclosures (box 5.1).

Information about borrowers. Sharing credit information enhances enterprise access to finance (Pagano 1993; Love and Mylenko 2003; Djankov et al. 2006). The extent of information asymmetry is directly associated with increased credit rationing (box 5.2). The amount of credit information available to banks depends on a country's credit information and payment systems. It also requires institutions that collect and distribute credit information, such as credit bureaus, and that ensure that good credit reporting systems promote both financial stability (accuracy of financial institutions balance sheets) and access.

A survey of 37 banks in MENA countries revealed that the lack of financial and information transparency constrains credit. ICA surveys indicate that enterprises with audited financial accounts have better access to bank credit. The indicators in *Doing Business 2010* also suggest that credit registries in the region are underdeveloped (figure 5.12). Information is scarce and barely shared between banks in countries such as Algeria, Morocco, Syria, and the Republic of Yemen.

Collateral legislation. Because credit markets have inherent information asymmetries, banks must protect themselves against default risk. Even in OECD countries with a developed institutional framework and extensive use of credit bureaus, more than 70 percent of credits are backed by a guarantee. International evidence suggests that reform of the legal framework for collateral can improve access to finance by strengthening creditor capacity to take possession of collateral in cases of default (Safavian and Wimpey 2007). By reducing the cost to lenders of using collateral (both registering it and subsequently executing claims), the cost barriers to lending to smaller firms can also be lowered.

Banks in MENA countries require a high level of guarantees. This overcollateralization is explained by creditors' lack of confidence in the institutions that are supposed to protect their rights, banks' inability to evaluate credit risk, and creditors' lack of information on borrowers.

BOX 5.2

Credit Rationing and the Availability of Credit Information

A financing gap arises when viable projects cannot obtain financing. Empirical evidence shows that banks reject many requests for financing of viable projects—firms are said to be credit constrained. Banks also apply widely different financing conditions for projects with similar risk profile and return. Credit rationing can be explained by asymmetric information and high transaction costs. Asymmetric information exists because banks lack credit data and adequate risk management systems to assess properly project viability and borrower creditworthiness. Banks resort to credit rationing—allocating credit based on quantitative criteria—rather than credit risk analysis. Banking system reform—strengthening bank risk management and credit risk analysis capabilities, supported by adequate information systems—can reduce the financing gap and generate better allocations of lending among borrowers (box figure 1).

BOX FIGURE 1

Banking Reform Can Reduce the Financing Gap

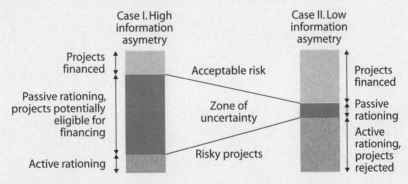

Source: Authors' report.

Financing gaps vary across countries. Constraints on access to finance are more pronounced in developing countries because their weak institutional frameworks cannot offset market failures. Credit rationing does not affect all firms equally. Newly formed small companies with local capital tend to experience greater credit rationing.

Sources: Beck, Demirguc-Kunt, and Martinez Peria 2006; World Bank 2007b.

FIGURE 5.12

Credit Information in MENA

(credit information index, Doing Business 2010)

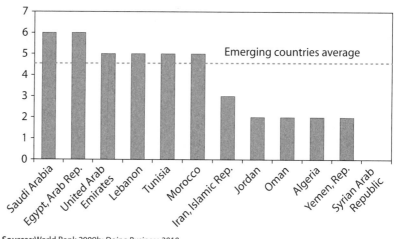

Sources:World Bank 2009b; *Doing Business 2010.*

A survey of banks in MENA countries showed that registration and execution of contracts seriously constrains the expansion of access to credit. Furthermore, according to the *Doing Business 2010* indicator, Legal Rights of Creditors, few MENA countries adequately protect creditors' rights (figure 5.13).

FIGURE 5.13

Collateral Legislation and Creditors' Rights in MENA

(extent to which difficulty of registration and execution of guarantees is a constraint to credit expansion)

(legal rights index, and Doing Business 2010)

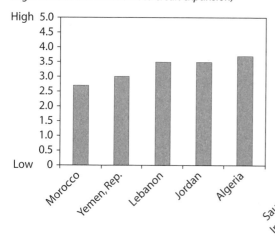

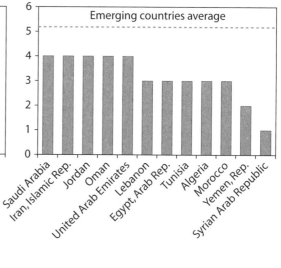

Source: World Bank 2008a, 2008d, 2009b, and *Doing Business 2010.*

Increasing financial accountability and improving governance. Disclosure and other good accounting and auditing practices promote sound credit markets. The current global financial crisis has reaffirmed the need for a solid financial infrastructure, including sound accounting and auditing standards, well-functioning payment and settlement systems, and well-designed corporate governance frameworks. The current crisis has shown the importance of the latter in terms of risk oversight by management and boards of banks and other financial institutions. Internationally accepted standards and practices offer numerous advantages. Financial reports facilitate international commerce, and efficient payment and settlement systems enhance investor confidence in companies and banks' ability to clear transactions efficiently, whereas proper documentation simplifies tax processes. Good corporate governance frameworks help broaden access while strengthening financial stability and preventing crises.

Corporate accounting and auditing are at a crossroads in the region. Many MENA countries have national rules and regulations on accounting and auditing based on international standards and practices. Some provide internationally recognized training in accounting and auditing, and professional organizations regulate accountants and auditor practices. Key stakeholders, however, have resisted reforms of accounting and auditing practices in many MENA countries. Several countries lack adequate legal and institutional arrangements to ensure that accounting and auditing follow international standards. In some cases accountancy profession laws are outdated—in Egypt the law dates to 1951. In other countries, excessively vague laws prove difficult to implement, as in the Republic of Yemen. Some laws fail to meet international standards, as in Jordan. Many regulators that have authority to monitor financial statements lack the capacity to do so. The current global financial crisis has underscored the crucial role of transparent financial reporting and enforcement of disclosure policies in providing markets participants with the required information to allow them to confidently make investment decisions.

Promoting Competition and Innovation in the Banking Sector

Market concentration. MENA countries have the world's most concentrated banking sectors. On average, the three largest banks control more than 70 percent of banking assets, compared with 55 percent in other emerging markets. Only Lebanon, Saudi Arabia, and Tunisia are below this level.

Number of commercial banks. Measured by entry, banks in MENA countries face only limited competition, except in Lebanon (figure 5.14) (Caprio,

FIGURE 5.14

Foreign Ownership of Banks in MENA
(percent of bank assets)

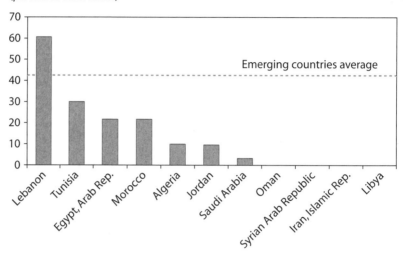

Entry into Banking, 2000–06
(number of applications)

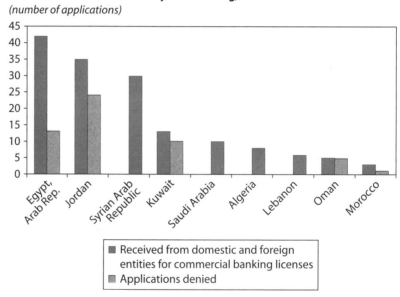

Sources: Database of Financial Sector Indicators, World Bank; IMF financial statistics.

Levine, and Barth 2008). This is true even in countries with good access to credit. Morocco has few commercial banks and limited entry. Jordan and Oman have highly concentrated markets in which the three largest banks hold 80 percent of banking assets. Their governments reject more than two-thirds of bank licensing requests. Saudi Arabia has a fairly open banking sector for locals but restricts entry of foreigners to 40 percent of a bank's shares.

Access to credit increased in many MENA countries despite barriers to entry and low competition in the banking sector. For access to further improve, however, governments must actively foster competition. Competition did not affect access to credit much during the early stages of banking development, when the stability of the banking sector and the quality of the market's institutional environment are more important. After these building blocks are put in place, more active measures are needed, with barriers to entry lowered, including those for foreign banks.

As the current global financial crisis has shown, the same competition that can broaden access to finance can also result in imprudent lending binges—and in systemic instability—if it is not accompanied by transparency and a strong and enforceable regulatory and supervisory framework (World Bank 2008d). Greater levels of competition are essential to encourage more banks and nonbank institutions to finance small and medium-sized enterprises. Strengthened regulatory capacity, better risk management practices, and more transparent information flows are needed to build the system's stability and ability to finance sustained growth.

Notes

1. The forthcoming World Bank flagship report on financial sector development in the MENA region will cover access to finance in the context of financial services and systems more broadly.

2. Algeria, Egypt, Morocco, Jordan, and Lebanon.

3. The definition of "credit-constrained" used in these estimations refers to those enterprises that have (1) made an application to obtain either working capital or investment credit over the past three years and have been declined because they lacked collateral (and not based on their financial statements or projections, nor because their application/business plan was rejected) or (2) decided not to apply for a loan because they did not have collateral to offer and assumed that they would be rejected on that basis.

4. *The Banker Database*, www.thebanker-database.co.uk.

5. Libya made the most progress in 2007 and 2008, by privatizing two of its five public banks.

CHAPTER 6

Reassessing the State's Role in Industrial Land Markets

Access to industrial land is a severe constraint to investment across MENA, the region where firms complain the most about this constraint. The issues are strikingly similar across countries. The diagnosis here points systematically to inefficiencies in the role of the state in land markets, to a lack of transparency, and to administrative and regulatory institutions that suffer from interference, discretion, and rent seeking. Although the enacted policies and the regulatory environment governing industrial land markets may be improved to reduce these inefficiencies, it is less with the policies than with the way in which the state applies them that the core of the problem lies.

The diagnosis is very similar across the region. State ownership of land and ineffective public regulation detach the supply of land from its market demand and thus from efficient use. Poor public policies produce artificial shortages and misallocations of public investment in land improvements. Land buyers are often treated unequally, and sales are often opaque. Small and medium-sized enterprises often lack large firms' access to land and related services.

To compensate for poor land market policies and institutions, many countries in the region develop industrial or special economic zones. But this approach introduces its own challenges and does not substitute for systemic reform. Many countries also use land price subsidies to encourage development. Neither efficient nor effective, the subsidies often invite land speculation. A better approach would be to create universal investment incentives and improve legal, regulatory, and public service quality in appropriate locations.

Most MENA countries lack a coherent asset management strategy for public land. Authority is often fragmented, overlapping, or confused. Land use planning is seldom guided by market demand and ignores opportunity costs. Land information systems are incomplete, outdated, and fragmented. As in other areas of the business environment, a lack of transparency is the norm. MENA governments must rationalize their land management policy and institutions. The supply of public land should be made more flexible and responsive to market demand, and authority decentralized to the local level. Land development generally is better entrusted to the private sector. Governments should not be involved in individual land allocation transactions, even when subsidies are provided to encourage investment. They should instead adopt a wholesale approach, whereas large industrial zones should be conceded to private developers and managers. Subsidies could still be embedded in retail prices if governments subsidize the large infrastructure development associated with these privately managed and operated zones.

The Low Access to Land in MENA Countries

The supply of public and private land and the government regulation of land are part of investor risk assessments of potential projects. In most MENA countries firms face many obstacles in the land market: in availability of good land, uncertainty over property rights, long delays in obtaining building permits and utility connections, and a lack of transparent procedures.

In Algeria, Egypt, the Islamic Republic of Iran, Kuwait, Morocco, Syria, and the Republic of Yemen public ownership of industrial land hurts business development, detaching land supply from market demand—creating shortages, mispricing land (thus inviting speculation), and often misallocating investment in land improvements. Most MENA countries lack coherent land asset management policies and strategies, and they fragment regulatory institutions and authority into multiple, overlapping, and sometimes contradictory rules and procedures for public land. Public land use planning is usually detached from market demand, and land information systems are often incomplete, outdated, and fragmented. But acquiring privately owned land is often equally problematic because of weak property rights and outdated supply-driven land use plans. *Doing Business* suggests that MENA countries have one of the most complex and expensive land registration system in the world (table 6.1).

TABLE 6.1

Registering Property (2009)

Region or economy	Procedures (N)	Duration (days)	Cost (% of property value)
OECD	4.7	25.0	4.6
East Asia and Pacific	5.0	97.5	3.9
Eastern Europe and Central Asia	5.7	59.7	2.2
South Asia	6.3	105.9	5.6
Middle East and North Africa	6.1	36.1	5.7
Sub-Saharan Africa	6.7	80.7	9.9
Latin American and Caribbean	6.9	70.4	3.6

Source: World Bank 2009b.

FIGURE 6.1

Access to Industrial Land Is Perceived More Often as a Major or Severe Constraint to Businesses in MENA Countries

(percent of firms rating access to land as a major or severe constraint)

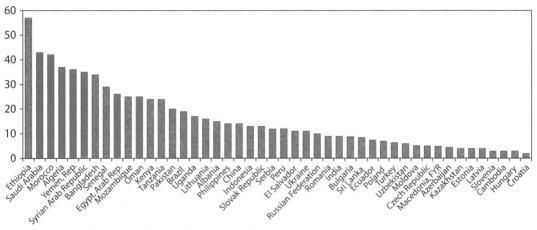

Note: Only private and domestic manufacturing firms are included.

Source: World Bank enterprise surveys, various years.

These issues are reflected in the perceptions of business owners about the access to land constraint—MENA countries surpass most other developing countries in the extent to which its business community complains about difficult access to industrial land (figure 6.1). About 37 percent of manufacturing firms in MENA countries identify access to land as a major constraint to doing business, according to the World Bank enterprise surveys. This result dwarfed responses from South Asia (17 percent), Latin America and the Caribbean (16 percent), East Asia and the Pacific (11 percent), and Eastern Asia and Central Europe (8 percent). The problem is likely much worse. Because World Bank enterprise surveys measure only the responses of firms that successfully addressed start-up constraints, they do not capture projects that never launched because of unavailable land.

Land buyers face an uneven bargaining field, where transactions lack transparency. If investors gain access to land, they face formidable land development controls. Issuing land subdivision or building permits is usually complex and time consuming, often associated with rent seeking, through extra-legal payments for timely service delivery. For example, *Doing Business* suggests that obtaining a warehouse building permit can involve 322 days of delay in Iran and 25 procedural steps in Egypt.

Investors in Egypt and Morocco wait more than three months for a building permit. More than a third of surveyed firms in Egypt reported paying a "gift" to municipal civil servants to obtain a building permit. Land and property tax systems in several MENA countries are also dysfunctional.

The exceptions to these issues tend to be in enclaves, such as free zones or special economic zones, where a centralized regulatory agency can be more efficient and less prone to rent seeking. For example, in Saudi Arabia firms in "industrial cities" secure utility connections faster than firms outside, but in most countries access to these enclaves is limited to certain investors or types of investment. Such restrictions might simply deter potential investors from participating in the market. Enterprise surveys also show that small and medium-sized enterprises have more difficult access to land than large firms.

Sources of Inefficiencies in Land Markets

Limited access to industrial land reflects discordant supply and demand. A frequent response to the difficulties of accessing land in MENA is to increase the supply of serviced land. Yet—as in Algeria, Egypt, Morocco, and to some extent Tunisia—a large stock of vacant industrial land already exists. In Egypt only 55 percent of serviced lands made available in public industrial estates have been allocated to investors. In Morocco, although 87 percent of serviced lands in public industrial estates have been allocated to investors, 508 hectares of vacant serviced industrial land are available, equivalent to about seven years of current estimated annual demand. In Tunisia the allocation rate of industrial land serviced by the Industrial Land Agency is 69 percent, and vacant land amounts to about 10 years of the average annual sales volume in recent years. In Algeria an estimated 15,000 hectares of public industrial land remains unused.

The real problem is linking supply and demand. The available supply of land for industrial investment does not match investors' various demands:

- Location near transportation infrastructure and labor markets
- Adequate land parcel sizes and planning to ensure future expansion
- Reliable utilities and access to roads
- Adequate industrial zone organization, maintenance, and management
- Affordable cost of land acquisition and more financing.

In Egypt the allocation rate of serviced land in industrial zones situated in the more desirable locations in Lower Egypt governorates is at least 65 percent, compared with only 17 percent in Upper Egypt.[1] In Tunisia, even though Grand Tunis and the coastal areas are estimated to account for 90 percent of the total demand for industrial land in the country, a third of the industrial lands serviced by the Industrial Land Agency since 1990 were in undesirable locations in the interior, in accord with a regional development policy.

Poor access to land and the discordant supply and demand have multiple dimensions. In a survey of Moroccan firms that acquired industrial land within the last three years,[2] 50 percent of firms flagged limited financing to acquire land as their main constraint, 44 percent cited the inability to expand, 42 percent the land price, 38 percent the poor quality of access roads, 31 percent the poor location, 18 percent unsuitable parcel sizes, 18 percent poor quality of electricity, and 6 percent poor water supply.

The Republic of Yemen illustrates the problems affecting firm entry into the land market. Detailed data from investment and land authorities reveal that of all investment projects licensed since 1992, 50 percent in Aden and 30 percent in Al Mukalla did not materialize because of a land-related problem. These problems included investors' inability to access the site, unsuitable sites, land disputes, and a lack of services.

Public interventions or institutional weaknesses that detach supply from demand create this discordance. The public owns vast areas of land in much of MENA. Yet relative to demand, the government releases land too slowly. So in Algeria, Egypt, and the Islamic Republic of Iran the land supply is highly inelastic, and some highly valued public land is idle because of inertia in the relevant public agencies. Algeria and Egypt divide control over public land among many uncoordinated government agencies—agencies that lack common procedures for land management and disposition.

In most of MENA multiple factors segment land markets: location (urban or rural), insecure property rights, land use, and regulating institutions. Land markets for investment and for other uses can follow very different rules and regulations. For example, different institutions may govern formal land markets in industry, tourism, agriculture, and commercial real estate development projects. Informal markets—where land is unregistered and development unregulated—also exist because of the rigidity of land use plans, the weakness of land registration systems, the steep cost of compliance with the formal system, and inadequate regulations. Informal land markets can be governed by customary rights, but they generally do not offer investors the security of title required to mitigate the risk of competing claims of ownership.

Finally, many governments and quasi-public agencies of varying efficiency own land or regulate it. Central government ministries and institutions, regional and local governments, free zones, special economic zones, and industrial zones all can control land. Disparate rules and procedures among these entities further segment the land market.

The Preference for Land Ownership versus Leasing: Historical Legacy or the Result of Policy Distortions?

Firms seeking access to industrial land prefer ownership over leasehold, elevating the investment cost. The highest percentage of land ownership reported by firms is in Syria (84 percent) and Egypt (81 percent), followed by Lebanon (73 percent), West Bank and Gaza economies (64 percent), Algeria (62 percent), Saudi Arabia (53 percent), and Jordan (52 percent). Only in the Republic of Yemen (48 percent), Morocco (47 percent), and Oman (37 percent) were there more firms leasing than owning land. In all countries except Saudi Arabia and Oman the percentage of large firms owning land exceeded the country average, reaching 100 percent in Syria, 84 percent in Egypt, Lebanon and West Bank and Gaza economies, and 70 percent in Jordan (figure 6.2).

Why do manufacturing firms prefer to own land, given the upfront capital cost and limited flexibility it imposes on relocation or expansion? First, land is used as collateral for construction finance. Because in several MENA countries leasehold and usufruct rights cannot be registered at the land registry, they cannot be used as collateral. In Lebanon the law does not provide for lease registration. Thus Lebanese agroindustrial companies, which prefer long-term leases, cannot get financing. In Egypt the law does not allow for the registration of usufructs or conditional ownership (*takhssiss*, another prevalent form of contract). Although the law allows for the registration of leases longer than five years, the

FIGURE 6.2

Ownership Status of Industrial Land in MENA Countries
(percent of firms owning their main site)

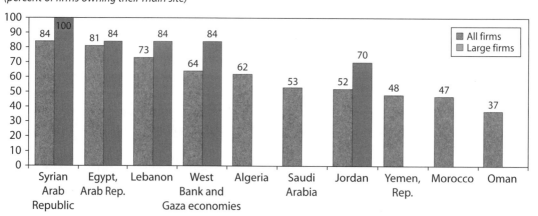

Note: Only private and domestic manufacturing firms were included.

Source: World Bank enterprise surveys, various years.

registries have no established procedures for doing so. In Morocco a land lease is not accepted as guarantee to get a loan.

Second, firms hope to take advantage of government subsidized land prices to take advantage of inflated land values, recover investment costs, and generate windfall profits. Land can then constitute a safety valve on firm exit. Subsidized land is often considered a fruitful investment for speculators, who envisage reselling their plots at market prices. In reaction, governments often impose very strict legal limits on the transferability of allocated plots—which imposes a constraint for exit for firms.

A Supply of Public Land That Is in Sync with Demand

Few MENA countries sell publicly owned and controlled land in response to demand. In Algeria, the Islamic Republic of Iran, and Syria the release of public land for investment and noninvestment or residential use fills a small fraction of existing demand, despite its abundant supply, because of the mismatch in the type and location of land released compared with that desired. The result is an artificial land shortage and a steep increase in prices.[3]

In Egypt the majority of the population lives on 5 percent of the national territory. The remaining 95 percent is publicly owned undeveloped desert. Five authorities affiliated with the agriculture, irrigation, tourism, industry, and housing ministries control 2.1 million hectares of land (equivalent to half of Egypt's total settled land area), but a large proportion of these lands lies untouched. Although 11,000 hectares of serviced industrial land are available for use (about 70 percent of the industrial land area made available over the past 25 years), 26.5 percent of manufacturing firms surveyed in the ICA believe that access to land is a major problem.

Other countries face the opposite problem. The Republic of Yemen chaotically distributed massive amounts of public land, especially in its southern governorates after national unification in 1990. Some land was distributed as restitution for nationalized property in the former South Yemen, some as conciliation to meet land acquisition demands of citizens from the North. Highly subsidized prices also caused extensive speculative and nontransparent dealings. In Al Mukalla the public land distributed during the 1990s could accommodate twice the city's current population of about 200,000. In Aden the land distributed between 1990 and 2004 could, at prevailing densities, accommodate the city's 600,000 inhabitants. In both cities the distributed land remains undeveloped and is not available for private development. Yet an investor seeking to access land for an investment project is either offered public land in a very remote and likely nonviable location or forced to buy land from a private owner. Land distribution that far exceeds real demand raises long-term concerns about sustainability.

In most MENA countries the large public sector role in land ownership and regulation makes land market supply unresponsive to private demand. Unable to retain the land sale or lease proceeds to finance their activities, land-controlling agencies lack the incentives to release land into the market. Agency employees have no performance-based incentives. In addition, pricing is detached from market forces. Governments sell or lease industrial land at below-market prices—sometimes even for free or at below-infrastructure cost recovery. High subsidies on industrial land prices encourage speculation. A large proportion of land parcels in public industrial estates—in such countries as Algeria, Egypt, Morocco, and Syria—remains undeveloped long after their allocation to investors. Low land prices are inadequate to finance government land servicing and development. Compounding this detachment of supply from demand, development policies subsidize investors to locate in underdeveloped regions, even when such areas lack the infrastructure or market access to attract or sustain competitive firms. Examples include Egyptian policy for industrial land in Upper Egypt, Tunisian pricing of industrial land in the interior regions, and Yemeni donations of public land to large investment projects (exceeding $10 million).

Contractual rules require governments to repossess distributed lands that lie undeveloped after three years, but governments do not enforce them. In the Republic of Yemen unclear legislation, missing land classification and land information systems, and the lack of public land registration cause frequent property disputes that pit the state against local communities or squatters. In this country and elsewhere investors often pay twice for land—once to the state and a second time to resolve a private claim on the land.

Pricing Issues

MENA countries maintain high subsidies on industrial land prices, fueling speculation. Overall land prices reflect existing market distortions. High urban land prices in Cairo and Alexandria reflect a scarcity of land for expansion (a problem of inadequate land use planning and public land management) and lack of legitimate titles (a property rights problem). By contrast, MENA countries tend to sell industrial land at highly subsidized prices. In Egypt government-fixed land prices in high-demand industrial zones are about 20–25 percent of the market price and about 50–60 percent of the infrastructure cost recovery (table 6.2). In Upper Egypt industrial land is free, although often without services. In Morocco the Hassan II Fund extends subsidies to eligible industrial investors that could

TABLE 6.2

Industrial Land Prices in Selected MENA Countries

(dollars per square meter)

Country	High-demand zones (in or near main cities)	Medium-demand zones (in or near secondary cities)	Low-demand zones (regional development areas)
Egypt, Arab Rep.			
Sale price, New Town industrial zones	16.6	12.3	0.0
Annual lease rate free zones	3.5	1.8	—
Annual lease rate industrial zones	—	—	—
Morocco			
Sale price, industrial zones	41.0	17.6	5.9
With Hassan II fund subsidy (50 percent option)	20.5	0.0	0.0
With Hassan II fund subsidy (100 percent option)	11.7	0.0	0.0
Annual lease rate, Tangier free zone	30.0	—	—
Annual lease rate, industrial zones	7.0	3.8	1.2
Tunisia			
Sale price, Industrial Land Agency industrial zones	34.3	19.0	3.8
Sale price, Enfidha private industrial zone	—	39.0	—
Annual lease rate, free zones	3.9	3.1	—
Annual lease rate, technopoles	3.8	3.8	—
Annual lease rate, industrial zones	—	—	—
United Arab Emirates			
Annual lease rate Ras Al Khaima free zone	4.0	—	—
Republic of Yemen			
Annual lease rate, Aden free zone	2.0	—	—

Note: — = not available.

Source: World Bank 2006.

reach up to 100 percent of the land price to a ceiling of $30 per square meter. In Tunisia land prices in high-demand Industrial Land Agency zones are fixed to recover the cost of infrastructure delivery (including administrative overhead), but these prices are about 40–50 percent below the market price. Algeria also had a long history of allocation of public plots at highly subsidized prices—before reverting recently to auctioned long-term concession contracts. These policies of subsidizing land reflect the desire of governments to encourage investment by lowering its fixed costs. The distortions that these policies induce on the functioning of land markets are large, however, and suggest that alternative policies should be explored to reduce investment costs.

Governments set industrial land price subsidies to offer competitive land prices to investors in high-demand areas and to attract investors to low-demand locations deemed priority areas for regional development. The first objective is usually driven by a goal of attracting investment and contributing to growth, yet it is founded on a misconception that the industrial land price is a major factor in firms' locating decision. Governments rarely introduce contractual provisions for subsidy recapture if the objective behind the subsidy—investment and job creation—fails to materialize. The second objective of regional development largely fails to attract firms to the least developed areas. The high vacancy rate in industrial zones in unattractive areas in southern Algeria, Upper Egypt, inland Morocco, and western and southern Tunisia implies that land price or availability alone is not enough to attract investment.

Highly subsidized land prices in Algeria, Egypt, and Morocco attract land speculation. Only a small fraction of the industrial lands that have been allocated to investors in Egypt (31 percent) and in Morocco (36 percent) are actually in operation. A large amount of the land is kept vacant for speculative purposes. In Tunisia, by contrast, where land subsidies are much lower than in Egypt or Morocco, the occupancy rate of allocated industrial land in Industrial Land Agency zones is 81 percent—reflecting a much less distorted land market. Because of the prevalence of speculation from high land price subsidies, governments are introducing measures to prevent land beneficiaries from deriving windfall profits from sales. Such measures are often not enforceable, however. For example, industrial land is rarely repossessed in Algeria, Egypt, or Morocco. Given the problem of speculation, it is surprising that vacant land is seldom taxed in several countries, including Algeria, Egypt, Lebanon, and Morocco.

Adding to the Inefficiencies of Public Land Supply: Persistent Issues with the Maintenance and Servicing of Existing Public Industrial Zones

Because many MENA governments have chosen to develop land through industrial enclaves, a key constraint to investment is the infrastructure quality in those zones. This includes the poor quality of access roads, water, and power, sanitation systems (at times nonexistent), security (often due to lack of zone fencing, poor street lighting from lack of maintenance, nonexistent management structures, and so on), and inadequate municipal waste collection. In Egypt the lack of maintenance has degraded the infrastructure of almost all mature industrial zones. Moreover, limited resources prevent servicing of many industrial zones in Upper Egypt. In 2001, after parceling industrial land for free to investors, the government scrapped its service delivery plans, eliminating the ability to recover the cost of infrastructure.

Publicly developed industrial zones in Morocco and Tunisia also suffer from poor infrastructure maintenance, prompting the Moroccan and Tunisian governments to launch major rehabilitation programs. In the 1980s the Moroccan rehabilitation program covered two-thirds of public industrial zones, with a government contribution equivalent to 45 percent of the total investment cost. In the 1990s the Tunisian program covered 23 percent of its target of 75 public industrial zones. Government contributions ranged from 50 percent of total investment costs in Tunis and coastal areas to 100 percent in the interior.

Inadequate management structures in publicly developed zones—the predominant share of industrial land available in MENA countries—are directly responsible for the deterioration of infrastructure. In Egypt industrial zones developed by the New Town Authorities and governorates have no dedicated management structures and no private-sector involvement (either tenants or specialized management companies). Zone maintenance is included only in the meager local budget. Industrial landowners and tenants thus suffer from serious neglect and often pay for maintenance and repairs, such as potholes and electricity repairs. Moreover, in governorate zones industrial landowners deal directly with the different utility providers—a pervasive problem due to the lack of privately developed zones and maintenance programs.

Tunisia, by contrast, has the only well-functioning management structure for publicly developed zones, although it still has problems. A 1994 law required each publicly developed industrial zone to develop a tenants' association, Groupement de Maintenance et de Gestion (GMG), to maintain and manage the zone. The association collects an annual fee of about $0.10–0.15 per square meter from the tenants. It has the power to collect maintenance fees, which are treated as tax obligations. It also can add uncollected fees to tenants' gas or electricity bills or pursue court proceedings. The government established GMGs in 60 percent of the zones developed by the Industrial Land Agency and local governments, but only half are deemed active. To be eligible for government zone rehabilitation funding, zones must have an active GMG. With active GMGs in only 30 percent of the zones, the model has problems but is still better than those in the rest of MENA. Tenants are often reluctant to pay for maintenance, arguing that it is the responsibility of the local authorities.

Private Markets Are Not Able to Compensate for These Artificial Shortages—Their Development Is Hindered by Ineffective Land Planning and Development Policies

Access to privately owned land is as problematic as access to public land. Land use plans are often ineffective, outdated, and unenforced. Land also is often informally converted from agricultural to industrial activities.

Land use planning is typically top-down and supply driven. Central government agencies prepare land use plans based on standards that do not reflect market demand or the opportunity costs of the land. Government plans typically adopt unreasonably high planning standards—especially for services and rights-of-way in land reserves. This leads to a low and inefficient land-use ratio (25–50 percent in Egypt's new towns and in Morocco). In many urban areas master land use plans are outdated and disconnected from the development reality on the ground. For instance, Sana'a's 1978 master plan has not been updated. Algeria, Egypt, and Morocco have recently begun reforming and streamlining planning practices. Because government reform of master plans is often long and cumbersome, a plan might be outdated by the time it is adopted.

In some MENA countries the enforcement of a master plan or land use plan is weak, so a large proportion of developments fail to obtain a building permit. The conversion of periurban and rural agricultural land to residential use or economic activity is prevalent in Algeria, Egypt, Morocco, Tunisia, and the Repubic of Yemen. In Morocco 43 percent of surveyed manufacturing firms were outside organized industrial zones, including some via illegal conversion of agricultural land. In the Republic of Yemen industrial development often unfolds in an ad hoc manner. For example, neighboring industries create industrial zones. Over time the largest private business groups have built private industrial estates that accommodate their different industries and share services such as water, power, and security.

Costly, cumbersome, and time-consuming development controls compound investors' problems. Because of subdivision rules, Moroccan developers face up to nine years of delays between acquiring land and developing it. In Egypt the delay to obtain the land subdivision permit can take two years. The average delay for Moroccan and Egyptian firms to obtain the construction permit is more than three months. In Tunisia the developer of a private industrial zone in Enfidha waited a year to obtain approval for a change in the zone's subdivision plan. Clearly, such long delays increase the transaction cost of development.

Inadequate Government Ownership and Regulation

Low access to land owes much to incoherent government policy toward the land market—through ownership and regulation. As the largest landowner, governments should respond to market requirements and allocate land well, but ineffective government institutions create further obstacles to efficient land use. For instance, in Egypt over 40 entities (line ministries, agencies, and local governments) control public land along sectoral and geographic lines. Among these entities, boundaries and jurisdictions are often unclear. Agencies rarely coordinate actions, and there is no consolidated land information system. Interagency disputes over public land thus are common. Overall, governments lack effective asset management practices for their land and property holdings.

Several countries do not adequately regulate the management and development of industrial zones. In Tunisia the regulatory framework did not address the difference between publicly developed and regulated zones and privately developed but publicly regulated zones. Private zone developers thus complain of an uneven playing field with the Industrial Land Agency, which they perceive as having an unfair advantage in the regulatory review process and in land pricing (the Industrial Land Agency is mandated by law to price at cost recovery). Saudi Arabia, however, has a model law governing the development and management of industrial zones, even if most industrial zones are public. Until recently Egypt lacked a regulatory framework. This created a conflict of interest for the government, which was at once landowner, zone developer, and regulator. The 2005 Industrial Development Authority did not address the development of industrial zones, so regulators must induce rules from an inadequate authorizing decree. The Republic of Yemen's law (Republican Decree no. 79 of 2005) governing the development, management, and operation of industrial estates provides for private participation but lacks key provisions, including a definition of private developers' rights and obligations and a process to establish an industrial estate on private land.

Many governments do not provide effective institutional support to the land market. Weak land registration systems—which in turn weaken the security of property rights—are a crucial constraint. With few exceptions (namely Jordan, Lebanon, and to less extent, Tunisia), land and property registration systems fail to account for the bulk of the land stock and property transactions.

A mix of demand- and supply-side problems contributes to the weakness of registry systems. In some countries high registration costs and a complex administrative process deter applicants from using the registry, as in Algeria, where registration costs 9 percent of the property value and takes 52 days to complete. Until recently in Egypt registration cost 12 percent of the property value, which meant that very few land and property transactions were recorded in the registry. Instead, people relied on the courts to enhance tenure security. When Egypt cut registration fees from 12 to 6 percent and then to 4.5 percent, the registry recorded a higher volume of transactions and thus increased government revenue. The reduction of fees in Egypt continued until 2006, when government capped registry fees at $350. Yet registration still takes more than six months. The poor quality of property maps and surveys for person-based deed registration systems in Algeria, Egypt, Morocco, and the Republic of Yemen further deters demand.

Weak land registration systems have many negative consequences. Land and property disputes create unnecessary litigation for unspecialized court systems. In Egypt, Morocco, and the Republic of Yemen, property disputes account for over 50 percent of primary courts' caseload. Most property cases take years to resolve (75 percent of cases in the Republic of Yemen take more than four years). In addition, Egypt's weak land registration system constrains the mortgage finance market by failing to create acceptable guarantees for lenders.

Getting the Incentives Right in Enclaves

Most MENA countries realize the time needed to reform the market and its governance. Yet many face myriad constraints to building functioning land markets. Vested interests pressure many countries to adopt a gradual "enclave approach" to reform, designating investment zones in which prevailing difficulties can be overcome—special economic zones in Egypt and Jordan, economic activity zones in Tunisia, and industrial zones in the Republic of Yemen. The perceived advantage of this localized approach is that it allows governments to introduce, test, and refine measures before applying them nationwide. In addition, it allows them an opportunity to confront a host of other challenges—regulatory, infrastructural, and institutional—on a limited basis where systemic reforms may not be possible.

However, an enclave approach and targeted government intervention can further exacerbate the segmentation and inefficiency of land markets. This is evident in countries that rely heavily on targeted interventions—extending various fiscal and nonfiscal incentives that differ by location, purpose (investment or noninvestment project), land use, sector, firm size, and other factors. Flagship foreign investors, strategic sectors, and projects of national significance, however ill defined, often receive more favorable treatment.

An enclave approach can proliferate investment zones—special economic zones, free zones, industrial zones, priority development zones, technopoles, and so on—outside the normal land market and national investment climate. Such zones have differentiated incentives, nontransparent subsidies, and separate institutional and regulatory frameworks. Egypt, Morocco, and to less extent Saudi Arabia and Tunisia possess different versions of this problem. In Egypt and Tunisia land price subsidies favor less-developed regions in agriculture, manufacturing, and tourism. Such targeted government policy is a challenge to reforming and harmonizing the overall land market.

Further risks from this approach include nonenclave investors feeling the playing field is tilted toward enclave investors. Enclave administrators (for example, the special economic zone authority) can conflict with local authorities, especially if the administration is a one-stop shop in a large zone. Here local governments are deprived of control over their prized land assets, sidelined from local economic decision making, and unable to regulate such activities. Local governments can also face mandates to deliver services to the zone—solid waste collection, access roads, water supply, overall security, traffic management, hospitals, and schools—often without adequate revenues to pay for these services. Similar tensions can occur with the line ministries whose prerogatives are ceded to the zone administration (for example, ministries of industry in industrial registration and regulation matters, and ministries of public works in building permit issuance).

These jurisdictional tensions exist, for instance, between the Aden Free Zone Authority and the Aden Governorate in the Republic of Yemen. Tensions also arise with the Yemen General Investment Authority over promoting and facilitating investment. In Egypt similar problems arise between the tourism zones in the Red Sea, managed by the Tourism Development Authority, and the Red Sea Governorate, which bears much of the infrastructure burden. The authority has deprived Egypt of all its valuable coastal property, and the governorate receives only limited revenues to provide services.

Subsidizing a single factor of production creates distortions and is an inefficient way to attract investment. Such subsidies, however, create opportunities for rent seeking and discretion in the allocation of cheap land ploys. Reforming the system will remove an important source of power and rent allocation that are often used in MENA to reward or maintain the loyalty of allies.

It is thus critical for governments to get incentives right. Some incentives other than land price are fiscally more efficient and more attractive to serious investors. For example, broad-based tax incentives, such as an investment tax credit or accelerated depreciation, are generally more efficient than subsidizing a single input, such as land. Politically and administratively feasible reforms that make the investment climate less costly and more predictable are preferable to distortionary incentives.

Power and Rent Seeking in Public Land Allocation and Regulation

A key impediment to MENA land markets is the strength and multiplicity of vested interests that influence land management policies and practices. In MENA countries land and real estate assets traditionally store and generate wealth. Because these countries have limited economic diversification and few alternative investment channels that can generate an equally high return on investment, land speculation is prevalent. Speculators and connected investors who have preferential access to subsidized land often become vested interests, influencing public land policy. Understanding the political dimension of land markets is a prerequisite to successful reform efforts.

The vested interests in land markets have strengthened over the last few years, along with the rapid growth of domestic and foreign real estate development investment and the construction boom. Real estate development investment exceeds $1 billion, booming in such cities as Dubai, Cairo, Alexandria, Tunis, Beirut, Sana'a, Algiers, and Casablanca.

Regional real estate development and investment companies—such as Egypt's Orsacom and Talaat Mostafa groups, Lebanon's Solidere, Qatar's Diar and Al Qodra, and the United Arab Emirate's Emaar and Nakheel—have become major players in regional urban land markets, producing large mixed-use developments with residential, retail, commercial, tourism, and office space. A few players (such as Emaar) have global operations. State funds (such as Abu Dhabi's) have also invested significantly in real estate development. Competition to attract such companies has prompted MENA governments to offer very attractive investment incentives, including free or very cheap land and tax holidays.

Many development agreements impose few obligations on the developer and throw all risk on the government. Developers build according to market demand, without any regulatory burden to invest in infrastructure. The land title is also often transferred upfront to the developer, so if demand does not materialize, the government might encounter difficulties in reclaiming the land in accordance with contractual agreements—especially if there are liens on the property by banks holding the land as collateral.

Vested interests can exert the most influence in public land management. Below-market pricing creates opportunities for rent seeking by the officials responsible for land pricing and land allocation decisions and by private sector "insiders" seeking to benefit from privileged access or preferential conditions of transfer. The chance for corruption grows with the gap between administrative prices and market prices. One recurrent example of such irregularities is the disposition of land and real estate assets during the privatization of state-owned enterprises.

Land market support functions are prone to corruption and preference. Recent regional reforms have sought to remove discretion from land registration. In Lebanon the automation of the cadastre caused rent seeking and extralegal payments to decline by greatly simplifying the process and enhancing transparency. The Yemeni cabinet recently approved a new land registration law that regulates and makes transparent the registration system. The land registry also has developed standard property transfer contracts for use by the notary publics to reduce deed forgery. So long as public policy preserves substantial rents through subsidy or artificial constraints on land supply, however, the risk of corruption and capture remains.

Changing land use from residential to commercial means a windfall profit for owners, which makes another target for rent seekers. Some investors or land speculators also seek access to undisclosed information—which areas in a city will be planned and serviced or which rural areas will be included in the municipal boundaries. Speculators use this information to acquire land from owners at preimprovement prices. In many MENA countries building permits and other land development regulations require "gifts" to officials for prompt service. Over a third of Egyptian firms reported paying gifts to municipal engineers during the building permit process.

The Way Forward

A pressing need exists to remove investment constraints from land markets. As the owner, enabler, and regulator of land markets, governments must improve their performance. Implementing such reforms is no easy task, however. Vested interests in the public and private sectors, who currently benefit from the mismanagement of public land assets and the weakness of market support institutions, will resist reform. Governments should attract qualified private developers to develop, manage, operate, and maintain industrial zones. They must guarantee investors access to well-located and well-serviced industrial land in professionally managed zones.

Strengthening and Reforming the Government's Public Land Management

Governments should develop an asset management approach to public land, including the following steps:[4]

- *Formulate an explicit and coherent public land management policy.* A critical foundation for public land asset management, this policy is based on economic efficiency, fiscal health, and environmental sustainability. It governs the disposition of public land to private interests, it leverages land assets to achieve policy objectives, and it requires support at the highest level.

- *Recognize the cost of fixed asset ownership and use.* Governments should move from a free-good to an opportunity-cost approach. This transforms a mostly supply-driven process into a more market-responsive one that reflects the opportunity cost of land.

- *Build land information systems.* Governments need to prepare a consolidated inventory of public land and property assets, with information on the location, use, and value of such assets.

- *Create accountability mechanisms and incentive structures.* Public land asset managers must be accountable for their performance. Incentive structures are also key to achieving efficient asset management.

- *Decentralize management responsibilities, strengthening central leadership and regulation.* The global trend of public land management in developed countries and emerging economies is toward decentralized land management. In Botswana, China, Indonesia, the Philippines, and Turkey, central governments delegate land use planning and allocation of private interests to local governments. Central governments retain responsibilities for establishing national policies, regulations, and monitoring. In MENA countries most public land management functions still rest with the central government. Local governments play a small role in setting land use, disposing of public land, and retaining the proceeds of land sale or lease for use in financing service delivery. Central oversight is generally weak and fragmented. To strengthen public land management, a two-step process is needed. First, moving away from fragmentation by unifying public land management functions in one ministry—ideally finance—will ensure efficient management, accounting, and valuation. Second, gradually decentralizing public land asset management will strengthen the central government regulatory capacity by enacting checks and balances, accountability measures, and performance incentives for local governments.

- *Allocate public land to the private sector.* Public land policies should specify how land rights are allocated and valued. The disposition of public land ought to occur through transparent market-driven processes, such as auctions, rather than obscure government sales. Auctions will curb the speculation prevalent in MENA. Public land disposition at below-market prices should be restricted to narrowly defined policy objectives, such as low-income housing. Even then, however, the government should use competitive allocation among developers. Although subsidies are occasionally needed to attract investment and create jobs, governments ought to become wary of ones that distort the land market through below-market pricing. Subsidies are also inefficient. They attract speculators without guaranteeing that the policy objective will be met and put the onus on governments to recapture land when subsidies fail. This adds an administrative burden and requires strong enforcement.

- *Improve accounting practices.* For their land assets, governments should move from cash accounting to accrual accounting, and from book value to fair market value.

Strengthening the Government's Land Market Support

Effective administration of property rights is critical to attracting investment. Many MENA countries must strengthen property rights legislation and administration systems to address the parallel formal and informal systems, as in Egypt, Morocco, and the Republic of Yemen. Governments should house land registry and survey functions under a single, preferably autonomous agency, as in Jordan, where authority is under the king's office,[5] and in Lebanon, where the functions are under a single (yet nonautonomous) Ministry of Finance.

Governments should also use both systematic registration (often extremely costly) and voluntary registration. Once lands and properties are recorded in the registry, governments must take pains to ensure that the registry is maintained and regularly updated. The act of registration must be legally conclusive. The price and quality of services are also critical to sustain demand for registry services. Governments should price subsequent property transaction registration fees at the lowest level needed to ensure that the authority recovers operational and investment costs, and governments should resist the temptation to couple land registration with other taxes on owners. These additional measures may deter registration (in the Republic of Yemen owners must pay the property transfer tax as a prerequisite to registration). A need will also be present to eliminate competing systems of land registration, such as the use of courts to examine the ownership title, the role of notary publics, and so on. All this will require public awareness campaigns.

Attracting Private Developers to Develop, Manage, and Operate Industrial Zones

Experience in MENA and elsewhere has shown that central and local governments are inefficient zone developers and managers. Relative to the private sector, governments lack:

- The incentives to efficiently develop zones and optimize infrastructure delivery,
- The specialized knowledge of zone development and marketing, and
- The finance required for development.

Publicly developed industrial and special economic zones have mostly failed to attract tenants and to provide for efficient management,

FIGURE 6.3

Master Developer Requirements to Invest in Industrial Zones
(percent of firms identifying each area as an essential requirement)

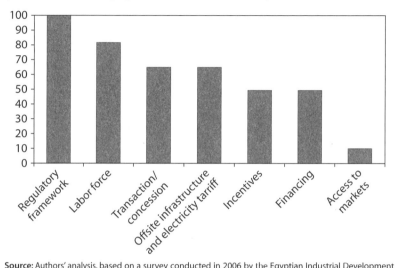

Source: Authors' analysis, based on a survey conducted in 2006 by the Egyptian Industrial Development Authority.

operation, and maintenance. Private industrial zone developers have identified the most essential requirements (figure 6.3).

Private zone developers emphasize clear and transparent regulatory frameworks as their top priority. This includes shedding light on rights, obligations, and procedures; interacting with government agencies; and acting as a single interlocutor or providing efficient one-stop shop services to their tenants. The available and affordable labor and off-site infrastructure are other key priorities because they provide competitive advantages for tenants. The structure of the concession agreement is also important, especially the ability to own the land or obtain a long-term lease (minimum of 49 years) that allows master developers to attract sub-developers or tenants. The incentive package is crucial. All operators in a special economic zone must receive similar incentives. Other issues include available financing and market access.

More generally, liberalizing land markets is the natural solution to the inefficiency of industrial land markets in the region, even if it includes privately owned or industrial park concessions. Governments should not be involved in individual land allocation transactions, even when subsidies are provided to encourage investment. They should instead adopt a wholesale approach, and large industrial zones should be conceded to private developers and managers. Subsidies could still be embedded in retail prices if governments use them in the large infrastructure development associated with these privately managed and operated zones.

True reform entails institutional changes that reduce discretion and arbitrariness and that increase credibility in land management decisions. Transparency needs to be introduced in decisions of land administration institutions, in the prices of transactions involving public lands, in the land registries, and in the management of public land assets. Reforms should give a larger role to private developers and managers in maintaining and administering industrial zones—as Jordan, Morocco, Tunisia, and the United Arab Emirates have piloted. Administrative reforms of the institutions in charge of land markets should increase the transparency of land allocations, prices and subsidies, and transactions involving public land. There is clearly a technical aspect to these reforms in simplifying and computerizing property registration procedures. The challenge of improving access to investable land, however, is deeply rooted in the political economy of each country, because more equitable access means reduced rents.

Notes

1. Some industrial zones in preferred locations in Lower Egypt are even full.

2. Survey conducted by the World Bank, in collaboration with the Ministry of Industry and Trade of Morocco, in 2007.

3. The Islamic Republic of Iran's National Land and Housing Organization—which has a monopoly over the land market—built a land inventory of 712,939 hectares between 1979 and 2002, including negotiated purchases from the private sector (7 percent), barren land, and the public/national land stock. Yet it released less than 10 percent of its inventory to the market during the same period, far short of demand. This artificial scarcity, coupled with the introduction of market-based pricing in 1994, steeply inflated land prices, which reduced construction and real estate investment.

4. This approach is described in Kaganova and McKellar (2006).

5. The agency also includes the public land management function, which should ideally be separate from the land registry. Combining both functions often leads to a perceived conflict of interest from placing the adjudicator of property rights and a landowner who may have a land dispute under one roof.

CHAPTER 7

New Industrial Policies: Opportunities and Perils of Selective Interventions

MENA countries, which have a strong tradition of state intervention in markets, have actively supported specific enterprise sectors with subsidies. Less attention has been given, however, to improving the overall business environment. Sectoral policies that focus on sector-specific public goods and regulations are often absent, even in the subsidized sectors. Recently many countries have put in place new industrial policies. These come on top of interventions favoring small and medium-sized enterprises, large (foreign) investors, young entrepreneurs, and other categories of firms.

Has state intervention promoted investment and economic growth in MENA? Unfortunately, no interventions have been subjected to rigorous evaluation or transparent cost-benefit analysis. The conclusions of this report suggest that intervention has not injected dynamism and investment but has instead reinforced a narrow set of entrepreneurial interests.

The new industrial policies may suffer from the same pitfalls. Although industrial policies may be needed to correct market failures—particularly in oil-rich countries where oil windfalls do not naturally push economies toward greater diversification and full employment—it is difficult to assess success or failure of those policies. The lack of evaluation has obscured the need to interrupt failing programs. Discretion and lack of transparency in the allocation of subsidies or credit lines fuel the impression that less deserving firms are often the beneficiaries. Successful exporters, large firms, or multinationals receive subsidies, protection, and privileges they do not need. Institutional processes that involve the private sector in reviewing policies and identifying priorities have been largely absent.

Industrial strategies and interventions can be effective only if the following prerequisites are in place:

- *A sound investment climate*
- *An institutionalized and inclusive process of consultation with the private sector in designing, monitoring, and evaluating interventions*
- *Transparent intervention subsidies, including clear identification of beneficiary firms*
- *Clear, measurable, and transparent indicators of each intervention's success*

- *Arm's length relations between the government and the private sector*
- *A public governance setup that binds the government to enough accountability to prevent capture and to shut down failing interventions*

Today no MENA country combines these features of successful interventions. Even if the recent industrial strategies tend to refer to these features when they are announced, in reality their implementation has so far suffered from the same pitfalls: limited transparency, no quantifiable and measurable objectives, no institutional mechanisms in place to spot failures, limited private sector involvement, and so on. The risks of reproducing past failures in industrial strategy remain very high because the conditions that undermined past interventions are still in place.

A Tradition of Subsidies and Selective State Interventions

In many MENA countries (as in other regions) industrial policies subsidize exporters, foreign investors, small and medium-sized enterprises, or particular sectors or activities. These selective interventions or sectoral "competitiveness" strategies, although justifiable at times, carry considerable risks.

In a region prone to government intervention, industrial policies have been gaining in popularity in recent years. Should MENA countries embark on a new wave of industrial policies and selective interventions? Should they expand existing ones? This chapter argues that, yes, justifications can be found for selective interventions and that these interventions may have been useful catalysts to diversify some emerging economies—particularly in East Asia. It also argues, however, that much international experience sounds a cautionary alarm: institutions, transparency, and safeguards need to be in place to prevent selective interventions from falling into the all-too-common trap of sustained failure. The chapter also argues that this "yes, but" answer is magnified in oil-rich countries, where both the justifications for intervening and the cautionary alarms are strongest.

To better evaluate the positive and negative attributes of industrial policies in MENA, the chapter documents where different governments have been intervening. Within a framework that categorizes interventions according to their justification, extent of selectivity, and subsidy content, the analysis

- Shows that most interventions in MENA have been of the sort most prone to failure and capture;
- Makes the case that justifications for some selective interventions may be very strong, especially in oil-rich countries;
- Sets out the explicit preconditions—overall investment climate, institutional prerequisites—for these interventions to succeed; and

- Argues that most MENA countries do not meet these preconditions, particularly the oil-rich, labor-abundant countries.

Given these findings, MENA governments that want to expand existing interventions or launch new industrial policies should carefully consider three factors that may influence their likely success:

- The institutional setup that guards against capture and ensures that failed interventions are identified early and interrupted or corrected
- The process of designing, implementing, and evaluating selective interventions in partnership with the private sector
- The mechanisms to ensure independent, transparent, and regular evaluation—including cost-benefit analysis—of the programs' performance and impact on beneficiaries

Also to be clarified is what this chapter cannot do. First, it cannot document the impact of any of the past interventions because there has not been a single rigorous evaluation of any of these programs. A fundamental message is that without a rigorous and transparent monitoring and evaluation framework, it will be difficult for any country to succeed with interventionist strategies, because the country will be unable to evaluate the impact of its policies—and to stop or correct failing programs.

Second, the chapter will not evaluate the justifications of ongoing interventions in MENA. Prointerventionists see market failures everywhere, whereas laissez-faire advocates perceive only pervasive government failure. The authors found no evidence of even rudimentary empirical justification for any MENA intervention. This absence of evidence that might support interventions matches the absence of any evaluation of the programs.

A Framework to Clarify a Controversial Debate

As in many developing countries, MENA governments are advancing new industrial policies to promote growth. Morocco is implementing sectoral interventions under the "Emergence Plan," while Algeria and Egypt are designing their own plans. Tunisia is launching sectoral competitiveness centers, a plan that—although not explicitly called an industrial strategy—is similar to Morocco's. Many Gulf countries have adopted long-term strategies that explicitly include sectoral development plans. Building on the successes of the Emirate of Dubai in diversifying its economy, Bahrain, Kuwait, Oman, Qatar, Saudi Arabia, and others are implementing sector-specific interventions, often in the form of subsidies, to diversify away from oil.

Before this recurring appearance of industrial policies, all MENA countries had a range of policies, mixing laissez-faire approaches with selective interventions of different sorts.[1] In the 1960s and 1970s more interventionist policies prevailed, in particular state ownership of firms, protection of selected sectors, and targeted subsidies. In the 1980s these widespread policies were largely abandoned in MENA and elsewhere.[2] Other selective interventions, however—surprisingly less controversial (export zones, small and medium-sized enterprise policies, technology parks)—have since spread parallel to market-oriented reforms.

Industrial policies based on selective sectoral interventions generate strong continuing controversy. With all but a few MENA governments enjoying large budget surpluses and with economic diversification lagging, especially in oil-rich countries, the political pressure to design new sectoral and enterprise support programs is high.

The pros and cons—whether "growth elixirs or growth poisons"[3]—thus need to be sorted out clearly. This chapter introduces a simple analytical framework showing which features make public interventions fundamentally different from one another—in their justifications and in their implications for instruments, risks, costs, and distortions—and which affect an intervention's likelihood of success.[4]

Despite the widespread use of industrial interventions, little rigorous evidence is at hand with which to assess the impact of these policies—probably because counterfactuals are hard to find. In MENA no intervention of note has been seriously evaluated. None has even been the object of a serious performance and cost-benefit analysis. The limited research on this topic offers unsurprisingly weak econometric estimates and ambiguous results (Nabli et al. 2004; Galal 2005, 2008).

Public policies for enterprise development differ in many ways:

- The criteria of selectivity (size, sector, ownership of firms, export orientation, age of firms)
- The extent of selectivity, ranging from neutral or horizontal interventions to very selective ones, to the extent of price subsidies and distortions, and to the fiscal implications
- The justifications for the intervention (types and extent of market failures)

The two aspects of public interventions that depart most from laissez-faire business policies are, first, the degree of selectivity (how much they target certain groups of firms), and second, the extent of subsidization (how many subsidies the corresponding policy instrument delivers to firms).

These two dimensions do not necessarily overlap. Selectivity and subsidies need not go hand in hand. Selective industrial policies need not use subsidies or taxes or protect targeted groups of firms. A government might focus its resources and political capital on putting in place a world-class business environment in a specific region (enclave) or for specific types of firms (exporters or foreign investors). These policies entail much selectivity but little direct intervention in market prices, unless the government also subsidizes those targeted investors in that same enclave by providing tax breaks, land, or energy subsidies. In some cases they might simply try to help preferred investors navigate difficult regulations and procedures, leaving others to their own devices.

Similarly, not all interventions based on price subsidies are selective. For example, a land policy that subsidizes the price of industrial land for all investors is not particularly selective.[5] Subsidized credit lines for enterprises may equally not target any specific type of firm. More often than not, however, and especially in MENA countries, interventions combine both types of instruments, subsidizing select groups of firms.

Using such a typology of interventions, any private sector development policy can be represented in one of four quadrants depending on how much it departs from a nonselective business environment policy (figure 7.1).

FIGURE 7.1

The Basic Framework: Government Subsidies by Degree of Firm Selectivity

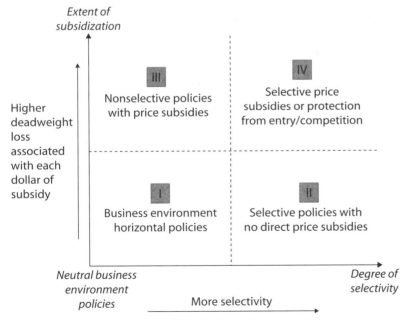

Note: Deadweight loss rises with each dollar of subsidy. These are the losses associated with distortions that subsidies generate, including those related to the raising of fiscal revenues to finance them. Horizontal policies refer to nonselective policies that improve the business environment for all firms, irrespective of their characteristic.

Source: Authors, based on Benhassine and Raballand 2009 and the framework described in text.

Quadrant I Policies: Business Environment Horizontal Policies

These horizontal policies focus on aspects of the business environment that are neutral to firm type and that do not affect prices or quantities. These include policies that affect market openness, macrostability, trade, and investment openness. They also include the quality of market institutions that protect private property rights, infrastructure, and free-functioning products and factor markets (labor, capital, and land).

This list of standard horizontal policies of business environment reform can be long enough and complex enough to absorb all the implementation capacity, political capital, and fiscal space a reforming government can have. This is one strong argument in favor of selectivity. It may just not be feasible for a government to significantly improve every aspect of the business environment for all firms. For example, the infrastructure for trade logistics may not be brought to world-class standards across all large countries such as Algeria, Egypt, or the Islamic Republic of Iran, where regional enclaves of world-class infrastructure logistics platforms can be developed.

Quadrant II Policies: Selective Policies with No Price Subsidies

Selective interventions not involving price subsidies can take many forms but are usually based on two types of justifications:

Type A. Those referring to the need to address sector-specific aspects of the business environment or sector-specific coordination failures, both of which require that sector-specific public goods or investments be publicly provided (such as regulations, institutions, or specific complementary public infrastructure investments).

Type B. Those calling for piecemeal enclave approaches to improve the business environment. Here selective interventions are justified on the basis that it is often not feasible to improve the overall business environment for all—and that a second-best solution is to create enclaves of good business environment for some categories of firms (either in a given location or for certain sectors or types of firms). The hope is that they will benefit the most promising sectors or areas for growth and eventually spread to the rest of the economy.

Arguments in favor of type A selective policies state that simply getting the business environment basics right does not mean the same thing for every sector or every category of firms. Many aspects of the business environment have to be tailored and are very specific, especially laws and regulations. In addition, institutions implementing and enforcing these regulations are usually also specific to the sectors at which they are aimed. Another example of sector-specific policies is public infrastructure investment. Many types of public investments (waste management, water connection, high-voltage electricity nodes, transport, and so on) inevitably demand planning based on sectoral or geographical considerations and naturally lend themselves to industry or location specificity.

The argument is that governments cannot be doing everything everywhere, and that they naturally tend to focus on either existing industries or those that they think have a potential in their country. They are basically "doomed to choose" (paraphrased from Hausmann, Rodrick, and Velasco 2006).

In their selective interventions, some MENA countries have adopted sector-specific strategies that include public investments, regulatory changes, and other sector-specific public goods. Tourism is a typical sector that requires specific public investments. Tourism-specific strategies are in place in Egypt, Jordan, Morocco, Oman, and Tunisia. Algeria is designing its own. Agribusiness is another sector for which some MENA countries adopted selective interventions that did not explicitly include subsidies. Developing phytosanitary control institutions and regulations, dedicating port logistics for perishable goods, and investing in public research institutes in agronomy are typical measures. Egypt, Jordan, Morocco, Saudi Arabia, Syria, and Tunisia have been pursuing such sectoral strategies for years—with most including subsidies of some sort.

The argument justifying type B selectivity states that some weak points in the business environment have no short-term remedy—either because of administrative capacity, fiscal constraint, or political reasons. The argument points to piecemeal enclave approaches as second best or transitory solutions. For example, infrastructure cannot be in good condition everywhere, and upgrades might need to be made in industrial zones that benefit a minority of particular firms (large firms, exporting firms). Another example is urban land reform—involving legal status, ownership, or tenure security—in which progress can be very slow, for either political or institutional reasons. Here governments facilitate particular investments, such as tourism infrastructure (Egypt's Red Sea resorts area and Morocco's Plan Azur development zones), by taking partial measures to clear legal and title-issuing difficulties.

Another example involves administrative reform of public institutions dealing with firms and investors. Because improving administrative services through comprehensive public service reform is often long and difficult (both politically and from a capacity standpoint), governments often create localized world-class administrative environments. The Aqaba Zone in Jordan and the Tangiers Free Zone in Morocco provide such an enclave environment (with good infrastructure and administrative services). Egypt's one-stop shop of Cairo is a best practice enclave for administrative reform. These enclaves are often geographically delimited (in special economic zones, for example) or dedicated to a limited group of firms (typically foreign investors or exporters, as in Tunisia).

Quadrant III Policies: Nonselective Policies with Price Subsidies

Policies in this quadrant involve market interventions that directly affect equilibrium prices and quantities. The usual justification for most of these interventions is the presence of some sort of market failure—typically in research, innovation, training, or other forms of human capital formation—or pollution abatement. With the exception of subsidized training programs (for example, in Egypt, Jordan, Morocco, Oman, and Tunisia), MENA countries provide very few subsidies in areas that traditionally justify them, such as research and development. Instead, they intervene in more controversial areas: credit markets (subsidized credit lines or public credit guarantee schemes), industrial land subsidies, and input price subsidies (particularly energy prices in oil countries). Subsidized credit lines with artificially low interest rates, for example, can undermine the development of competitor financial institutions and can send a signal that loan repayment is not a priority.

Quadrant IV Policies: Selective Price Subsidies or Protection from Entry and Competition

Usually grouped in industrial policies, the most common interventions include selective policies that offer some sort of subsidies, protection, or tax breaks. The justifications for these are similar to the ones in quadrant III, except that they assume that these market failures are specific to certain groups of firms. For example, some technology-intensive sectors are thought to exhibit externalities. Also, exporters or foreign investors are often thought to exhibit some type of externalities on the rest of the economy (for example, through learning).

Interventions in quadrant IV most often offer a mix of policies with different justifications. For example, most technology parks rest on an assumption of clustering (agglomeration) externalities. Yet they are usually coupled with investment subsidies or tax breaks. Some sectors or certain types of firms (large ones, for example) are not only subsidized and sheltered in business environment enclaves but are also protected from trade or entry competition. The usual justification is an infant-industry argument that new sectors need support and protection in the early stages of their development when much experimental learning is thought to take place.

In recent years this argument has been slightly twisted to take into account the growth of global foreign direct investment and trade. Now it is said that a country has comparative advantages in a number of sectors, but to benefit from them, it needs to give tax breaks and subsidize input prices to be cheaper than competitors and attract large-scale foreign direct investment. This claim is based on the premise that large international investors make investment decisions based solely on input-cost comparisons, requiring countries to compete on that basis. Countries that recently embarked on industrial policies (Algeria, Egypt, Morocco, and Saudi Arabia) conducted exercises to identify promising products and then designed dedicated sectoral strategies comprising selective investment subsidies.

Private Sector Policies in MENA—A Legacy of Disproportionate Interventionism

Policies that mix selectivity and subsidies (mirroring quadrant IV) are the most common in MENA—but also the most prone to failure, especially when the overall business environment is poor. A review of private sector development policies conducted as a background to this report showed that basically all MENA countries traditionally have been very active interventionists, even where the scope and means of interventions have evolved. Moreover, many of them have relied, and still rely, on quadrant IV interventions while their investment climate (quadrant I) remains poor. As shown in previous chapters, this is particularly so in oil-rich, labor-abundant countries. Market-oriented sectoral strategies that do not involve subsidies (quadrant II) are also rare, and subsidies are most often selective. This disproportionate reliance on quadrant IV interventions is also coupled with poor institutional mechanisms to support these interventions and guard against their pitfalls.

Selective policies providing subsidies can range from targeting particular products (for example, consumer electronics, or even more selectively, DVD players) to particular sectors or particular categories of firms based on characteristics other than their activity. Typical selectivity criteria in MENA include the following:

- *Size.* Almost all countries in the region have programs targeted at small and medium-sized enterprises, however defined. Some entail subsidies to capacity building and investment (as in Algeria, Egypt, Jordan, Lebanon, Morocco, Syria, and Tunisia). Others include subsidies for training (as in Egypt, Jordan, Morocco, and Tunisia). Some include subsidized credit lines to buy equipment (often donor-funded, as in Egypt and the Maghreb). Soft loans from state-owned industrial or agricultural development banks were popular throughout the

region in the 1960s, 1970s, and 1980s, but as elsewhere, those in
credit markets for small and medium-sized enterprises failed. Only
Oman and Qatar still have such programs in place. Most countries
also provide generous incentives to large firms—especially large
(often foreign) strategic investments (see below).

- *Export orientation.* As in many developing countries, programs to support exporters are present throughout the region. Egypt and Jordan
  have recently developed qualified industrial zones for garment and
  other exporters, which are exempt from import tariffs and have free
  access to the U.S. market. Tunisia has an older program providing
  generous tax and tariff exemptions to exporters and subsidies to
  support entering foreign markets. A few years ago Morocco launched
  a free zone in Tangiers, and its industrial strategy explicitly calls
  sectoral export-processing zones "Mediterranean Maquiladoras."
  Saudi Arabia provides various subsidies to non-oil sectors with potential for exports (particularly agribusiness).

- *Ownership type (state- or foreign-owned).* Many countries in the region
  have been, or still are, favoring state-owned enterprises. From the
  1960s to the 1980s, even early reformers such as Jordan, Morocco, and
  Tunisia protected state-owned firms in selected strategic sectors, supporting them with government-backed loans from state-owned banks
  or giving them monopolies in certain markets or in access to imported
  inputs. In some countries such selective policies continue, even where
  explicit support and monopolies have largely been disbanded. Significant parts of the industrial and sometimes banking sectors in Algeria,
  the Islamic Republic of Iran (the *bonyads*), Iraq, Libya, Syria, and the
  Gulf Cooperation Council countries are still state or parastatal owned.

  Another type of selective support is targeted to foreign investors.
  All but a few countries (Libya, for example) have eliminated provisions from their investment codes that distinguish between foreign
  and locally owned firms. In practice, however, the competition to
  attract foreign direct investment is fierce, taking the form of special
  incentives. Many countries have discretionary provisions in their
  investment codes to provide such incentives for large, strategic
  investors. The Hassan II Fund in Morocco, for one, provides subsidies to such investments through the Investment Directorate agency.
  The *régime dérogatoire* provides room for deal-specific incentives in
  the Algerian investment code. Egypt, Jordan, Libya, Qatar, and Saudi
  Arabia have similar legal provisions. These special incentives—which
  can be very generous—are not explicitly targeted to foreign direct
  investment, but in practice most large, strategic investments are
  foreign in origin.

- *Firm age.* Algeria, Egypt, Morocco, Oman, Tunisia, and other countries have programs to support start-up firms or even young entrepreneurs. More widespread are tax incentives for new investors. Two main categories of fiscal incentives are available in almost all MENA economies. First, in the investment phase most countries offer fairly wide-ranging exemptions from duties, customs, and indirect taxes on items related to the investment project. Second, nearly all countries offer a corporate tax holiday, in many cases extendable in case of supplementary investments. The most generous of such schemes is in Egypt (tax holidays of up to 20 years).

- *Technology or research and development content.* Dubai, Egypt, Morocco, Oman, and Tunisia have clusters of technology-oriented firms. Algeria, the Islamic Republic of Iran, Saudi Arabia, and Syria are planning to develop their own. Surprisingly, however, research and development subsidies are rare in the region. Tax deductions are available for some research and development spending in a few countries (Morocco, Syria, and Tunisia), but no MENA country has yet embarked on any major program to spur private research and development—leaving most applied research to publicly driven state universities.

- *Geographical location.* To spur regionally balanced growth, many MENA governments provide special incentives, such as subsidized prices for public industrial land in less-developed locations in Algeria, Egypt, Jordan, Lebanon, Morocco, Oman, Saudi Arabia, and Tunisia. Sometimes geographical incentives take the form of a regulatory exemption for investors in a given region. Examples include easing limits on employing expatriates (Kuwait, Lebanon, and Qatar), exemption from land acquisition formalities (Algeria and Morocco), waivers of import quotas (Qatar), and a preferential capital accounts regulation for foreign investors in specific locations (Syria).

Some interventions combine different selectivity criteria. One popular intervention, the special economic zone, is spreading throughout the region (see chapter 3). It provides many kinds of enclave incentives for certain types of firms (such as exporters or information technology firms) in certain geographical locations. Is this a good development? With scarce data and nonexistent evaluations, special economic zones might appear as business environment havens that benefit only a small part of the economy. They can, however, also put useful pressure on other government agencies to match zone performance. For such pressure to be productive, transparent benchmarking of the performance of public entities inside and outside these zones should be made available. Special economic zones should also be explicitly designed as part of a broader reform agenda and evaluated as such.

Without formal evaluations of these interventions, definitive conclusions regarding the potential benefits and risks of industrial policies are not yet possible. The next section assesses those benefits and risks in the context of what we do know with certainty—that there are institutional priorities that should be addressed first.

Assessing Risks of Industrial Policy Interventions

Three types of risks are associated with selective interventions: the opportunity cost of selectivity, the distortions and waste associated with selectivity and subsidies, and the political economy risk of state capture associated with policies that exclusively benefit special interest constituencies. These risks are particularly high in MENA countries, where political and economic relationships have mostly omitted safeguard institutions and policies.

The Opportunity Cost of Selectivity

The more selective a policy, the more likely it will concentrate resources as well as administrative capacity on a targeted group of firms. However, the more selective the policy, the higher the opportunity cost of forgone benefits from conducting more neutral policies that could benefit a broader range of firms. The same argument that justifies selectivity (limited administrative capacity and political capital to reform) can be turned on its head: the more selective governments are, the less they will invest in broader policies and the smaller the segment of the economy that will benefit from these interventions.

At least two factors affect this opportunity cost. First, the policy's extent of selectivity influences both the benefits and the opportunity costs. In view of this, the highly selective recent industrial policies in some MENA countries (for example, in Algeria, Morocco, and Saudi Arabia) that target specific activities or products deserve careful scrutiny. Policies in other countries favoring exporters, for example, entail less selectivity and therefore fewer opportunity costs.

Second, the quality of the overall business environment is key. On the benefits side, it is easy to argue that selective policies will have limited impact if the overall business environment is poor. In other words, as long as a critical mass of structural policies in quadrant I are not put in place, selective interventions are very likely to fail. In fact, the better the business environment, the lower the opportunity costs of conducting selective policies and the larger the benefits of selectivity. Here, what is hard to assess is the critical mass of general business environment reforms that need to be in place. A judgment call can be made only when the overall business environment is poor. For example, in Algeria, the Islamic Republic of Iran, Libya, Syria, and to less extent Egypt, the impact of industrial policies is very uncertain because of the deficient business environments of these countries.

Distortions and Waste Associated with Selectivity and Subsidies

Selectivity inevitably introduces distortions between beneficiary and nonbeneficiary firms, especially when the boundary between them is permeable and hard to draw. These distortions can be significant in small and medium-sized enterprise interventions, targeted interventions for technology-intensive sectors, or new firms. Firms or public officials can abuse the selection criteria. Even without abuse, unless the targeting aligns perfectly with economic efficiency, firms will be encouraged to alter their behavior (for example, to remain small enough to qualify as a small and medium-sized enterprise) in ways that are not always econom-ically beneficial.

Similarly, channeling subsidies inevitably leads to a waste of resources either because of spillage, poor targeting of subsidies, or poor mecha-nisms to administer the subsidies. Waste rises when subsidies are coupled with selective interventions.

Other features affect the risk assessment of subsidized or selective programs. Of course, the state's administrative capacity and the quality of its governance will directly affect the waste and distortions associated with selective and subsidized interventions. Lower costs of raising taxes (in resource-rich countries) reduce the cost of subsidized interventions, especially when subsidies are prevalent and not selective (quadrant III). Market failures in the economy—which are hard to identify and quantify with the available analytical tools—increase the benefits of subsidized or selective programs.

Last, the type of instrument used to administer subsidies will affect the level of waste: price subsidy compared with demand mechanisms that use matching grants, quality of carrot-and-stick features and measurabil-ity of outcomes, administrative allocation of supply-side or demand-side subsidies, and so on. The literature on industrial policies has focused extensively on the effectiveness of carrot-and-stick instruments in East Asia (Evans 1997 and references therein; Rodrik 2004), attributing their success to the credibility of the stick and to measurable, verifiable, and unambiguous targets that trigger both rewards and penalties. The political aspects of the government-private sector relationship are key determinants of credibility, and design, governance, and administrative capacity determine the clarity of measurement.

Political Economy Risks

Selective policies, by definition, exclusively benefit special constituencies. This has political implications if the private sector is involved in policy making and has political influence on the government.

During the design phase of selective interventions, the state faces a tradeoff between detaching from specific groups of firms or listening to the private sector and tailoring policies to the needs of those firms. The risk of being captured by special interests in the second is countered by a serious risk of being detached from market reality in the first. A government that engages in sectoral policy making faces a difficult balancing act.

Once selective policies are in place, the narrower the interests of the constituency and the higher the risk of getting caught in sustaining and increasing selective support. Many homogenous constituencies are, after all, better organized politically and have stronger advocacy interests. This is precisely why selective policies that, at the outset, do not involve direct subsidies or protection (quadrant II) get dragged into quadrant IV. A risk exists that new sectors—which selective policies have transformed into constituencies—will pressure the state for protection or subsidies. Similarly, selective, subsidized programs run the risk of strong demand from other sectors to extend subsidies and protection to other parts of the economy.

Many carrot-and-stick interventions are unsuccessful because of the political forces working on economic policy. In theory, government financial support for a sector should be conditional on a performance measure and should be discontinued if clear and measurable targets are not reached. The problem is that granting the carrot is easy and politically rewarding to governments (even if waste occurs), whereas administering the stick is costly, and the justification for action is hard to verify. Typically, sunset clauses built into sectoral-support policies get deferred indefinitely under pressure from the very constituencies that these policies have supported and created.

Nabli et al. (2004) illustrate how the slow pace of change of public interventions to promote private sector development in MENA is due to the "privileged networks" of firms created in the industrial strategy era of the 1960s and 1970s. These networks, advocacy groups supporting the status quo, sometimes employ a well-organized and unionized workforce (state-owned enterprises) or have business leaders who, collectively, have strong influence on policy making (state capture by private interests). Networks of privilege now strive to use the present reforms to reorganize their rent seeking and slow the reform process.

The severity of this political economy risk varies according to the state of governance and politics in a country. The nature of private sector constituencies, their relation to the state, and the state's ability to shield itself from capture by private interests puts such interventions more or less at risk. In particular, government commitment to retreat from policies that prove unsuccessful and to assess success or failure independently will be determined by how much it is captured by the private constituencies it is supporting.[6]

When public officials meet businessmen to design selective policies, two things need to be examined in any given country: the nature of the existing private sector actors and the capacity of the state to avoid capture by private interests.

What are the preferences of existing private sector actors and the constraints they face? Are they homogenous or conflicting? Which are the most powerful and better organized? How strongly do they influence government?

Even if there is no risk of state capture and both the government and the private sector are genuinely engaged in designing an optimal growth strategy, the economy may end up focusing on the wrong sectors. Why? Because the amount of information generated in the market will be dominated by the largest, most vocal, and best-organized existing sectors. Because weak or small sectors cannot voice their preferences and constraints, private sector development policy making—even if derived from a well-designed public-private dialogue—will likely favor large and more-established sectors. The situation worsens when selective policies are in place and capture kicks in, because beneficiaries of these policies may get their constituency even more politically reinforced.

Private sector organizations (also called business membership organizations) are an important channel of communication between government and the private sector. They can be more or less developed depending on the sectors and more or less captured by the most influential firms in every sector—particularly in the early stages of development or when the economic structure is not diversified (oil economies). In such cases the state-business relation is often captured by business membership organizations that represent only a narrow group of influential firms.

This is costly in two respects. First, the type of information and advocacy that the government gathers from the private sector is biased and can lead to a suboptimal policy prioritization. Second, these business membership organizations limit the ability of the state to partner with sector associations to implement effective interventions with credible carrot-and-stick instruments. However, active organizations representing the business community are an important ingredient of good private sector development policy making. What is needed is for all types of businesses to be represented and for the business membership organizations to be diverse and open to entry. Short of that, the risk is that the few existing business membership organizations be captured by narrow interests.

The governance and capacity weaknesses of the private sector also increase the cost and risk of failures of these policies. The problem is that
weak public and private sectors prevail in many countries where these
interventions are most needed (as in oil economies).

The second political economy risk is the capacity of the state to avoid
capture by private interests, while responding to the specific constraints
that sectors face. That is difficult to assess, but external accountability
mechanisms, past government efforts to cut support to failing sectors,
and the overall quality of public governance are important elements that
can determine the capacity of the state to shield itself from capture.

Should Oil-Rich Countries Intervene? Yes, but the Risks of Failure Are Higher

The temptation to design strong industrial policies is very high in oil
economies that struggle to diversify outside the low-employing oil sector. In most oil economies big push industrial policies were tried in the
1960s and 1970s, relying on state-owned enterprises and coupled with
very limited trade openness. All types of quadrant IV policies were tried
(subsidized credit lines for priority sectors, investment subsidies, input
price subsidies, protection from entry, and public investment in selected
sectors) at the expense of not addressing the quadrant I business environment. These efforts generally failed, most likely because of inefficiencies in state ownership, excessive protection and distortion in the
economy, and the lack of mechanisms to correct failed interventions. A
general set of evidence that these policies failed in MENA simply lies in
the poor performance in terms of export, diversification, and productivity documented in chapter 3.[7]

The ability of oil economies to credibly implement carrot-and-stick
strategies and especially to enforce the penalties for failed interventions
remains questionable. Given their very loose budget constraints and
strong political pressure to continue to support failing programs, the
extent of fiscal resources often masks the real costs of interventions,
making it harder to spot failures in oil-rich countries. Such strategies are
also unlikely to succeed in oil-rich countries simply because many of
them suffer from governance issues.[8]

Even if the political economy risks of intervening are much higher in oil
countries, and the waste and distortions more likely to last, the case is
strong for intervening to spur economic diversification. Norway, and to
less extent Indonesia, have used dedicated sectoral policies (not necessarily
involving subsidies) to spur infant sectors, but they have done so in the context of a good, open business environment and wise macromanagement of

Dutch disease, an important part of any diversification strategy. For such programs to succeed, a combination of sound macropolicies to limit the competitiveness damage by the oil rents, a certain degree of openness, and a good business environment (all quadrant I policies)[9] are needed. If these are in place, sectoral policies to initiate diversification are probably justified.

A Final Cautionary Note: Industrial Policies Could Succeed if the Right Conditions and Processes Are in Place

Sectoral policies or industrial policies—whether they include such selective interventions as subsidies or focus only on sector-specific regulations and public goods—may be justified, even more so in oil-rich countries where market pressures do not naturally push economies toward greater diversification. Governments could focus on successful approaches if they had good information on what was working and what was not.

However, the risk of such strategies failing or being captured by the beneficiary constituencies is very high unless governance, transparency, and institutional arrangements are strong. The reasons past interventions failed to produce sustained growth still apply in the region: no systematic and transparent evaluation of interventions, no transparent costing of benefits awarded to firms, and no institutional process involving the private sector in reviewing sectoral policies and identifying priorities.

Governments should focus on putting in place the prerequisites to maximize the effectiveness of interventions and to spot and correct inevitable failures. These prerequisites include the following:

- A sound investment climate (including sector-specific public goods and regulations)
- An institutionalized and inclusive process of consultation with the private sector in designing, monitoring, and evaluating interventions
- Transparent intervention subsidies, including clear identification of beneficiary firms
- Clear, measurable, and transparent indicators of each intervention's success
- Arm's length relations between the government and the private sector
- A public governance setup that binds the government to prevent capture and to shut down failing interventions

Today no MENA country really combines these features of successful interventions. The basic ingredients of sound governance are in general too weak in most of the region to allow for effective interventions to have sufficient impact. Issues of transparency in outcomes, evaluation, and commitment to interrupt unsuccessful interventions remain prevalent in most countries. In such circumstances the prospects for industrial policy interventions are poor. The risks of failure and capture remain very high because the weaknesses that undermined past interventions are still in place—and those weaknesses are generally more prevalent in oil-rich countries, which may need industrial policies the most.

Notes

1. The industrial policies pursued by most MENA countries between the 1960s and 1980s were very different from the current ones in that they relied heavily on central planning and state-owned enterprises. Although present policies are still called industrial policies, they are often heavily focused on services (such as information technology, offshoring, and tourism), rather than exclusively targeting industry.

2. Even though privatization of state-owned enterprises in MENA lagged behind other regions (for example, Latin America), economic strategies that protected state-owned enterprises in emerging industries were abandoned.

3. Pack (2000), using a rather weak econometric identification strategy, controversially argues that these policies explain very little, if any, of the success of East Asian economies.

4. For a more detailed and conceptual introduction to this framework, see Benhassine and Raballand (2009).

5. It is selective to an extent because the subsidy is targeted to the industrial sectors, not to agriculture and services. Among industrial firms, however, it is not selective.

6. For a more complete analysis of these statements, see Evans (1997), Maxfield and Schneider (1997), and Nelson and Finger (2004).

7. More specific analysis of the poor performance of selective interventions in MENA can be found in Galal (2005) and Nabli et al. (2004). For a recent collection of papers on industrial policies in the MENA region, see Galal (2008).

8. The correlation between natural resource endowment and weak governance, well established in the empirical literature, is discussed in chapter 9.

9. Note that the minimum level of quadrant I policies needed before any intervention can have a chance to work is arguably higher in oil than non-oil economies.

Designing Credible Private Sector Reforms Informed by Political Economy Realities

"Why a seminar on the knowledge-based economy? Our economy is totally based on 'knowledge.' To do anything in our country, you have to know *someone."*

Participant at a high-level seminar on the knowledge-economy in the region (2008)

So far, this report has shown that weaknesses in the business environment relate, in great part, to the discretionary allocation of rents to the private sector, the arbitrary implementation of rules by public agencies, and the distortionary role of many MENA states when intervening in markets or regulating them. That lowers the credibility of reform efforts in the eyes of investors. Changing this requires altering the relationship between policy makers and the beneficiaries of privileges. Political leaders can enhance credibility with investors, public administration staff, and the broader public by dismantling the web of rent-creating and -sharing opportunities that weakens the regulatory and administrative functions of the state in many areas of the business environment. This is the topic of the last part of this report.

Chapter 8 first shows why the needed reforms have been slow in coming to the MENA region. Looking at the political economy of state-business relations, it argues that both the demand for reform (by the most vocal, dominant private sector) and the supply (the incentives of the political leadership to conduct deep institutional reforms) are weak. The narrow coalition favoring the status quo has nevertheless evolved in some countries where the private sector has grown more diverse—especially in non-oil economies.

Informed by a political economy perspective, chapter 9 stresses that private-led growth strategies and policy reforms will gain in credibility and sustain their impact only if they explicitly address core governance issues. This will require a change in the way that policy making is conducted—enabling in particular a broader coalition of private sector businesses to engage in the design and evaluation of policies. It will also require institutional reforms that limit discretion in the way rules are applied to firms—focusing in particular on transparency, accountability, and greater autonomy of all market institutions.

Although each country context will dictate the mix of priority actions that will have the greatest impact on investor expectations, the chapter argues that governments of the region should redefine their private sector development strategies and policy making along very similar principles, aiming to (1) increase business entry and competition and reduce rents, (2) reform institutions to level the playing field, and (3) foster open policy making based on inclusive partnerships with the private sector.

CHAPTER 8

Institutions and State-Business Alliances Constraining Reforms and Credibility

The political economy in most of the MENA region—which reflects both the demand for reform and its supply—has limited the willingness and ability of policy makers to conduct reforms that address the deep-rooted institutional and governance issues in a credible manner.

On one hand, the supply of quality reforms has been hindered by policy-making institutions that lack credibility of commitment. The region lacks the institutions that would limit the discretion and arbitrariness of public officials. In well-performing democracies, those institutions include political checks and balances, independent judiciaries, and institutionalized political parties, but institutions matter in nascent or nonestablished democracies, too.

Fast-growing nondemocracies in East Asia exhibit starkly different institutional arrangements than slower growing nondemocracies. In the former, larger groups of citizens (organized in an institutionalized ruling party or civil service, for example) can act collectively to limit discretionary decisions by the political leadership. In the latter, they cannot.

For historical reasons MENA countries have found themselves largely in the latter group. Most governments in the region rely on the relationship between their political leaders, higher levels of the public administration, and a narrow group of allies, including key private sector entrepreneurs. Political leaders and high-level public officials retain discretion over the allocations of publicly controlled rents, rather than entrusting such allocations to institutions that are protected from interference. This undermines the credibility of state policies and reforms—and of promises of future reforms—for most investors not connected to the political elite. It also explains the insufficient response of the private sector to reforms in the region.

On the other hand, demand for reform has also been weak. The most vocal private sector generally has not been in favor of reforms that would affect its dominant position. In transition countries where the private sector has grown more diverse and was able to advocate for change (such as in Eastern Europe), pressure on policy makers to extend the reforms has grown. At least until recently, this has not been the case in the region, especially in oil-rich countries or countries where the private sector voice is muted. This is due in part to the inability of a more developmental and less rent-seeking private sector to both organize and freely advocate for change. It has also been due to a tacit alliance between politicians and the more prominent members of the private sector to maintain the status quo. Recent economic liberalization measures have given rise to new private interests more eager for reforms to enhance competitiveness and growth—exporters in particular. Indeed, the diversity of the private sector is increasing in the region, especially in non-oil countries, as is the capacity of these new private constituencies to advocate for change.

The fundamental reform challenge for many MENA governments goes deeper than the technical obstacles to reforming large public agencies, discarding policies that create rents, withdrawing the state from productive activities, and strengthening the state's capacity to provide the legal and regulatory framework for markets and service provision. The most formidable roadblock is the inability of governments to forge credible relationships with entrepreneurs outside a narrow group of businesses. Indeed, credibility is at the heart of the governance problem that impedes reform and blunts its impact. At the same time, these governments maintain deep-rooted ties with that narrow group, who resist some of the very reforms that would encourage faster economic growth and more employment.

This chapter aims to understand the political economy factors that affect the incentives and ability of MENA governments to conduct far-reaching institutional reforms that would change the status quo. It is divided in two parts. The first tries to understand what constrains the supply of such reforms—what in the political settings of MENA countries limits the ability of their governments to credibly commit their institutions to reform and limit the ability of political leaders to interfere in a discretionary way in how rules are applied. To do that it will contrast the political regimes in the region—both oil and non-oil countries—with the political systems in some countries in East Asia to emphasize what differs in the incentives of political leaders.

The East Asian comparison was chosen because these governments share some important characteristics with MENA countries politically and in terms of their starting position before their periods of sustained growth. Both lacked strong public accountability mechanisms supported by democratic electoral systems, but there is a strong contrast in how public institutions were developed, empowered, and used. Comparing MENA with a region that was able to conduct such reforms and grow quickly while not progressing as much in the area of political openness offers a new angle to understand the current status quo. It also offers new routes to policy making in the area of private sector development—routes that would signal more credibly a commitment for change, while taking into account these political economy constraints.

The second part looks at the demand for reform that emanates from the private sector. It argues that such demand is not as strong as one may expect given the discretionary nature of the business environment, because channels for effective demand have been controlled in large part by the interests benefitting from the status quo. A "virtuous circle" can emerge, however, where initial reform creates new interests that in turn become key advocates of further growth-oriented reform. This dynamic has been increasingly important in more reforming countries—Egypt, Jordan, or Morocco, for example—where the private sector has grown more diverse, more vocal, and more organized over the years.

Weak Supply of Reforms: Policy-Making Institutions That Lack Commitment and Credibility

MENA's weakness in attracting private investment is linked to the lack of rule-based institutions that are insulated against discretionary interference by political leaders, that limit their power, and that hold them accountable. Such organizations—such as an independent bureaucracy—to which substantial power is entrusted, and that can operate by established rules independent from discretionary central leadership decisions, are institutionalized. The key argument in this chapter is that in economically successful nondemocracies—as in East Asia—either the ruling party, the civil service, or other organizations are institutionalized, holding the political leadership accountable and restraining its power. In contrast, MENA countries have resisted institutionalization, weakening the credibility of the state for both investors and the public administration.[1]

The Link between Credibility and Institutionalization of Policy Making

Key characteristics of institutionalization in East Asia included transparent promotion and recruitment schemes, the delegation of substantial authority to low levels of the organization, and the simple fact that intraorganizational coordination and information flows were substantially free. The effect of institutionalization in East Asia was not only to improve the performance of an institution such as the public administration, but also to limit the ability of political leaders to violate the rules governing the institution and to resort to arbitrary behavior favoring political supporters. MENA countries exhibit less institutionalization because establishing institutions of this kind limits discretion and access to rents, especially where high natural resource rents are available.

Institutionalization of political parties. Although rulers in nondemocracies are often supported by political parties, it is less common for rulers to allow these parties to be institutionalized—that is, to allow party members to coordinate in limiting the power of the political leadership and hold it accountable for its actions. Institutionalization also imposes limits on the ability of political leaders or high-level public officials to act arbitrarily or to allocate rents and privileges in a discriminate fashion. This encourages investment by members of the organization or their allies, even those lacking personal connections to political leadership or high-level officials.

Recent research shows that greater institutionalization of the ruling party is associated with higher investment. To circumvent data limitations, this research relies on the assumption that the older a ruling party is, holding constant the years in office of the leader of a country, the more likely it is to be institutionalized. A large, positive association can be found between the age of the ruling party and private investment (figure 8.1) (Gehlbach and Keefer 2008). Of course, specific country

FIGURE 8.1

The Effects of Ruling Party Institutionalization on Private Investment

(percent of private investment in GDP)

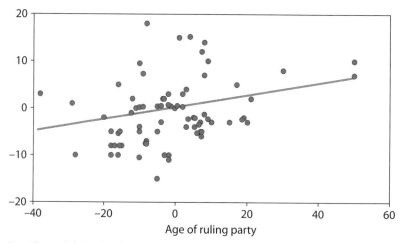

Note: The graph depicts the effect of age of ruling party on private investment after controlling for leader years in office; the years the country has been nondemocratic; the rate of replacement of key actors; ethnic, religious, and linguistic fractionalization; the distance of major trading partners; the fraction of the population that is young or rural; total population and land area; and real purchasing power parity-adjusted income per capita. Negative numbers can be interpreted as investment rates or party ages that are "below average," positive numbers as "above average."

Source: Authors' analysis based on data from Gehlbach and Keefer 2007.

examples may differ from this econometric finding, but overall the relation between party institutionalization and private investment is robust.

Such a relationship could be fortuitous: parties that foster more economic growth may simply last longer. However, the results control for the years in office of the leader and the length of the nondemocratic episode. None of these are significantly related to private investment, and yet all should be if the results were simply the result of more investment leading to more political stability.[2]

Chinese economic success exhibits close links with institutionalization. The policy reforms that China undertook starting in the 1980s are well known (from liberalizing agriculture to allowing foreign direct investment), but the success of many of these reforms required high levels of trust between leaders and lower-level officials. For example, the reinvestment of profits from township and village enterprises required village and township heads to believe that they could retain the profits that they earned from township-village enterprises.[3] Numerous reforms were introduced that enhanced credibility between leaders and lower-level officials, including greater information dissemination among officials and transparent, performance-based promotion schemes (Manion 1992; Wong 1992; Edin 2003; Manion 2004; Li and Zhou 2005; Whiting 2006). Because leaders could credibly offer officials rewards in exchange for economic growth, they had an incentive to promote private investment. Indeed, officials were promoted based largely on their achievement of employment and growth objectives.

MENA's lack of institutionalization. Institutionalized ruling parties or bureaucracies are not characteristic of the MENA region. In many countries the political and economic elite are members of the ruling party and membership in the party (or ruling party coalitions) is an important criterion for bureaucratic advancement. Whereas in institutionalized ruling parties the party offers a transparent career path for the ambitious, in MENA this is not so. Political leaders generally remain the hub of centralized decision making, delegating little and promoting and rewarding members of the party, the bureaucracy, or other decision-making organizations at their discretion. Personal ties to the political leaders play a large role in these decisions. In several cases, power is passed down not through the party, but through closeness to the leadership circles.

Owen's (1992) review of the evolution of parties in select Arab countries indicates the absence of party institutionalization, even where the ruling party was apparently prominent. Parties had many of the trappings of institutionalization, but their leaders retained discretion over power and benefits rather than subjecting them to the rules and organization of the party. Rulers were careful to avoid party organization that would permit party members to threaten their rule. Key to this was establishing competing organizations that also reported to the political leaders. Recruitment and promotion, rather than being based on merit or on commitment to the ideological principles on which parties were founded, is based largely on regional and sectarian considerations.

By nature, most of the monarchies of the region are also weakly institutionalized. Most of the decision-making power remains in the hands of the leader—leaving little influence to parliamentary politics—and thus promoting and recruiting public officials are generally geared toward rewarding allegiance to the leader and his close circles. High-level public officials at the central and local levels retain significant discretionary power in such systems because they are accountable only to the leader or close allies.

These qualitative comparisons are systematically reflected in a quantitative difference between MENA countries and faster-growing countries in East Asia (figure 8.2). In 2004 all three subsets of MENA countries had parties more clearly dominated by the party leadership (in the sense that the leader's tenure was close to or greater than the party's age) than in middle-income nondemocracies, all East Asian nondemocracies, and the larger East Asian nondemocracies.

Transitions from one leader to another are also revealing about ruling party institutionalization. In MENA transitions have generally followed

FIGURE 8.2

Party Institutionalization in MENA and Comparator Countries, 2004

(number of years: party age minus leader tenure)

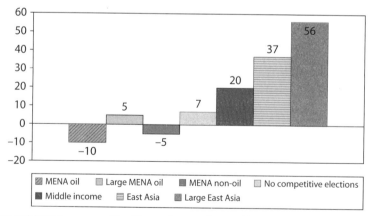

Note: Each bar is the average of the difference between the age of the ruling party and the number of years the leader has been in power. In countries where there is no ruling party, as in some Gulf states, this number is negative. The yellow shows the average for all countries that have no competitive electoral processes.

Source: Authors' analysis based on the *Database of Political Institutions* (available at go.worldbank.org/2EAGGLRZ40 and described in Beck et al. 2001).

the death of the previous leader. This has often accompanied at least a change in the name of the ruling party—if not its wholesale dismantling or the creation of competing parties that are loyal to the leadership. In East Asia, by contrast, party institutionalization is reflected in regular leadership transitions before the death of incumbents.

Another sign of the weak institutionalization is the lack of cohesion between stakeholders and mobilization around a clear long-term economic strategy in many MENA countries—reflecting in part the lack of consensus around growth. Few countries in the region have devised a long-term growth strategy. Sectoral ministries often have strategies, but rarely are they part of a consistent comprehensive plan. Coordination and cohesion between ministries is often weak—generally reflecting divided political elites. Tunisia and the Emirate of Dubai may stand as exceptions here, but in general a common long-term economic goal—a strong feature of the East Asian growth successes—is rare in the region.

Institutionalization of Bureaucracies

Singapore's institutionalized bureaucracy. Party institutionalization is not the only (or even the preferred) strategy for political leaders to make credible commitments to private investors. Leaders can also institutionalize the civil service. In general, this implies undertaking the same measures that are part and parcel of public sector reform (meritocratic and transparent recruitment, rule-bound and transparent decision making, and accountability for performance).

The best example of this is the Singaporean civil service, which has all of the attributes of institutionalization. First, it is structured to provide a high level of public services, which requires ample ability to coordinate within and across ministries. Second, it ties its promotion and compensation standards to successful service provision so that coordination is rewarded. By 2006, 40 percent of average civil service compensation and 50 percent of senior civil service compensation were performance-based.[4] These ratios are higher than other public sectors worldwide and most private sector employment contracts.

Third, Singapore has entrusted substantial decision-making authority to civil servants, decentralizing authority. For example, in the early 1980s community policing was introduced, generating substantial police-community interaction and endowing police with substantial discretion to prevent and tackle crime in their patrol areas. Workplace and food safety regulators were allowed to defer prosecution for firms in violation. More broadly, the Block Vote Budget Allocation system introduced in 1989 set a target of total expenditure for each ministry as a percentage of national income. Following budget approval, each ministry could then spend according to stated objectives but could freely shift funds and manpower between programs and activities. In particular, the budgeting process allowed ministries to use unexpected surpluses from one area to achieve objectives in other areas without going back to the legislature or cabinet for approval.

Balancing such discretion, performance standards are transparent, which is a result of significant investments in management information systems. The Singapore Government Management Accounting System was introduced in 1992. This computer-based information and analytical system allowed exact costing of public sector activities. This made results-based budgeting possible. It was introduced in 1994, linking budgets and compensation to precise performance and cost targets (Jones 1999).

The institutionalization of the Singaporean civil service encourages investment for two reasons. The first (well-known) reason is that investor risks are lower when they face a predictable, high-quality public administration. The performance contracts that characterize the Singaporean civil service condition promotion on economic growth. Their success depends, however, on the credibility of promises of bonuses and promotions in exchange for performance for civil servants. The second reason is that the institutionalization of the public administration or the party allows those promises to be credible (Gehlbach and Keefer 2008). The characteristics of the Singaporean civil service make it difficult for the government to renege on its promises to compensate administration officials for treating investors well. Internal transparency and stability allow the civil service to coordinate a response to government if it reneges on these promises.

Singapore is, indeed, exceptional in its ability to attract private investment. Its ratio of private investment to GDP is 10 percentage points higher than in the average nondemocracy.[5] Of course, the government needed motivation to make these promises in the first place—growth. As a tiny and physically vulnerable state lacking natural resources, Singapore's pursuing sustained export-led growth may have been the only sustainable option for its leaders to maintain credibility with citizens.

MENA's lack of an institutionalized bureaucracy. In MENA's public sector, there is little sign of the meritocracy, information flow, and coordination that characterizes the Singaporean equivalent. Performance-based contracts are nearly unknown, promotions are largely seniority based, and recruitment is heavily clientelist.

For example, the World Bank's flagship publication on governance in the MENA region reported that appointments to the civil service in many countries in the region, including Algeria, Egypt, Morocco, and Syria, are based on demonstrations of loyalty rather than merit

(World Bank 2003a). Loyalty to one's immediate superiors as a basis for recruitment leads to a personalized, rather than an institutionalized, civil service. After the reunification of North and South Yemen, large-scale public employment was key to winning political loyalty in the Republic of Yemen. Loyalty to the political leadership, their inner circles and close supporters and allies is crucial to advance in the public sector in constitutional monarchies such as Jordan, Morocco, and Oman, as well as in republics such as Algeria, Egypt, Syria, or Tunisia.[6]

An oversized and noninstitutionalized civil service is also a strategy that rulers who lack credibility can use to defuse opposition to the regime. Direct employees of a regime and their families are likely to believe they will lose out if the regime fails and are therefore unlikely to support opposition (Robinson and Verdier 2002). Others, observing that public sector workers—a significant fraction of the population—support the government, see their chances for successful opposition as unlikely. Although there is no comprehensive, up-to-date data on the public sector wage bill in MENA, the available information points to much higher spending than in comparator countries (table 8.1).

TABLE 8.1

The Public Sector Wage Bill in MENA and Comparator Countries, 2001–05

Country	Year	Percentage of public wages per gross domestic product
Algeria	2001–05	7.5
Bahrain	2001	16.0
Egypt, Arab Rep.	2001–05	7.8
Jordan	2001	19.0
Kuwait	2001	16.0
Lebanon	2001	10.0
Morocco	2001–05	12.0–13.0
Syrian Arab Republic	2001–05	9.5–11.0
Tunisia	2001–05	12.0
Indonesia	2005	1.3
Malaysia	2005	5.2
Philippines	2005	5.5
Thailand	2005	5.9

Source: Authors' compilation based on data from the Unified Survey and *World Development Indicators*.

In 1997 MENA countries had much larger government workforces and offered more generous compensation to government workers (Schiavo-Campo, de Tommaso, and Mukherjee 1997). In Algeria, Bahrain, Egypt, Jordan, Lebanon, Morocco, Syria, Tunisia, West Bank and Gaza economies, and the Republic of Yemen, total government employment averaged 8.4 percent of the labor force (3.3 percent of the population), the average government wage was 3.4 times GDP per capita, and the total government wage bill was 9.8 percent of GDP.

By contrast, figures for Latin America were 4.7 percent of the labor force (1.9 percent of population), a lower average wage of 2.5 times GDP per capita, and a total wage bill of 4.9 percent of GDP. Among East Asian countries, these numbers were lower still. In China 2.8 percent of the labor force, or 1.7 percent of the population, were employed by the government for a total wage bill amounting to 3.8 percent of GDP, with average wages amounting to 1.3 times GDP per capita. In Singapore, with its much-vaunted and famously well-paid civil service, 2.0 percent of the labor force, or 0.9 percent of the population, were government employees, and the total wage bill was 4.6 percent of GDP. Although salaries in Singapore are high, they are only 2.1 times GDP per capita.

These larger expenditures in MENA do not translate into greater efficiency, because administration quality is not higher than in comparator countries. On the contrary, given a lack of institutionalization, leaders cannot easily monitor or contract with the public sector to induce high performance. Shirking is easier when institutionalization is low.

Such high spending on public sector employment to maintain political stability explains why public sector reform is historically difficult in MENA countries. It is, however, successful in serving its main purpose: compared with all nondemocracies, the non-oil MENA countries (excluding Lebanon) exhibit much greater political stability, a difference that is even more striking if one focuses only on middle-income countries. The average tenure of leaders of the non-oil MENA countries was about 15 years in 2000, 10 years for all other nondemocracies, and just over 8 years for the 12 nondemocracies with similar incomes per capita. Political stability—proxied by the fraction of years in which a leader of a country was replaced—was less than 2 percent from 1990 to 2004 for the non-oil MENA countries and more than 8 percent for other nondemocracies. Although investors have few institutional guarantees in MENA, political stability means that leaders in the region have had more opportunity to build credible personalized ties with investors than is usual. Still, the circle of investors benefiting from these ties is small.

The major decision political leaders must make, then, is to determine the size of the circle to which the leaders can make credible commitments. At one extreme, unelected leaders can make themselves, their close relatives, and their close allies the center of entrepreneurial activity in the country. Because leaders have no reason to expropriate themselves, this approach solves the credible commitment problem but limits investment to a small group. This may work in small countries and may explain why some smaller states of the Gulf Cooperation Council (GCC) have created a more business-friendly environment—with the United Arab Emirates leading the way and Bahrain, Oman, and Qatar catching up (box 8.1). The political economy of these countries—where government leaders may often be the business leaders—does not, however, offer a viable model for imitation in other larger MENA countries, where the political economy is more complex.

BOX 8.1

The Gulf Cooperation Council: Exception to the Resource Curse?

Recent empirical work distinguishes governance in GCC countries from other resource-rich states. In GCC countries progress in business environment reforms was faster because of supply and demand factors. On the demand side:

[T]he private sector, which included mostly entrepreneurs either from the ruling families or close associates, was supportive of reforms favoring the private sector. The state-owned enterprise sector expanded significantly, but it was not meant to substitute for the private sector; it was a rather practical response to the need to recycle the oil revenues into wealth creating activities. There were no opposing interest groups.

On the supply side, credibility was ensured by the immense wealth controlled by the political leadership:

The regimes did not even need any specific political institutional arrangements to ensure their credibility. The relative wealth of the rulers and the readily available rents at the governments' disposal to sustain the regimes were enough to ensure against expropriation.

Especially in the small GCC countries, the lack of institutionalization that other MENA countries face was absent because the circles close to the political leadership (often their extended family members) are large enough to form a class of entrepreneurs immune to expropriation because of their connectedness, and also large enough to develop the private sector country-wide. This peculiarity cannot be replicated in larger countries where the network of connected entrepreneurs is smaller relative to their economy, and/or where natural resources are not as large, per capita.

Source: Nabli, Silva-Jauregui, and Aysan 2008.

The Determinants of Reform: What Prevents Political Leaders from Strengthening Institutionalization in MENA?

Why do not more countries institutionalize to pursue economic growth? The willingness of political leaders to institutionalize to boost investor confidence depends on an essential tradeoff. Leaders can make credible promises to many investors only if these investors believe they can hold political leaders and public officials accountable to these promises. The stronger the mechanisms of accountability,[7] however, the smaller the rents that these political leaders can derive from the economy. The more credibility that these leaders gain by giving power to their constituents, the less rent they can control and allocate. For a political leader that gains support from distributing large rents to a relatively small circle of political clients, getting more credibility by giving more power to larger parts of society is costly—as they have to give up part of the rents that rewards their support base.

This tradeoff suggests several circumstances that might make institutionalization more or less desirable. For example, it is attractive when the returns to private investment are high and the rents in the absence of private investment are low (such as in China or resource-poor Singapore or Taiwan, China). Another important factor that affects the costs and benefits of institutionalization—one that is especially relevant in MENA—is the availability of resource rents, which acts as a disincentive to reform (Box 8.2).

Finally, the decision to institutionalize and promote a favorable investment climate to a larger group of firms also depends on the ability and willingness of various constituents—in particular the private sector itself—to pressure for reform.

Weak Demand for Reform: A Private Sector That Has Yet to Become an Agent of Change

The extent to which institutions of the private sector are supportive of policy and institutional changes that stimulate entry and growth will also affect the willingness of political leaders to reform. Unfortunately, a dominant private sector in most MENA countries has had ample reason to support a status quo that brought it high rents. This section reconciles the apparent contradiction that the private sector is both an obstacle and a key to the success of job-creating reforms. To understand the relation between government and business in MENA and their shared interest in the status quo, it is important to understand the historical genesis of the dominant private sector in the region. The story varies from country to country, but common traits form today's legacy.

BOX 8.2

Oil Rents, Foreign Aid Rents, and the (Dis)Incentives to Institutionalize

Oil revenue presents governments with tremendous opportunities, but it leads rulers to rely on redistribution rather than investment and growth to ensure political stability. This keeps incentives to institutionalize low, because natural resource rents are high, and unaccountable control over them is key to maintain support and allegiance. Also, the returns to private investment are likely to be low in sectors such as manufacturing, because the resource rents reduce their competitiveness through higher real exchange rates (Dutch disease).[8] Earlier chapters have noted that in the MENA region non–oil-exporting countries have generally made faster progress on reform and economic growth than oil exporters over the long term. Oil wealth can affect economic performance in different political systems (Eifert, Gelb, and Tallroth 2002).

The abundance of rents can allow such states to maintain a high level of redistribution, ensuring stability and a long planning horizon. In fact, it would be hard to identify an oil exporter in the region without an inflated public sector, subsidies, and protected inefficient enterprises in the public or private domain.

In a few countries, foreign aid has played the same role as oil rents in affecting the incentives of political leaders to reform. The interaction between foreign aid and autocracy can have similar effects to those of oil. Egypt and Jordan, for example, have historically received large amounts of foreign assistance that have been delinked from development objectives. Before 1990 foreign aid was 8.7 percent of gross national income in Egypt and more than 18 percent in Jordan.

The Lasting Influence of Old Business Elites

The heritage of the private sector policies over the last few decades is reflected today in the nature and characteristics of the private sector. Although new entrants have made the private sector much more diverse over the years, in every country a large group of dominant entrepreneurs remain who emerged and expanded during the years of protection and state-led policies. Most have since diversified, but old family entrepreneurs emerged thanks to the restrictive environment or the partial liberalization episodes that rewarded insiders and politically connected individuals. Notwithstanding a few country specificities and nuances, the pattern of entrepreneurship across the region's modern economic history is consistent. Mirroring changes in policy paradigms and economic strategies over the years, one can identify four similar phases in each country: colonial, state-led, partial liberalization, and diversification.

Colonial era. Some family businesses emerged during the colonial era, mostly in trade and small industrial sectors, and some prospered after independence when they were tolerated. Often these were traditional merchant families that expanded—typically in agribusiness—at a time of rising infrastructure and agricultural investment by European settlers. More often than not, and depending on their participation in the nationalist movements, these businesses and their owners' assets were expropriated after independence, as in Algeria, Egypt, Libya, and Syria. In other cases such as in the GCC countries, Lebanon, Morocco, and Tunisia, traditional merchant and industrial families formed the core business elite in the early postindependence years. This is also the case for the Islamic Republic of Iran. In both groups of countries, the private sector was also made up of microenterprises in small trade and services. In the large infrastructure sectors—transport, oil and mining, and banking—no local private sector presence was found. Only international corporations were present and dominant in these sectors.

State-led. A new set of entrepreneurs grew out of the opportunities during the state-led period, starting in the 1960s. Governments in almost all countries in the region embarked on ambitious economic programs of strong state intervention in all sectors of the economy, with nationalizations and investments in newly formed state-owned enterprises in priority sectors—often in heavy industry, but also in light manufacturing. This was the case in then-socialist countries Algeria, Egypt, Iraq, and Syria, and in more mixed economies such as the GCC countries, Jordan, Morocco, Tunisia, and the Republic of Yemen.

The private sector was largely repressed in this period, but niches of opportunity remain in the "shadows" of state dirigisme. The breadth of these niches varied between countries, but the business opportunities for the few entrepreneurs exploiting them were large. This was a time of record growth and public investment. It was also a time of heavy regulation in all sectors. The combination of the two enabled a network of businessmen to expand in monopolistic and protected environments.

The beneficiaries of these policies are usually still in the business scene today, constituting a large part of the current business elite. As opposed to the experience of other economies in transition, changing policies and increasing openness have usually not driven previously protected and privileged entrepreneurs out of business. This has important implications today for the relationship between the state and the private sector. Because the old business elite remains very prominent in private sector organizations and in formal and informal advocacy groups, the public-private dialogue in most MENA countries is affected.

Partial liberalization. That same group of businesses as well as new entrants embraced the opportunities offered by the first wave of partial liberalization. Facing the limits of the state-centered model, most countries opened at least partially to the private sector in the 1970s (Infitah in Egypt) or the 1980s. The wave of liberalization arrived only in the 1990s in Algeria, Libya, and Syria. During this partial opening, connections to the decision makers remained strong in most countries, a necessary condition of entry in most sectors. Not all firms needed such support, but the most important projects were subject to all sorts of licensing requirements. The private sector that could emerge and expand still depended on strong ties to the administration. Many public servants and heads of state-owned enterprises also turned into private entrepreneurs. Some used their connections and sectoral knowledge to invest in the newly opened sectors, often thanks to generous credit lines from public banks.

Diversification. With the opening to trade and investment, the 1990s were a time of further growth through diversification in newly opened sectors for the family groups, who acted as connected first movers. They were not the only ones, because new entrepreneurs emerged in all activities. Today, the private sector in most MENA countries reflects this diversity, even if the old business elite—now heading diversified family conglomerates—still dominates the formal business organizations and the informal policy advocacy channels. As an example, these four phases played out in shaping the private sector in Morocco today (box 8.3).

BOX 8.3

The Genesis of Business Elites in Morocco

Colonial era. In Morocco many dominant business families emerged during the protectorate era between the 1920s and mid-1950s. Large old trading families from the Fes region could sustain and expand their precolonial era trade business into new sectors such as transport and agribusiness by linking to the European settlers' modern economy. By the time of independence (1956), however, more than 95 percent of registered Moroccan companies were still foreign owned. The redistribution of European settlers' assets into Moroccan hands at independence marks the first wave of Moroccan capitalism. Independent Morocco adopted a relatively private sector–friendly policy, which led to the expansion of prominent family entrepreneurs who bought the firms left by European settlers at discounted prices.

This first wave of entrepreneurs (two-thirds of them still originating from Fes) diversified over the years into large family groups active in many sectors, eventually forming a large part of today's business elite. In parallel, the private sector flourished in the late 1950s and 1960s in the small service sectors.

(continued)

BOX 8.3 (continued)

State-led. With the development of new state-led economic strategies in the 1960s, the prosperity of the business elite started to depend in greater part on its proximity and connectedness to the state and the leadership circles of the kingdom. This also coincided with the emergence of a second wave of politically connected entrepreneurs. With the introduction of import licensing requirements, entry licenses in protected sectors, directed and subsidized credit from state-owned banks to priority sectors, selective investment subsidies, discretionary allocation, and discounted sales of public land plots, many prominent businessmen used their proximity to the political elite to secure exclusive sources of business growth. The story is all too common: protectionist import-substitution policies of the 1960s and 1970s protected a largely rent-dependent class of connected entrepreneurs from foreign competition.

Partial liberalization. The third wave of politically connected entrepreneurs arose from the Moroccanization policy launched in 1973. Foreigners were forced to sell their assets—primarily enterprises and real estate—to Moroccan nationals. In 1970 there had been about 5,500 foreigners active among a total of approximately 8,000 business managers in the country. The political objective of the time was to strengthen the social and nationalistic base of the regime. More than 1,500 firms and 400,000 hectares of irrigated rural land changed hands in two years. The Moroccanization benefited three social groups: employees of the formerly foreign-owned firms, high-ranking public officials, and the politically connected elite. Protection and political connections sustained the business success of many of these new entrepreneurs.

Diversification. In the 1980s and accelerating in the 1990s increased competition from imports led to a shift of the traditional business elite away from no-longer-protected tradable sectors toward nontradable sectors, in which many activities were still heavily regulated. This is the era of the rise of construction and real estate tycoons, who depended on their privileged access to large public procurement contracts (for social housing programs, in particular). It is also the era of the rise of business leaders in regulated sectors such as retail, telecoms, banking, and other services. It coincided with the era of privatizations, some of which benefited a few connected businessmen, as in banking.

In this decade of increased openness, a new brand of Moroccan entrepreneurs emerged in more competitive sectors: exporters, small and medium-sized investors in high-tech industries, offshoring, textile and garments, and supplying the growing auto industry. The private sector is now very diverse even if the old business elite still dominates the large firms. This new diversity is reflected in the network of sectoral and regional business membership organizations, which often compete in their advocacy on divergent interests. Entrepreneurs in competitive sectors form an increasingly active advocacy group for further liberalizing reforms.

Source: Authors' synthesis based on Leveau (1985), Tangeaoui (1993) Benhaddou (1997), Catusse (2008), Greenwood (2008), and various Moroccan press reviews.

Although countries across the region have reformed at different times and paces, the business elites share similar characteristics in the way that they emerged—their privileged relation to the states that often ensured their prosperity and to the successive waves of new entrants. Today, these large family-owned firms coexist with a considerably much more diverse private sector, made up of a new wave of younger firms that entered the market under a more open and competitive environment.

State-Business Alliances That Favor the Status Quo

In contrast to the arguments earlier in this chapter, which emphasize the political incentives of leaders to nurture a vibrant private sector, other research has pointed to the private sector itself as the source of distortions that block new entry. Firms "capture" the state, by shaping the laws and influencing policies to their own advantage, in return for (illicit financial) support to public officials, resulting in policies that are inimical to the investment climate and competition (see, for example, Desai and Pradhan 2005; Kaufmann 2005). In such economies, influential firms face fewer problems than their competitors, but are also less innovative. So the firms that dominate resources in a captured system do not use them to the full advantage of the economy.

In fact, alliances between the state and small privileged circles of businessmen are widespread in MENA. A review of state-business relationships in seven MENA countries shows how alliances between privileged businessmen and governments are strong, exclusive, and often decades old. For these countries, loyalty to the leader or membership in an elite group allied to the leader brings access to economic benefits. This group often makes up much of the dominant private sector. In none of these cases are either the rewards or the allegiances institutionalized in the ways seen in East Asia.[9]

Institutionalization of a civil service or ruling party, in combination with economic policies designed to remove barriers to entry, innovation, and investment, is one way to mitigate the effects of capture. Another is to institutionalize and open up organizations in the private sector itself. This type of open private sector institutionalization has also been lacking in the region.

Weakly Institutionalized and Inclusive Private Sector Organizations and Consultations: Two Private Sectors

Business associations in much of MENA tend to be poorly institutionalized. Advocacy for reforms has not yet found much support from generally weak, unrepresentative, or nonindependent business associations.

Depending on the country, the most prominent of these are either government controlled or are dominated by large prominent firms that favor the status quo and use the associations as a vehicle to pursue narrow interests over more broadly beneficial growth-oriented reforms. The "new" private sector of recent entrants and smaller firms has yet to organize to better advocate for change. In many countries it is constrained to do so because independent organizations are either not allowed (as in at least five countries) or effectively barred from freely voicing its criticisms of government policies. This phenomenon is by no means confined to MENA. Mancur Olson in his 1965 seminal work originally warned of business associations as "distributive coalitions" often pursuing narrow self-interest and rents (Olson 1965).

A 2007 survey of some of the most important business organizations in MENA showed that their policy advocacy priorities are often considerably narrower than the growth priorities expressed by the majority of enterprises. The expressed agenda of these business associations suggests that incentives and subsidies figure prominently in their priorities. Many business associations in the region place priority on specific support of particular sectors or on benefits granted by the state. At the same time, each country has a pressing policy agenda that, in many cases, does not figure in the top priorities of the leading business associations. The survey asked business associations about their top three advocacy priorities (left column in table 8.2). Their answers can then be compared to what firms—mostly small and medium enterprises—surveyed independently reflect as their top three constraints (right column). Highlighted in yellow in the table are the few topics where the two concur.

Enabling the entry of new investors and allowing more private voices to be heard will progressively shift the balance from the rent-seeking private sector that favors protection and the status quo to the developmental private sector that favors competitiveness and growth. The private sector in MENA countries has already grown more diverse. In countries where this is allowed, new business associations have emerged—some representing new young entrepreneurs, as in Algeria or Syria; some from specific regions or sectors, as in Algeria, Jordan, or Morocco; and some representing distinct categories of firms such as small and medium-sized enterprises or exporters, as in Egypt.

The recent election of the head of one of the most important business associations in Algeria (Forum des Chefs d'Entreprises) illustrates the changing times and the emergence of younger, more reform-oriented business elites. Although many expected the incumbent to be reelected without any competition, a young entrepreneur ran for the presidency of the forum. He was able to challenge the existing open-vote rule and change it to secret ballot. The campaign led to public debates,

TABLE 8.2

Advocacy Priorities of Business Associations Do Not Match the Top Constraints of Enterprises

	Top three advocacy priorities of main business associations	Top three growth constraints of enterprises
Iran, Islamic Rep.	1. Support to specific sectors/industrial strategy	1. Regulatory policy uncertainty
	2. Tax incentives for investment, govt. support	2. Macroeconomic uncertainty
	3. Reduced corporate taxes	3. Cost of financing
Algeria	1. Tax incentives for investment, govt. support	1. Anticompetitive practices/informal competition
	2. Regulatory barriers	2. Access to land
	3. Support to specific sectors/industrial strategy	3. Access to financing
Egypt, Arab Rep.	1. Support to specific sectors/industrial strategy	1. Macroeconomic uncertainty
	2. Regulatory barriers	2. Corruption
	3. Tax incentives for investment, govt. support	3. Anticompetitive practices/informal competition
Jordan	1. Regulatory barriers	1. Macroeconomic uncertainty
	2. Support to specific sectors/industrial strategy	2. Corporate tax rates
	3. Infrastructure	3. Regulatory barriers
Lebanon	1. Regulatory	1. Corruption
	2. Tax incentives for investment, govt. support	2. Cost of financing
	3. Support to specific sectors/industrial strategy	3. Corporate tax rates
Syrian Arab Republic	1. Tax incentives for investment, govt. support	1. Corruption
	2. Support to specific sectors/industrial strategy	2. Corporate tax rates
	3. Infrastructure	3. Electricity
Yemen, Republic of	1. Infrastructure	1. Macroeconomic uncertainty
	2. Reduced corporate taxes	2. Corporation tax rates
	3. Training subsidies	3. Corruption
Morocco	1. Training/education system	1. Cost of financing
	2. Support to SMEs	2. Corporate tax rates
	3. Reduced corporate taxes/judicial reform	3. Access to land

Note: Highlighted in yellow are those areas that were cited in *both* groups as priority constraints. The contrast between the two columns must be interpreted with care, because both groups were not responding to the exact same question. Business associations were asked about their advocacy priorities—policies that reduce constraints to businesses, but also government proactive policies. Firms were asked to rate different constraints to their development. The list of constraints proposed to both groups was identical.

Source: Survey of the main business associations in each country and World Bank enterprise surveys.

conferences, and public events—a first in the region. The incumbent ultimately won the election by a comfortable margin, but this first successful electoral competition in a major business association set a precedent and is likely to influence positively the future governance and management of the association.

These new voices are often more vocal in demanding further pro-growth reforms. If entry barriers continue to be lowered, these private constituencies will grow even more diverse, and pressure for reform will increase, creating a kind of "virtuous circle." Even partial reforms can trigger a self-sustaining dynamic process: the entry of more new players increases the support for further reform, leading to even more new entrants, which can eventually change the political economy of each country.

However, it is important, first, to note that the absence of institutionalized dialogue between the public and private sector leaves ad hoc mechanisms as the main means through which private sector demand can be expressed. These channels will tend to favor those with personal access to political leaders—the incumbent firms that are already large and influential. Further, to the extent that these same parties assume the leadership of state-sanctioned business associations, they tend to pursue the same narrow interests.

Public-private consultative mechanisms have been used by many successful fast-growing economies to enhance dialogue and consensus between policy makers and the private sector. The high-level "deliberative councils" of several East Asian tigers figured heavily in accounts of the strong consensus behind economic reforms in the 1990s. This sparked great interest in business-government consultation as a part of market-oriented reform. Since then, in a number of countries systematic consultation of affected parties has been incorporated into both the formulation of new laws and regulations and the reform of existing ones. In Australia, Canada, Great Britain, and the United States consultations with businesses on regulatory reform have become a standard procedure. In Vietnam consultations with the business community were credited with a major change in the enterprise law, which led to unprecedented levels of business registration.

Several features of the best-functioning consultative institutions distinguish them from business groups common in the MENA region. First, they are transparent both in their internal organization and in the way that they are governed. Second, entry into the institutions is not reserved to dominant firms. Third, government interaction with these firms is transparent and concerned with the substantive decisions government makes regarding the private sector. These characteristics yield several benefits:

- They improve the informational basis on which government acts by letting it know the costs and reaction of businesses to existing and proposed reforms.

- They improve business community compliance with laws and regulations by improving the information businesses have about regulation and increasing the community's sense of ownership in regulatory changes.

- They may reveal more efficient or acceptable ways to achieve government goals.

- They may generate more political support for (or dampen opposition to) growth-oriented reforms.

The lesson from this discussion is straightforward. Business associations, in the context of a formal consultative arrangement with government, can encourage investment. They cannot do this, however, if the legal and regulatory environment prevents new firms from entering (to take part in such consultations), or if the rules of association, determined by currently dominant firms or the political leadership of a country, exclude new entrants.

What Can Reformers Do to Change the Political Economy Status Quo?

Although the political economy of many MENA countries does not appear to be entirely encouraging for private sector development, it does not need to be a permanent regional feature. If even some barriers to entry are lifted and dynamic new entrepreneurs enter and create jobs, the demonstrated link between liberalization and growth can encourage political actors to take the risk of allowing broader institutionalization and even more entry. In several countries, including Egypt, Jordan, Morocco, and Tunisia, interests favoring liberalization and growth-oriented policies have begun to emerge as a counterbalance to defenders of the status quo.[10] Globalization and regional integration create stronger incentives for exporters and traders to work together to seek complementary liberalizing reforms and raise the political costs of non-reform (for example, faster job loss), as well as the political rewards of reform. Economic diversification creates conflicting interests within the private sector, such that multisectoral business associations will not survive if they insist on defending the interests of any one sector and will in the end press for policies that benefit overall prosperity (Pinaud 2007).

More generally, as noted above, reforms that remove barriers to entry and competition not only reduce rents available to the state to allocate, but also expand the constituency for further reform, including institutionalization in the public and private sectors (in the form of more representative business associations). Competition motivates firms to push for efficiency-enhancing reforms so they can compete better.

Competition, where unavoidable, leads industries to seek to become more competitive. In a 1997 study, Turkish business associations in protected industries tended to lobby for more protection. By contrast, those in competitive (and export-oriented) industries tended to lobby for broadly beneficial, competitiveness-enhancing economic reforms (Biddle and Milor 1997; Pinaud 2007). As a complement, reforms that enhance access to economic information (including the distribution and impact of public services) can empower reform advocates in policy debates.[11] Reformers, even within recalcitrant states, can seek opportunities to expand entry that broaden the constituency for reform.

Understanding the political economy of the region, although clearly sobering, can assist reformers to be more strategic in sequencing and focusing reform efforts, with a long-term view toward strengthening the interests of government and the private sector toward deeper reform and greater institutionalization. The next chapter considers measures that take into account the challenges imposed by the political economy. It provides options for proponents of reform (whether public or private) who may not yet have persuaded all (or even most) of the beneficiaries of the status quo. These policy recommendations are articulated around three pillars aimed at making MENA government commitment to private-led growth more credible: (1) reduce opportunities for rent seeking and fostering competition, (2) reform institutions to limit discretion and rent-seeking opportunities, and (3) strengthen stakeholder mobilization through open and institutionalized consultative policy making, anchored in a clear long-term growth strategy.

Notes

1. This finding is developed in the unpublished background paper for this report by Philip Keefer (2007). Substantial sections of this chapter are drawn from that paper.

2. Also, in the language of econometrics, the results are robust to using that component of ruling party age explained by whether the transition to nondemocracy was led by the military (that is, using the nature of the transition as an instrument for ruling party age). Chang and Golden (2008) find, as well, that personalized autocracies are more vulnerable to corruption than institutionalized autocracies. Boix and Svolik (2008) make similar arguments.

3. Che and Qian (1998) also argue that this credibility problem needed to be solved for township-village enterprises to succeed.

4. See the Vibrancy, Opportunities, and Growth Web site of the Public Service of Singapore and its information on the variable

component of civil service compensation at https://app.vog.gov.sg/StaticContent/FAQ.aspx#5.

5. This regression controls for income per capita to take into account diminishing returns to investment in richer countries with larger capital stocks. Consistent with this, higher income countries attract significantly less investment, all else being equal.

6. For reviews of the political systems and their history in selected countries of the region and the role of state-business relations, see Luciani (1990) and Heydemann (2004); Willis (2002) for the Maghreb countries; Leveau (1985), Tangeaoui (1993), Benhaddou (1997), Catusse (2008), and Greenwood (2008) for Morocco; Roberts (1992) and Dillman (2000) for Algeria; and Wilson (1987) and Wiktorowicz (2000) for Jordan.

7. More generally, this applies to the more institutionalized the political parties and other decision-making bodies.

8. This is similar to the arguments in Acemoglu and Robinson (2008) about the conditions for nondemocratic leaders to accede to democratization.

9. A recent review of the political economy of Algeria, Egypt, Syria, and Tunisia observed these alliances and concluded: "Together, the strengthening of a new ruling coalition composed of former state capitalists and a rent-seeking urban and rural elite, along with deliberalization measures to conceal emerging forms of crony capitalism, bode ill for the development of competitive multiparty politics" (King 2007, p. 446).

10. "In Morocco, the existence of a well-connected protectionist elite paradoxically spurred a cohesive class identity among emerging small exporters, galvanizing them to lobby vigorously for their interests and enabling them to gain increasing influence over policy-making" (Cammett 2007, p. 137).

11. In their seminal work on political capture in Eastern and Central Europe, Hellman and Kaufmann (2001) propose "competition and transparency" as the antidotes.

Rethinking Private Sector Policy Making in MENA

Governments need to make their commitment to private sector–led growth more credible and introduce fundamental institutional reforms. This will require a change in the way policy making is conducted. Decision making needs to be more open and inclusive. This chapter presents a three-pronged strategy that can be adapted to each country context:

- *First, reduce the opportunities for rent-seeking and foster competition. Governments can encourage entry in all sectors of the economy by removing formal and informal barriers to competition and by promoting transparency. This is a prerequisite for reducing rent seeking and fostering the emergence of a more diversified private sector that will, in turn, pressure for more pro-growth reforms.*

- *Second, reform institutions. Greater transparency and accountability of public institutions that interact with the private sector and regulate markets is urgently needed. Strong rule-bound public institutions must be built, with substantial decision making power over economic outcomes. Holding each agency more accountable to measurable outcomes is essential to shift incentives of public officials away from discretionary implementation of the rules and improve administrative service to investors.*

- *Third, mobilize all stakeholders around a dedicated long-term growth strategy. A new form of partnership is needed between the government and all stakeholders—inside the different parts of government and with the private sector especially—to develop stronger reform alliances and broader participation in designing, implementing, and evaluating policies.*

Short of such a fundamental shift, investor expectations that governments are committed to reform will remain weak. The returns on the reforms over the next few years will be lower if the investors—especially domestic ones—do not believe the changes are real, deep, and set to last.

What Should Be Done Differently to Change Investor Expectations?

The true challenge for policy reformers is to pursue strategies that prioritize, sequence, and design reforms in a way that strengthens support for the policies and reinforces their credibility. Engineering reforms in a way that ultimately overcomes the status quo is needed to assure investors—local and foreign, large and small—that things are really changing. Changing expectations is vital to success. Only when private sector actors believe that reform is really addressing core governance issues can the process actually produce the desired response and results. Thus the signal that reforms send matters at least as much as their policy content.

Reform strategies need to focus on making investors confident that things are really changing in a sustainable way. Some reform strategies may be appealing but are less useful from a credibility standpoint. For example, wide-ranging policy reforms may be helpful. If, however, investors fear unequal and discretionary implementation, then broad reforms need to be accompanied by wide-ranging administrative reforms for transparency and accountability. Only then will investors have confidence that even-handed implementation will be sustained.

The mix of policies that will carry the greatest credibility for investors varies by country. How to signal that "change is real" is usually common knowledge among local stakeholders. Some policies that might persuade investors in one place could have no impact in another. What serves as an effective signal of credible commitment to reform in one country has little sway in a different context.[1] But local investors, policy makers, civil society, and the public usually share common knowledge about what would signal a fundamental change. They may have conflicting opinions on whether such change is desirable, but they know what real change would entail.

In some countries in the region a necessary starting point will be to dismantle the conflicts of interest between political leaders and private business. In others it will be to open the banking sector to more competition and reduce the dominance of state-owned banks. In almost all countries it will mean reducing opportunities for rent seeking in public land markets or opening sectors that remain closed to (foreign or domestic) competition.

The main message of this report is that increasing credibility of private sector policies—and in turn the response of investors—requires audacious comprehensive strategies that should rest on three pillars: (1) increased business entry and competition and reduced rents, (2) institutional reform to level the playing field, and (3) inclusive partnerships and more open policy making. Although reform progress varies across the region—notably between oil-rich, labor-abundant countries and the rest—these three policy priorities apply to all countries, but the way each is implemented will strongly depend on the country context. As chapters 5, 6, and 7 have shown, the policy implications of increasing competition, reducing rents, reforming institutions, and including stakeholders in policy making take different forms in each area of the business environment. In each area the emphasis and policy content may differ between the three pillars.

First, Reduce the Major Traditional Channels of Rent Allocation and Foster Firm Entry and Competition

Start by reforming the basics. This applies particularly to oil-rich countries outside the Gulf Cooperation Council (GCC)—Algeria, the Islamic Republic of Iran, Libya, and Syria, for example—that have had the budgetary means to delay these standard reforms and protect failing (public or private) industries and banks. A priority for them will be to catch up with the rest of the region's more advanced reformers. Short of that, other low-grade reforms or interventions will have little impact on investor expectations.

These basic standard reforms include the following:

- Increasing openness to competition, particularly foreign competition, through trade and investment. Opening protected sectors, such as retail, services, and real estate, which are protected from foreign entry in some Algeria, Egypt, Gulf countries, and Tunisia, for example; reducing tariff bands and nontariff barriers; removing protection of state-owned firms by enforcing hard budget constraints and exposing them to open competition; and eliminating antiexport biases, such as the explicit surrender requirements on exports still in effect in a few countries (such as in Algeria, where 50 percent of export receipts need to be surrendered) will foster more openness and competition and will unravel many bastions of rent.

- Removing formal and informal barriers to new entry by eliminating requirements that give discretion to public officials to exclude some investors—such as sector-ministry approvals in effect in many activities in Algeria, Egypt, Syria, and Tunisia. Other barriers include high minimum capital requirements and restrictions on foreign ownership in certain sectors, in effect in Algeria, some GCC countries, the Islamic Republic of Iran, Libya, and Syria. The most important policy initiatives to develop small businesses should focus on easing entry and formalization to increase competition.

- Improving the governance of the banking sector, by increasing entry and competition among all banks—public and private—and reducing state ownership where still dominant. For example, Algeria, the Islamic Republic of Iran, Libya, and Syria should invest political capital to pursue privatization transactions that would reduce the dominance of public banks. Open and transparent competition in that process will be essential to increase the value of the transactions and to attract the most reputable international banks. Even more important, however, it signals a change in the way business is carried out with government. Beyond privatization, all countries should increase banking competition and reduce the room for abuse—for example, by limiting the credit that single borrowers can receive from public banks, by publicizing public bank portfolios and all troubled loans, by removing branching restrictions, and by improving the independent supervision of all banks.

- Removing the conflicts of interest between politicians and businessmen, or at least making them more transparent. That is a difficult agenda, but the first steps would be for reformist political leaders to send strong signals that things are really changing in this area. The presence of political leaders and their families in private markets hurts competition and creates serious conflicts of interest. It also prevents other investors from believing that the rules of the game are fair—no matter the extent of the reforms promoting openness. Particularly in countries that have made the most reform progress but where these conflicts of interest still hinder competition, bold steps by politicians to divest their current shares in major ventures (often in protected sectors) and to declare their assets would be a break from the status quo. A minimal alternative would be to increase transparency about these ventures and make them public.

Second, Reform Institutions by Anchoring Elements of Public Sector Reform in Key Agencies

Beyond getting the basic reforms right, reducing arbitrariness in policy implementation is crucial to convince investors that reforms will really affect them in a positive way. This is no easy task, because it must attack the basis of discretion that traditionally underpinned domestic politics. Reformers often have only partial control over the areas on which they can act, particularly for heterogeneous governments where a few reformist ministers coexist with reform opponents. Even if reforms are limited to certain institutions or even certain regional or sectoral enclaves, such as export processing zones or sectoral clusters, they should credibly address core public governance issues that plague these institutions.

This agenda could be started one institution at a time, focusing on ones in which discretion and arbitrariness are highest. In some countries, this could be the tax authority, customs, or the land administration. In others it could be the licensing and inspection agencies, the business registration office, or the investors' one-stop shop. The most successful reforms that have improved individual institutions have combined a change in written rules with a redesign of processes and renewed attention to institutional capacity and incentives. A good example is the reform of the Cairo one-stop shop (box 9.1).

BOX 9.1

Cairo's One-Stop Shop

Slow business startup. By 2001 Egypt faced a serious challenge in attracting investment. Foreign investment had fallen to less than 1 percent of GDP, and total private investment was stagnant, at just above 10 percent of GDP. One deterrent was the administrative delay, discretion, and uncertainty surrounding business startup, which could involve as many as 78 governmental entities and 349 services for approvals, permits, and licenses. Two hundred regulations governed business licensing, and the process took an average of 34 days (and up to 140).

False start. In 2002 a presidential decree established a one-stop shop under the General Authority on Free Zones and Investments (GAFI). The one-stop shop would assemble officials from "all relevant government entities in one place" to provide "all investment-related services": approvals, permits, and licenses necessary to start and operate a business. Yet this first effort faced major challenges. The one-stop shop had limited power and authority. It could not override existing complex and often inconsistent procedures. The staff lacked knowledge, training, and authority to grant approvals or licenses. The mind-set of public officials was unchanged. Its scope was limited to serving only investors entitled to GAFI-administered incentives.

Fresh start. In 2004 a new government launched dramatic reforms of taxes and tariffs. A new chairman of GAFI was appointed to transform the General Authority from a regulator of investments into a promoter and facilitator of investment.

New authorization. A new 2004 investment law consolidated procedures for registration and licensing for most businesses under GAFI, empowering it to obtain licenses and approvals required for the establishment and operation of a project. A new modern one-stop shop was under construction in Cairo. With strong support from the government (prime minister and minister of investment), semiautonomy, and a dedicated internal revenue source, the new chairman of GAFI established the new Cairo one-stop shop in temporary headquarters in late 2004. Red tape, delays, and corruption were reduced in several ways.

Deregulation and streamlining. The 2004 Investment Law merged GAFI and the Companies' Law and unified several establishment legal procedures. GAFI's team reviewed startup procedures to "eliminate every step and constraint that has no reason—and to eliminate duplication." Over 40 procedures were eliminated under this rationale, and others were streamlined to cut costs and delays.

Co-location. By 2006 the Cairo one-stop shop housed representatives of 32 agencies. Nine officials have on-the-spot approval authority.

Reengineering. To limit the points of contact and reduce opportunities of corruption, GAFI management decided to reengineer the office so investors interact only with

(continued)

BOX 9.1 (continued)

the front office. The approvals are now done in the "back office" by officials who have no contact with applicants. In the Cairo one-stop shop, each investor (or investor's representative) is assigned a single GAFI officer who walks the investor through the entire registration process. All services are provided through one window where required documents are submitted. Perhaps most important, all required payments are made at a single bank window in one transaction. Most opportunities for speed payments were eliminated.

Restaffing, reskilling, and remotivating. A combination of new and existing staff was used in the new one-stop shop. New staff were taken on to deal directly with clients in the "front office"—where client orientation and excellent investor-relation skills were at a premium. Many other posts used existing staff. A culture of professionalism dedicated to client service and performance was encouraged. A new promotion system was introduced, one that is based on merit and qualifications, instead of the old seniority-based system. Nonperforming staff were made redundant or reassigned. Eight heads of departments out of 12 were new appointees. Consultants were recruited but the GAFI management was careful not to create a parallel system—trying instead to promote people from within. The management took advantage of GAFI's autonomous financial structure to raise salaries 30 percent across the board. They also put in place an incentives system of up to 20 percent of salary. To increase output (and justify the higher salaries), the workday was extended by 1.5 hours. Staff compensation and promotion became increasingly linked to performance monitoring.

Decentralization. Decision authority was delegated to some one-stop shop officials.

Limitations. The one-stop shop did not solve all investor headaches. Some projects still require prior approval from other authorities. The investment law did not give the one-stop shop jurisdiction over some start-up necessities such as utility connections, fire extinguishers, local construction permits, tax cards, and some licenses. There were problems regarding cooperation from lawyers, notaries, and the Commercial Registry, and there were challenges to raise investor awareness of the one-stop shop—many people did not know about it.

Achievements. By 2006 the one-stop shop reduced the business registration time from an average of 34 days to 3. Responding to this and complementary reforms, the number of registrations greatly increased, as did foreign investment. Subsequent to the establishment of the Cairo shop, GAFI established similar facilities in Ismailia, Assuit, and Alexandria.

Source: Authors' analysis and interviews of GAFI management conducted in 2007.

The goal of reforming institutions that interact with investors or regulate markets is to instill a culture of equitable and effective public service to businesses, exempt from discretion and interference. The means to achieve this goal in every institution lie largely in standard public sector governance reforms and entail the following steps:

1. *Simplifying regulations to reduce the room for discretionary behavior by public officials.* This institutionalized process should continually evaluate and review regulatory and administrative barriers. It would:

- Systematically reduce the number and complexity of administrative steps in every significant interaction between businesses and public officials;

- Ensure that laws and regulations are clear and publicly available, with little room for interpretation; and

- Systematically introduce simplified, reengineered electronic processes (e-government) in administrative interactions that allow it.

2. *Increasing transparency and access to information for greater accountability in every public institution that interacts with the market.* MENA remains the one region of the world that has made the least progress in the accountability and transparency of their public institutions. Improving access to information is an essential starting point to improve both.[2] It is also an essential ingredient to restore market confidence in governments and their policies and increase the credibility of reforms. Information on all laws, regulations, and directives should be published and available on the Internet. Timid attempts have been made to develop legal portals in some MENA countries, but they are largely incomplete and undeveloped— with a few exceptions such as Tunisia. Simple rules should increase incentives for more transparent and publicly available information on laws and regulations. For example, in Canada if a regulation is not published, its violation is not punished. Information on tax incentives and other benefits granted to firms should also be public. In the longer term freedom of information and sunshine legislation can help shift a culture of secrecy to one of accountability.[3] Giving citizens legal recourse to obtain information can help.

Measures include the following:

- Launching independent, regular, and publicly available measurement of the performance of public agencies in contact with the private sector. This would help instill a culture of accountability in these institutions.

- Opening access to business information from various institutional databases—and introducing freedom to conduct independent surveys and research.

- Systematically publishing information on transactions involving privatizations, public land transactions, subsidies, and procurement tenders—particularly information on the beneficiaries—and on court decisions on commercial litigation.

- Creating a unified interagency enterprise identification number to link the firm-level databases of all public institutions that deal with businesses—and making most of it open and accessible. No MENA country has implemented one so far, even if initiatives to do so are ongoing in Algeria, Morocco, and Tunisia. Doing so could be a major step toward more transparency. This reform would also reinforce the state capacity to monitor fraud and enforce the law. It will therefore facilitate eliminating many cumbersome regulations aimed at preventing such frauds (such as ex ante approvals). This measure would only be effective, however, as a complement to other reforms. In particular, if the core issues of discretion and preferential treatment are not addressed, the effect of this reform could even be negative as it would strengthen government capacity to exercise discriminatory control over the private sector.

Implementing such measures—a task that is technically feasible in the short term using modern information technology tools of e-government—would signal a serious and significant drive toward increased transparency and accountability (and a radical change from the status quo almost anywhere in MENA). These measures are difficult to reverse. Even if they are implemented partially and applied to just a few institutions, they will begin to have an impact. Transparency is contagious: pressure on other institutions to follow suit will quickly increase.

A middle-income country that has made significant strides in the area of access to public information is Mexico. The measures implemented by the Federal Institute of Access to Public Information could serve as a benchmark for MENA countries to imitate (box 9.2).

3. *Reforming incentives in public agencies and encouraging institutional innovations to improve service delivery to businesses.* Rewarding effort for effective public service and discouraging discretion in key institutions that affect the business environment in MENA should form the core of private sector strategies. Performance-based compensation in public institutions is a characteristic of high-performing countries in East Asia. These reforms are part of core public administration and civil service reform agendas that could be initiated one institution at a time. Areas to start with include the customs, the tax authorities, the industrial land administrations, and the agencies regulating investment approvals and business entry.

Useful and politically acceptable, initial measures could include reforming reward mechanisms in new institutions (such as one-stop shops) or implementing pilot administrative reforms in enclaves (such as special economic zones or individual agencies). Reform cannot stop there, however.

BOX 9.2

The Federal Institute of Access to Public Information in Mexico

Following a widespread public debate, Mexico passed the Federal Law of Access to Public Information in 2002. It established an independent body with the required autonomy and authority to enforce the law within the departments and agencies of the executive branch, to review those cases in which authorities deny citizens information, and to determine whether the requested information is public, reserved, or confidential.

In 2007 a constitutional amendment assured citizens that "All information in possession of any public authority, entity, or organ, in the federal, state or municipal level, is public and may only be restricted temporarily and for reason of public interest in the terms established by the Law." Every state in Mexico enacted similar state-specific laws. The disclosing parties (compelled to divulge information) established by the law, are the following:

a. The Federal Executive, the Federal Public Administration, and the Attorney General's Office
b. The Legislative Branch comprising the House of Representatives, the Senate, and the Permanent Commission, as well as any instrumentalities thereof
c. The Judicial Branch and the Federal Judiciary
d. Autonomous constitutional entities
e. Federal administrative courts and any other federal entity.

The law has empowered citizens to investigate and, in some cases, to denounce specific instances of corruption or bad behavior of public institutions. Citizens can now access information on financial accounts of public (or partially public) trust funds. They can access information such as procurement bids (including government contractor information) and beneficiaries of public subsidies.

The law does not compel private enterprises to disclose information. However, information on firms in Mexico is centralized, and all agencies where businesses are registered share firm-level databases. All are linked to the INFOMEX system, which provides detailed firm-level information.

Source: Federal Institute of Access to Public Information.

Innovative piecemeal reforms that include incentives for staff in key agencies would create a momentum of wider public sector reform. Like transparency, innovations in public agencies can be contagious. To facilitate this worthwhile contagion, any piecemeal public sector reform should be explicitly designed (or subsequently used) as the vanguard activity in a broader and more comprehensive public sector reform. The criteria for evaluating these enclave and piecemeal reforms should measure when, how, and to what extent they are being extended to other parts of the public administration.

4. *Introducing systematic, independent, transparent, and regular evaluation of any selective public intervention, including industrial policies.* Public interventions supporting select groups of firms (exporters, small and medium-sized enterprises, or specific sectors) should include features that will guard against failure and rent seeking:

- Measurable objectives, outcomes, and selection criteria would form the basis of a monitoring system for the intervention. Monitoring reports should be public and, where possible, the subject of consultation with relevant stakeholders.

- Systematic publication of information on beneficiary firms and the subsidies.

- Independent access to data and surveys to evaluate and monitor interventions. When feasible, impact evaluations should be built in at the start of any intervention.

These reforms are politically difficult, and implementation takes time. Their fate is thus uncertain, and the cycle of positive expectations they could generate may be slow to take hold. It is thus all the more important for reformers to complement their reform efforts by increasing supportive alliances with stakeholders.

Third, Building Reform Alliances and Institutionalizing the Reform Process

Cohesion between stakeholders and mobilization around a clear long-term economic strategy is lacking in many countries—reflecting in part the lack of a consensual commitment to growth. Sectoral ministries often have strategies, but rarely are they part of a consistent comprehensive plan. Coordination and cohesion between ministries is often weak—generally reflecting divided political elites. Consequently, reformers are often in the minority in a system skewed toward the status quo. In these situations only broad and vigorous coalitions can sustain successful reform efforts. Alliances need to be created across internal governmental boundaries as well as between the government and different elements in civil society—in particular with representative private sector organizations.

Specifically, governments of the region will need to rethink the way they organize and interact when they design and implement private sector policies. They should do so by taking the following steps.

1. *Improving government cohesion and interministerial coordination.* Poor coordination is symptomatic of low-performing decision-making

processes and divided political elites. It hurts the effectiveness and credibility of reform programs, because most private sector policies involve more than one ministry or agency (for example, industrial land reforms, regulatory simplification, and industrial strategies). This coordination problem is severe in many MENA countries. It is very hard to tackle because it often has political roots—especially when coalition governments are in place to reflect political divisions, regional balances, or different constituencies.

No single blueprint exists to ensure better governmental coordination. It takes more than the multiministerial committees that abound in the region. Some countries have formed superministries that agglomerate many sectors to solve their coordination issues (Malaysia and, more recently, China and France are good examples). Others have relied on politically strong institutions or ministries with the clout to bring other government constituencies along (Ireland and Singapore). Chile adopted a multiministerial economic board, as did South Africa to develop its accelerated and shared growth initiative—a board led by its deputy president.

All these expedients reflect a common reality: the locus of coordination needs to be a politically strong institution (often embodied by a politically strong official) that has explicit and visible political backing from the top leadership of the country. The teams of reformers matter as well—particularly when headed by champions who enjoy high credibility, competence, and political weight. In a recent review of successful reform episodes, governments systematically "relied on a small, dedicated team of experts to get the job done. These teams brought to bear world-class skills along with direct access to the top level of government and a large development budget. That combination of skills, access, and resources gave them the clout to steer an ambitious reform agenda through vested interests and layers of government" (Criscuolo and Palmade 2008: 78). Egypt's significant recent reform can be attributed to a reform team embodying such features, as can an earlier reform episode in Dubai. Many observers have attributed the Tunisian government's effective pursuit of multisectoral reforms to the strong cohesion and coordination capacity of successive, stable governments. Few other countries in MENA share these essential ingredients.

2. *Building partnerships between governments and other stakeholders, especially the private sector.* No matter how well organized and cohesive reform alliances within governments are, they cannot pursue and sustain reforms effectively without alliances outside the public sphere. Accordingly, early reforms might include expanding these alliances in their objectives. Because the danger of capture by incumbent private interests is real, organizers of public-private alliances need to concentrate on

ensuring that new constituencies emerge from the reforms. Emphasizing reforms that increase entry and competition is one way to expand support in the private sector. Another way is to get more systematic information out to constituencies likely to mobilize (dynamic business associations, consumer groups).

Public-private consultation in the design, monitoring, and implementation of reforms needs a strong foundation in society at large. Specifically, organized partners in the private sector can bolster the credibility of reforms and reformers. Concretely, this requires the following:

- Freedom for the private sector to organize in independent organizations, to raise funding from members, to obtain economic and policy information, to inform open policy debates, and to advocate for policy reforms. Such freedoms are not granted by law or in practice in at least six MENA countries. When these freedoms are granted, it is up to the business community to engage in more active and organized advocacy. The government should have no active role in this area other than to remove barriers to entry to encourage the emergence of new private sector constituencies. This is where the private sector in many MENA countries bears part of the responsibility for the weak dialogue with governments—it is often poorly organized and unrepresentative, and its advocacy capacity is weak. It will be up to the new generation of entrepreneurs to change that.

- An institutionalized, transparent, and inclusive process for private sector consultation in identifying policy issues, designing reforms, and monitoring and evaluating implementation. This requires a high level of transparency and business associations that can partner with governments in continual consultations.[4]

3. *Mobilizing all stakeholders around a clear long-term growth strategy.* Institutionalizing a reform process requires that it be part of a clear long-term strategy with measurable objectives, action plans, and responsibilities. Few MENA countries have communicated such a plan. None is available on any government Web site in the region.[5] By contrast, Web sites from Ireland, Malaysia, and New Zealand offer inspiring examples of the type of information that strategic communication for private sector policy making involves.[6] Communicating the reform strategy, its implementation, and its evaluation should be an integral part of any successful private sector reform effort.

4. *Addressing the concerns of reform "losers"—the influential and the vulnerable.* Reforms that aim to promote greater entry and exit of firms and more dynamism to the private sector will inevitably lead to transitions with many winners, whose benefits are diffuse, and a smaller number of

losers, whose losses may be substantial. Among the losers, those that benefited from rents and privileges are often well organized and able to oppose reforms. They may need to be co-opted or accommodated to enable reforms to progress. Just as reformers should seek to mobilize and empower their allies, they must consider how to bypass, neutralize, or co-opt their opponents. For example, China's market-oriented reforms applied a dual track approach that kept the beneficiaries of the old system insulated while at the same time it opened up a new system based on free entry and competition.[7]

Many vulnerable groups in the labor market may also suffer from increased dynamism of the private sector. New skills will be in demand, and others will be in decline. Although compensating losers may seem necessary only for influential producers and labor unions, in fact, social justice concerns demand even greater attention to the vulnerable, who may lose out because of inevitable adjustments involved in economic transformation. Accompanying reforms with improvements in social safety nets and labor market policies can soften the blow to those who lose jobs.

Looking Forward: Unlocking the Region's Private Sector Potential

MENA is at a crossroads. Private-led growth has increased and created jobs recently. Reforms have progressed throughout the region, although at different paces. Despite the current global economic crisis, signs of positive expectations about the future and increased attractiveness to foreign investment are visible in almost every country. The coming years will be crucial for the region's economic future. Will the growth revival of recent years and private sector enthusiasm be strengthened beyond the current crisis and sustained? That will depend on the ability of each country's political leadership to commit credibly to change the deep-rooted status quo by pursuing difficult reforms that reduce discretion and inequities in the investment climate.

Despite the complex political economy of each country, opportunities are immense to advance toward sustained growth. Recent reforms that have tackled privileges and rents show the way forward. Examples can be found in almost every country. Recently successful experiences with regulatory and institutional reforms have reduced entry barriers in Egypt, Libya, Morocco, and Saudi Arabia. Several are leading the way in some areas—banking in Morocco, tax reform in Egypt, business entry in the Republic of Yemen, e-government in Dubai, and customs in Tunisia. Successful liberalization stories abound, such as for telecommunications in Algeria. These reforms have allowed many new businesses to enter the market and have created more diverse constituencies, ones demanding further reform. In Egypt, Jordan, Morocco, the United Arab Emirates, and other countries this new diversity of private sector actors is creating a dynamic of change, pressuring for more reforms.

All these scattered reform successes show that the key to stronger private sector–led growth is within reach. Yet it will take political will—and time—to support sustained reforms that credibly address the real issues holding the region back and meet the expectations of investors and the public. It will take a renewed and stronger commitment to long-term growth, one that mobilizes all stakeholders. The region's policy makers know the challenges and how crucial a stable and transparent climate for private investment is to growth, job creation, and social stability in their countries. MENA countries are endowed with strong human capital, good infrastructure, immense resources for some, and much creativity and entrepreneurship everywhere. The economic and social payoff of embarking on a more ambitious private-led growth agenda could thus be immense for all.

Notes

1. For example, Mody and Saravia (2006, abstract) argue that IMF programs work as commitment devices only in select contexts, where they are viewed as "likely to lead to policy reform" and when "undertaken before economic fundamentals have deteriorated significantly."

2. As the current financial crisis painfully reminds us, transparency, access to information, and effective regulation are essential ingredients of functioning markets—and no country is immune to deficiencies when these fail. The origins of the financial crisis are identified by many authors as such failures having taken place in the United States.

3. For more information on the fundamentals of freedom of information acts, see Mendel (2004).

4. For good practice principles and examples, see Herzberg and Wright (2006).

5. A notable exception is the portal of the government of Dubai (www.dubai.ae), which includes a 40-page summary of the 2015 strategic plan. This summary, however, falls short of providing any information on the implementation or evaluation of the strategy.

6. See www.entemp.ie, www.miti.gov.my, and www.nzte.govt.nz.

7. "The approach, based on the continued enforcement of the existing plan while simultaneously liberalizing the market, can be understood as a method for making implicit lump sum transfers to compensate potential losers of the reform" (Lau, Qian, and Roland 2000, abstract).

References

Acemoglu, Daron, and James A. Robinson. 2008. "Persistence of Power, Elites and Institutions." *American Economic Review* 98 (1): 267–93.

Beck, Thorsten, George Clarke, Alberto Groff, Philip Keefer, and Patrick Walsh. 2001. "New Tools in Comparative Political Economy: The Database of Political Institutions." *World Bank Economic Review* 15 (1): 165–76.

Beck, Thorsten, and Augusto de la Torre. 2006. "The Basic Analytics of Access to Financial Services." Policy Research Working Paper 4026. World Bank, Washington, DC.

Beck, Thorsten, Asli Demirguc-Kunt, and Maria Soledad Martinez Peria. 2006. "Banking Services for Everyone? Barriers to Bank Access and Use around the World." Policy Research Working Paper 4079. World Bank, Washington, DC.

Benhaddou, A. 1997. *Maroc, les élites du royaume: essai sur l'organisation du pouvoir au Maroc.* Paris: L'Harmattan.

Benhassine, Najy, and Gael Raballand. 2009. "Beyond Ideological Cleavages: A Unifying Framework of Industrial Policies and Other Public Interventions." *Economic Systems* (forthcoming).

Biddle, Jesse, and Vedat Milor. 1997. "Economic Governance in Turkey: Bureaucratic Capacity, Policy Networks, and Business Associations." In *Business and the State in Developing Countries*, ed. Sylvia Maxfield and Ben Ross Schneider. Ithaca, NY: Cornell University Press.

Boix, Carles, and Milan Svolik. 2008. "The Foundations of Limited Authoritarian Government: Institutions and Power-Sharing in Dictatorships." Mimeo, Department of Politics and Woodrow Wilson

School of Public and International Affairs, Princeton University, Princeton, NJ.

Bolaky, Bineswaree, and Caroline Freund. 2004. "Trade, Regulations, and Growth." Policy Research Working Paper 3255. World Bank, Washington, DC.

Cammett, Melani. 2007. *Globalization and Business Politics in Arab North Africa: A Comparative Perspective.* Cambridge: Cambridge University Press.

Caprio, Gerard, Ross Eric Levine, and James R. Barth. 2008. "Bank Regulations Are Changing: For Better or Worse?" Policy Research Working Paper 4646. World Bank, Development Research Group, Finance and Private Sector Team, Washington, DC.

Catusse, Myriam. 2008. *Le temps des entrepreneurs? Politique et transformations du capitalisme au Maroc (Broché).* Paris: Maisonneuve & Larose.

Chang, Eric, and Miriam A. Golden. 2008. "Sources of Corruption in Authoritarian Regimes." Department of Political Science, University of California at Los Angeles.

Che, Jiahua, and Yingyi Qian. 1998. "Institutional Environment, Community Government, and Corporate Governance: Understanding China's Township-Village Enterprises." *Journal of Law, Economics, and Organization* 14 (1): 1–23.

Commission on Growth and Development. 2008. *The Growth Report: Strategies for Sustained Growth and Inclusive Development.* Washington, DC: World Bank. Also available at http://www.growthcommission. org.

Criscuolo, Alberto, and Vincent Palmade. 2008. "Reform Teams: How the Most Successful Reformers Organized Themselves." Public Policy for the Private Sector Note 318. World Bank, Washington, DC.

Dennis, Allen. 2006a. "The Impact of Regional Trade Agreements and Trade Facilitation in the Middle East and North Africa Region." Policy Research Working Paper 3837. World Bank, Washington, DC.

———. 2006b. "Trade Liberalization, Factor Market Flexibility, and Growth: The Case of Morocco and Tunisia." Policy Research Working Paper 3857. World Bank, Washington, DC.

Desai, Raj M., and Sanjay Pradhan. 2005. "Governing the Investment Climate." *Development Outreach* 7 (2): 13–15.

Dillman B. L. 2000. *State and Private Sector in Algeria: The Politics of Rent-Seeking and Failed Development.* Boulder: Westview Press.

Djankov, Simeon, Oliver Hart, Caralee McLiesh, and Andrei Shleifer. 2006. "Debt Enforcement around the World." NBER Working Paper 12807. National Bureau of Economic Research, Cambridge, MA.

Dobronogov, Anton, and Farrukh Iqbal. 2005. "Economic Growth in Egypt: Constraints and Determinants." Middle East and North Africa Working Paper 42. World Bank, Social and Economic Development Group, Washington, DC.

Dollar, David, and Aart Kraay. 2001. "Trade, Growth, and Poverty." Policy Research Working Paper 2615. World Bank, Washington, DC.

Edin, Maria. 2003. "State Capacity and Local Agent Control in China: CCP Cadre Management from a Township Perspective." *China Quarterly* 173: 35–52.

Eifert, Benn, Alan Gelb, and Nils Borje Tallroth. 2002. "The Political Economy of Fiscal Policy and Economic Management in Oil Exporting Countries." Policy Research Working Paper 2899. World Bank, Washington, DC.

Evans, Peter B., ed. 1997. *State-Society Synergy: Government and Social Capital in Development.* Berkeley: University of California Press.

Frankel, Jeffrey A., and David Romer. 1999. "Does Trade Cause Growth?" *American Economic Review* 89 (3): 379–99.

Galal, Ahmed. 2005. "The Economics of Formalization: Potential Winners and Losers from Formalization in Egypt." In *Investment Climate, Growth, and Poverty*, ed. Gudrun Kochendorfer-Lucius and Boris Pleskovic. Washington, DC: World Bank.

Galal, Ahmed, ed. 2008. *Industrial Policy in the Middle East and North Africa: Rethinking the Role of the State.* Egyptian Center for Economic Studies. Cairo: American University in Cairo Press.

Gehlbach, Scott, and Philip Keefer. 2008. "Investment without Democracy: Ruling Party Institutionalization and Credible Commitment in

Autocracies." Department of Political Science, University of Wisconsin, Madison.

Greenwood, Scott. 2008. "Bad for Business? Entrepreneurs and Democracy in the Arab World." *Comparative Political Studies* 41 (6): 837–60.

Haddad, Mona. 1993. "How Trade Liberalization Affected Productivity in Morocco." Policy Research Working Paper 1096. World Bank, Washington, DC.

Haddad, Mona, and Ann Harrison. 1993. "Are There Positive Spillovers from Direct Foreign Investment?" *Journal of Development Economics* 42 (1): 51–74.

Hallward-Driemeier, Mary, Giuseppe Iarossi, and Kenneth L. Sokoloff. 2001. "East Asian Manufacturing: Market Depth and Aiming for Exports." World Bank, Development Research Group, Washington, DC.

Harrison, Ann E. 1994. "Productivity, Imperfect Competition and Trade Reform: Theory and Evidence." *Journal of International Economics* 36 (1–2): 53–73.

Hausmann, Ricardo, Lant Pritchett, and Dani Rodrik. 2005. "Growth Accelerations." *Journal of Economic Growth* 10 (4): 303–29.

Hausmann, Ricardo, Dani Rodrik, and Andres Velasco. 2006. "Getting the Diagnosis Right: A New Approach to Economic Reform." *Finance and Development* 43 (1): 12–15.

Hellman, Joel, and Daniel Kaufmann. 2001. "Confronting the Challenge of State Capture in Transition Economies." *Finance and Development* 38 (3): 31–35.

Herzberg, Benjamin, and Andrew Wright. 2006. "The Public-Private Dialogue Handbook: A Toolkit for Business Environment Reformers." World Bank, Small and Medium Enterprise Department. http://publicprivatedialogue.org/tools/PPDhandbook.pdf.

Heydemann, Steven. 2004. *Networks of Privilege in the Middle East: The Politics of Economic Reform Revisited.* London: Palgrave Macmillan.

International Monetary Fund. 2008. "Socialist People's Libyan Arab Jamahiriya: Staff Report for the 2008 Article IV Consultation." IMF

Country Report 08/302. International Monetary Fund, Washington, DC.

Jones, C. Stuart. 1999. "Hierarchies, Networks and Management Accounting in NHS Hospitals." *Accounting, Auditing and Accountability Journal* 12 (2): 164–88.

Kaganova, Olga, and James McKellar, eds. 2006. *Managing Government Property Assets: International Experiences.* Washington, DC: Urban Institute Press.

Kaufmann, Daniel. 2005. "Click Reset Button: Investment Climate Reconsidered." *Development Outreach* 7 (2): 16–18.

Keefer, Philip. 2007. "Beyond Legal Origin and Checks and Balances: Political Credibility, Citizen Information, and Financial Sector Development." Policy Research Working Paper 4154. World Bank, Washington, DC.

Kinda, Tidiane, Patrick Plane, and Marie-Ange Véganzones-Varoudakis. 2007. "Firm-Level Productivity and Technical Efficiency in MENA Manufacturing Industry: The Role of the Investment Climate." CERDI, Etudes et Documents, E 2008.19, Université d'Auvergne, Clermont-Ferrand, France.

King, Stephen J. 2007. "Sustaining Authoritarianism in the Middle East and North Africa." *Political Science Quarterly* 122 (3): 433–59.

Klinger, Bailey, and Daniel Lederman. 2004. "Discovery and Development: An Empirical Exploration of 'New' Products." World Bank Policy Research Working Paper 3450, November. World Bank, Washington, DC.

Lau, Lawrence J., Yingyi Qian, and Gérard Roland. 2000. "Reform without Losers: An Interpretation of China's Dual-Track Approach to Transition." *Journal of Political Economy* 108 (1): 120–43.

Lederman, Daniel, and William F. Maloney. 2003. "Trade Structure and Growth." World Bank Policy Research Working Paper 3025. World Bank, Washington, DC.

Leveau, Rémy. 1985. *Le Fellah marocain, défenseur du trône.* 2nd edition. Paris: Presses de la Fondation Nationale des Sciences Politiques.

Li, Hongbin, and Li-An Zhou. 2005. "Political Turnover and Economic Performance: The Incentive Role of Personnel Control in China." *Journal of Public Economics* 89 (9–10): 1743–62.

Love, Inessa, and Nataliya Mylenko. 2003. "Credit Reporting and Financing Constraints." Policy Research Working Paper 3142. World Bank, Washington, DC.

Luciani, Giacomo, ed. 1990. *The Arab State*. London: Routledge.

Manion, Melanie. 1992. "Politics and Policy in Post-Mao Cadre Retirement." *China Quarterly* 129: 1–25.

———. 2004. *Corruption by Design: Building Clean Government in Mainland China and Hong Kong*. Cambridge, MA: Harvard University Press.

Maxfield, Sylvia, and Ben Ross Schneider, eds. 1997. *Business and the State in Developing Countries*. Ithaca, NY: Cornell University Press.

McMillan, John, and Christopher Woodruff. 2002. "The Central Role of Entrepreneurs in Transition Economies." *Journal of Economic Perspectives* 16 (3): 153–70.

Mendel, Toby. 2004. "Legislation on Freedom of Information: Trends and Standards." PREM Notes–Public Sector 93. World Bank, Washington, DC.

Mody, Ashoka, and Diego Saravia. 2006. "Catalysing Private Capital Flows: Do IMF Programmes Work as Commitment Devices?" *Economic Journal* 116 (513): 843–67.

Nabli, Mustapha K., Jennifer Keller, Claudia Nassif, and Carlos Silva-Jauregui. 2004. "The Political Economy of Industrial Policy in the Middle East and North Africa." Papers by Chief Economist. World Bank, Washington, DC.

Nabli, Mustapha K., Carlos Silva-Jauregui, and Ahmet Faruk Aysan. 2008. "Autoritarisme politique, crédibilité des réformes et développement du secteur privé au Moyen-Orient et en Afrique du Nord." *Revue d'économie du développement* 22 (3): 49–85.

Nelson, Douglas R., and J. M. Finger. 2004. *The Political Economy of Policy Reform: Essays in Honor of J. Michael Finger*. Amsterdam: Elsevier.

Olson, Mancur. 1965. *The Logic of Collective Action: Public Goods and the Theory of Groups.* Cambridge, MA: Harvard University Press.

Owen, Roger. 1992. *State, Power and Politics in the Making of the Modern Middle East.* London: Routledge.

Pack, Howard. 2000. "Industrial Policy: Growth Elixir or Poison?" *World Bank Research Observer* 15 (1): 47–67.

Pagano, Marco. 1993. "Financial Markets and Growth: An Overview." *European Economic Review* 37 (2–3): 613–22.

Palmade, Vincent. 2005. "Industry Level Analysis: The Way to Identify the Binding Constraints to Economic Growth." Policy Research Working Paper 3551. World Bank, Washington, DC.

Pigato, Miria. 2009. *Strengthening China's and India's Trade and Investment Ties to the Middle East and North Africa.* Washington, DC: World Bank.

Pinaud, Nicholas. 2007. *Public–Private Dialogue in Developing Countries: Opportunities and Risks.* Paris: OECD Development Centre Studies.

Roberts, Hugues. 1992. *The Algerian State and the Challenge of Democracy.* Oxford: Blackwell.

Robinson, James Alan, and Thierry A. Verdier. 2002. "The Political Economy of Clientelism." CEPR Discussion Paper 3025. Centre for Economic Policy Research, London.

Rodrik, Dani, ed. 2003. *In Search of Prosperity: Analytic Narratives on Economic Growth.* Princeton, NJ: Princeton University Press.

Rodrik, Dani. 2004. "Industrial Policy for the Twenty-First Century." CEPR Discussion Paper 4767. Centre for Economic Policy Research, London.

Sachs, Jeffrey D., and Andrew M. Warner. 1995. "Natural Resource Abundance and Economic Growth." Development Discussion Paper 517a. Harvard University, Harvard Institute for International Development, Cambridge, MA.

Safavian, Mehnaz, and Joshua Wimpey. 2007. "When Do Enterprises Prefer Informal Credit?" Policy Research Working Paper 4435. World Bank, Washington, DC.

Schiavo-Campo, Salvatore, Giulio de Tommaso, and Amitabha Mukherjee. 1997. "Government Employment and Pay: A Global and Regional Perspective." Policy Research Working Paper 1771. World Bank, Washington, DC.

Schneider, Friedrich. 2005. "Shadow Economy around the World: What Do We Really Know?" *European Journal of Political Economy* 21 (3): 598–642.

Schumpeter, Joseph. 1942. *Capitalism, Socialism, and Democracy.* New York: Harper and Brothers.

Tangeaoui, Saïd. 1993. *Les entrepreneurs marocains: pouvoir, société et modernité.* Paris: Editions Karthala.

Whiting, Susan H. 2006. *Power and Wealth in Rural China: The Political Economy of Institutional Change.* New York: Cambridge University Press.

Willis, M. J. 2002. "Political Parties in the Maghrib: The Illusion of Significance?" *Journal of North African Studies.*

Wilson, John S. 2003. "Trade Facilitation and Global Economic Prospects: Beyond the WTO Agenda." Presentation, September 25, Transport and Urban Development Division, World Bank, Washington, DC.

Wilson, Mary C. 1987. *King Abdullah, Britain and the Making of Jordan.* New York: Cambridge University Press.

Wiktorowicz, Quintan. 2000. "The Salafi Movement in Jordan." *International Journal of Middle East Studies* 32: 219–40.

Wong, Christine P. W. 1992. "Fiscal Reform and Local Industrialization: The Problematic Sequencing of Reform in Post-Mao China." *Modern China* 18 (2): 197–227.

World Bank. 2003a. *Better Governance for Development in the Middle East and North Africa: Enhancing Inclusiveness and Accountability.* MENA Development Report. Washington, DC: World Bank.

————. 2003b. *Trade, Investment, and Development in the Middle East and North Africa.* MENA Development Report. Washington, DC: World Bank.

————. 2003c. *Unlocking the Employment Potential in the Middle East and North Africa: Toward a New Social Contract.* MENA Development Report. Washington, DC: World Bank.

————. 2004a. *World Development Report 2005: A Better Investment Climate for Everyone.* Washington, DC: World Bank.

————. 2004b. *Algeria: Legal and Judicial Review.* Washington, DC: World Bank.

————. 2005. *Economic Growth in the 1990s: Learning from a Decade of Reform.* Washington, DC: World Bank.

————. 2006. *Doing Business 2007.* Washington, DC: World Bank.

————. 2007a. *Doing Business 2008.* Washington, DC: World Bank.

————. 2007b. "Export Diversification in Egypt, Jordan, Lebanon, Morocco, and Tunisia." Middle East and North Africa Region Report 40497-MNA. World Bank, Washington, DC.

————. 2007c. *Middle East and North Africa Region 2007 Economic Developments and Prospects: Job Creation in an Era of High Growth.* Washington, DC: World Bank.

————. 2007d. *Lebanon: Legal and Judicial Review.* Washington, DC: World Bank.

————. 2008a. *Doing Business 2009.* Washington, DC: World Bank.

————. 2008b. "Morocco Investment Climate Assessment." World Bank, Washington DC.

————. 2008c. *The Road Not Traveled: Education Reform in the Middle East and North Africa.* MENA Development Report. Washington, DC: World Bank.

————. 2008d. *Finance for All? Policies and Pitfalls in Expanding Access.* Washington, DC: World Bank.

————. 2008e. *Global Economic Prospects 2009: Commodities at the Crossroads.* Washington, DC: World Bank.

————. 2009a. *World Bank Research Digest* 3 (2). Special issue on the financial crisis.

————. 2009b. *Doing Business 2010.* Washington, DC: World Bank.

Zagha, Roberto, and Gobind T. Nankani. 2005. *Economic Growth in the 1990s: Learning from a Decade of Reform.* Washington, DC: World Bank.

Index

Boxes, figures, notes, and tables are indicated by *b*, *f*, *n*, and *t*, respectively.